D1010619

Eco-efficiency

Eco-efficiency

The Business Link to Sustainable Development

Livio D. DeSimone and
Frank Popoff with the
World Business Council for
Sustainable Development

The MIT Press
Cambridge, Massachusetts
London, England

Second printing, 1998

This book was set in Palatino by Omegatype Typography, Inc.

Printed and bound in the United States of America.

Library of Congress Cataloging-in-Publication Data
    DeSimone, Livio D.
      Eco-efficiency : the business link to sustainable development /
    Livio D. DeSimone and Frank Popoff with the World Business Council
    for Sustainable Development.
          p.   cm.
      Based on various activities of the Council, including expert
    meetings in Europe (Antwerp 1 in November 1993 and Antwerp 2 in
    March 1995) and in the United States (Washington, D.C., in November
    1995),
      Includes bibliographical references and index.
      ISBN 0-262-04162-6 (alk. paper)
      1. Sustainable development.   2. Economic development—
    Environmental aspects.   3. Social responsibility of business.
    I. Popoff, Frank.   II. World Business Council for Sustainable
    Development.   III. Title.
    HC79.E5D4637   1997
    338.98—dc21   96-49857
                                                            CIP

Never Rust™, Post-it®, Safest Stripper™, Scotch-Brite™, Scotchtint™, and Siverflux™, are trademarks of 3M.

Fiberex™, High-Performance™, and Renewal by Andersen™ are trademarks of Andersen Corporation.

Sirene® CM is a trademark of Novartis Agro Ag.

Crest® and Pump & Spray are trademarks of Proctor and Gamble.

Azurel™ is a trademark of Dow Europe S.A.

Invert™ is a trademark of the Dow Chemical Company.

Broadstrike™ and Sentricon™ are trademarks of DowElanco.

Aquabase® is a trademark of ICI.

Raid™ is a trademark of S.C. Johnson and Son Inc.

Powermiser® is a trademark of Nordyne.

Meridien™ is a trademark of Northern Telecom.

DryView™ is a trademark of Imation.

Responsible Care® is a registered service mark of the Chemical Manufacturers Association in the U.S.

Therminox Ultra™ is a trademark of Novo Nordisk.

AS-400® is a trademark of IBM.

Pronatur® is a trademark of Pronatur.

Contents

Foreword

Maurice Strong

It is a very special honor to have been invited to provide the foreword to *Eco-efficiency: The Business Link to Sustainable Development* by Livio DeSimone and Frank Popoff, two executives recognized for their leading-edge thinking on issues of sustainability.

Back in 1992, I had the unique experience of being present at the creation of the concept of eco-efficiency during the Earth Summit. In just five years, eco-efficiency has moved from a vision to implementation. Discussed in board rooms, debated by policy makers, and promoted by NGOs, it is an idea whose time has not only come—but one whose contribution will help society move along the path to sustainable development.

As both a businessman and now an international public servant, I have first-hand experience of the exciting and important potential eco-efficiency provides. The worldwide adoption of eco-efficiency by governments and the widespread practice by business is just under way, but all those who are experiencing it know how fundamental it is becoming to how we think and act about sustainable development.

Evidence of the evolution of eco-efficiency from concept to concrete action is growing day by day:

- Eco-efficiency workshops have been conducted in many parts of the world;
- UN agencies, the OECD, the European Commission, and many national governments are promoting awareness of eco-efficiency on all continents;
- the WBCSD global network is introducing the idea to developing countries and economies in transition;

• and important manuals and managerial guides are being published by the business community.

Eco-efficiency is truly far-reaching. It can help developed countries improve their resource productivity, encourage developing countries to reach their full potential without depleting their material resource heritage, and provide governments with the essentials to develop innovative and pragmatic policies that energize and enable society to become sustainable.

In my current capacity as special advisor to the UN Secretary-General I can foresee the fundamental and crucial role eco-efficiency will play for today's generation to achieve a sustainable future. And that means it can help everyone—individuals, businesses, and governments—achieve responsible attitudes.

Weaving eco-efficiency into the very fabric of how businesses, governments, NGOs, and consumers think and act is essential if we are to reap the vast rewards of this concept and tool. Of course it will take time, but the progress we have achieved so far tells me we have every reason to be optimistic as to how quickly the idea will spread, how fast it will be implemented, and how much it will contribute.

Views of Business Leaders

Samuel C. Johnson is chairman of S.C. Johnson & Son, Inc. (better known as SC Johnson Wax). Fortune has called him "America's leading corporate environmentalist," for reasons that are clear from the company case study in chapter 6.

"My grandfather once used a white-flannel test to sell the company's wax. After polishing and shining a customer's floor dressed in a smart white suit, he sat down and got them to pull him over the newly waxed floor. When he got up, his backside was clean, not a speck of dirt.

"My dream is to be able to conduct an environmental white-flannel test around our offices and factories to show that they operate behind a "clean" ethic while producing goods.

"We aggressively seek out eco-efficiencies—ways of doing more with less—because it makes us more competitive when we reduce and eliminate waste and risk from our products and processes. And it saves us money. By developing products that are as safe as possible for people and the environment, we improve our market share. Of course, we're making tough decisions all the time that weight the human positives of our products against their potential environmental impact. We're always looking for cleaner, greener solutions. This is going to become increasingly important as customers become more sophisticated and demanding in this regard.

"But our actions aren't just about business. When my grandchildren first saw the big snapping turtle in the pond where I used to play and fish as a boy, they glowed with the same wonder and awe as I did. Without sustainable development, it's going to be a less satisfactory planet for my grandchildren to live in. For me, those are the stakes."

Percy Barnevik, president and CEO of ABB Asea Brown Boveri, is often cited as Europe's most respected corporate leader. He has always placed great emphasis on taking early action to anticipate long-term trends, whether this be investing in transitional economies or taking the environment seriously (see ABB case study in chapter 6).

"On the threshold of the twenty-first century, the earth is home to about 6 billion people striving to improve their quality of life. As our numbers continue to grow, there are few challenges as daunting as providing people in every part of the world with the tools they need to achieve their sustainable development goals.

"Energy—both human energy and the energy we tap from nature—drives development. Yet in many countries lack of electrical power hampers progress in agriculture, urban development, and industry. They need an abundant, affordable, and reliable power supply—but with as minimal environmental impact as possible.

"Achieving this balance is among our top corporate priorities. Our products and systems boost efficiency and reduce emissions, from the largest power plants to the smallest electrical relay, from transmission lines stretching across entire continents to mass transit systems running across town, from pulp and paper mills to steel plants. We want people to know that, when they choose ABB products and services, they get technological excellence aimed at delivering high performance with low environmental impact.

"ABB believes that the innovative powers of entrepreneurial business can provide eco-efficient solutions to many of the world's environmental challenges. We intend to play an important role in meeting those challenges—and in so doing to safeguard and develop our long-term prosperity."

Erling Lorentzen is chairman of Aracruz Celulose, a $2 billion turnover Brazilian producer of paper pulp which is setting world-class standards for sustainable production from natural resources. He also chaired a two year multi-stakeholder WBCSD study of the environmental impacts of the paper cycle, from forest to final disposal.

"Living and working in Latin America gives a different perspective on sustainable development from Europe or America. You realize that

poverty is one of the world's leading polluters. That's why development is essential for sustainability, because you can't expect people who
don't eat a proper meal to be concerned about the environment. However, this development has to be eco-efficient so that we preserve our
natural heritage and leapfrog some of the pollution problems experienced in the North.

"Our starting point is a good understanding of what our environmental impacts are. That's why we led the study on sustainable paper
cycles. We have to get the facts—whether good or bad—on the table to
elevate the debate to the highest level.

"Our study shows that paper can be sustainable—and that companies moving in this direction will get a competitive advantage. There'll
be fewer customers for the products of companies who aren't seen as
environmentally progressive. The discipline of eco-efficiency also
means that we're continually getting more productive in our use of
resources. And the pride our staff have in our policies means higher
morale and better performance from top to bottom of the organization."

*Tadahiro Sekimoto is chairman of the board of NEC Corporation. NEC estab-
lished an environmental department in 1970 and has a reputation as one of the
most environmentally progressive organizations in Japan.*

"We all know that environmental damage in one area may have grave
consequences for not only the people who live there but the whole world.
Such damage could even sow the seeds for the destruction of humanity.
We sincerely believe that the global environment is a legacy for the entire
human race. I have been trying to address this idea for the last ten years.

"Global environmental issues raise a contradiction between the
needs of humanity and the earth. When people start achieving economic development and prosperity, energy consumption increases.
This is a major cause of environmental deterioration, such as the greenhouse effect.

"If we approach the problem simply by protecting the earth's environment, we face the dilemma of having to sacrifice material wealth to
achieve spiritual wealth. To tackle environmental issues, we need to
understand how to overcome this dilemma. The basis for solving these
issues exists in reconciling economic activities with planet earth. Our
mission is to take up this challenge.

"Thus, we place our faith in human knowledge, and, in particular, the application of technology. We are committed to achieving sustainable development by providing environmentally conscious products, that is, pursuing eco-efficiency and contributing to society by fully utilizing our technological ability. We must tackle environmental problems with the belief that economic development and the global environment can coexist."

Stephan Schmidheiny is chairman of several holding companies involved globally in high technology, construction materials, retailing, marketing and services, real estate, housing, and forestry. He is the founder of the Business Council for Sustainable Development, a predecessor body to the World Business Council for Sustainable Development (WBCSD), and author of several books on business and sustainable development.

"Eco-efficiency is plainly and simply the 'business end' of sustainable development.

"I want my various companies to be efficient overall. If they add a great deal of value to goods and services while using small amounts of resources and producing little or no waste and pollution, then they are efficient from an ecological point of view. In societies that appropriately punish waste and pollution, they will also be efficient from an economic and financial point of view. They will be highly competitive.

"Thus business leaders concerned with the quality of the planet on which their children will live, and with the 'total quality' and competitiveness of their companies, have a two-pronged eco-efficiency agenda. They will make their own enterprises eco-efficient. They will also work with other entrepreneurs to improve market conditions and policies so that markets reflect environmental as well as economic realities—and thus reward the more eco-efficient firms."

Björn Stigson is executive director of the World Business Council for Sustainable Development, the leading advocate for business on sustainable development issues (see Introduction).

"The WBCSD has a special relationship to 'eco-efficiency' ever since Stephan Schmidheiny put this concept forward in his 1992 book *Changing Course*. It is both a management concept and a tool used by business—but not exclusively—to make measurable progress toward sustainability.

"Eco-efficiency catches at a glance the balance business strives toward: sound ecology and profitable operations. Quite simply, it is about doing more with less, and being environmentally responsible.

"As an evolving concept, it has shifted from 'resource productivity' to becoming a significant driver of innovation, underpinning the move from product to service, from individual to sectoral accountability, and even beyond to governments and consumers who start recognizing its value.

"I am grateful to Dow and 3M for bringing together collective thinking and experience on this subject. It is an important step forward, yet not the ultimate. With our members, we will continue to set forth thoughts on how the practice of eco-efficiency can be enhanced through both voluntary action and enlightened government policies and incentives. Why? Because it makes good business sense and it is the right thing to do."

John B. Maree, the chairman of Eskom, Africa's largest electrical utility, is one of southern Africa's most respected business leaders. For the past six years he has also stood firmly at the helm of the Industrial Environmental Forum of southern Africa signaling the commitment of corporate leaders to sound environmental management. John Maree acquired his love and understanding of the environment as a child on the great open plains of the Karoo, a harshly beautiful but fragile area deep in the heart of South Africa.

"Sustainable development is an imperative in South Africa as we reconstruct our new democracy. It is now widely accepted that the top national priority is to stimulate capital investment, growth, and job creation. Without that we will not achieve a politically stable and equitable society.

"We must address the hopes and aspirations of the less privileged members of our society in practical ways. The changes taking place in our country must be seen to result in positive changes in their everyday lives.

"However, development must take due consideration of the constraints of our rich but fragile environmental base. Only through eco-efficiency and the optimization of human, capital, and environmental resources will we be able to offer all our people and future generations the hope of a better quality of life.

"Eskom has striven to be a leading corporate citizen in all facets of its operations. It is committed to bringing electrical power to as many people as possible to stimulate development and education and to raise the potential quality of life. We have already made good progress toward ensuring that schools, clinics, and other vital services are connected to reliable energy sources. We have set ourselves challenging targets for the rapid electrification of homes, no matter how humble, and must ensure that electricity remains affordable.

"Eskom has also played a leadership role through the Industrial Environmental Forum in developing appropriate environmental management practices and promoting them throughout the southern African business community."

Ed Falkman is chairman of Waste Management International plc, a part of WMX Technologies, the world's leading environmental services organization. The company operates in twenty countries worldwide providing a range of environmental services to millions of municipal, commercial, and industrial customers. Ed chairs the Environment Commission of the International Chamber of Commerce and the WBCSD Working Group on Sustainable Production and Consumption.

"For almost twenty years I have focused on providing services that have improved the quality of life, health, and the environment for people in countries across the globe. Having spent extensive time in Africa, the Middle East, and South America during my youth, I learned early on that throwing money at environmental problems alone is not likely to solve them. Leadership is fundamental, particularly in leveraging existing resources—human or otherwise—to achieve environmental improvements. The selection of cost effective technological solutions is also key to meeting the aspirations and needs of industry and communities. I see our role at WMI as helping leaders to organize their resources and select appropriate technology in order to deliver high quality, efficient, and affordable environmental services that make a real contribution to the goals of sustainable development.

"I can also give testimony to the fact that our customers are embracing the concepts of eco-efficiency in the way they do business. We see less waste being generated, more wastes being reused or recycled, and greater emphasis on the conservation of energy and natural resources. This is creating new dynamics in the marketplace, which I believe will transform the way my company operates in the future. I am convinced as I look forward to the next twenty years that our destiny is to become more of a resource and materials management company."

Acknowledgments

Although for practical reasons our names appear as the authors of this book, much of the credit for its content belongs to others. Its origins lie in the World Business Council for Sustainable Development's working group on eco-efficiency, which we had the good fortune to chair. The group's mission was to transform into action what was then a vision, eco-efficiency, by providing examples of how it had improved the economic and environmental performance of companies. As part of its activities, it convened two expert meetings in Europe (Antwerp 1 in November 1993 and Antwerp 2 in March 1995) and one in the United States (Washington, D.C., in November 1995). A list of all the participants at these meetings, and of working group members, is located at the end of the book.

We are especially grateful to Allen H. Aspengren, eco-efficiency manager of 3M, and Peter James, director of the Sustainable Business Centre, for their inputs to the preparation of this text, and to the anonymous reviewers of MIT Press for their comments on early drafts. Thanks are also due to the members of the WBCSD editorial steering group, consisting of Paul Adams, Frank Bosshardt, Claude Fussler, Jan-Olaf Willums, and Ben Woodhouse, and all those like Peter Hindle, Jane Hutterley, Ross Stevens, Clement Malin, and Judith Mullins who read drafts of the manuscript and submitted some of the best-practice examples reproduced in the text. We have also cited a number of company examples from various publications of the UNEP Industry and Environment Programme, which provides invaluable assistance on cleaner technology to many companies around the world, and from *Tomorrow* magazine, which has a close working relationship to the WBCSD. In addition, we would like to acknowledge the valuable contribution made by the WBCSD Working Group on Sustainable Production and Consumption (SP&C), chaired by Ed Falkman, chairman of Waste Management International. Some of the ideas, concepts, and case studies referenced throughout the text are drawn from their publication "Sustainable Production and Consumption: A Business Perspective" (Geneva: WBCSD, 1996). A list of the SP&C Working Group is located at the end of the book. Finally, the WBCSD Secretariat has provided direction and administrative support during the many years in which this project has been under development.

Given that this book is the product of a collective effort and draws upon many published sources, it has been difficult to check every detail within it. But we hope that we have avoided any errors of fact or unsubstantiated assertions. We also hope that we have reflected the views of the members of the WBCSD and other environmentally proactive companies—although ultimately we are solely responsible for all opinions expressed in the following pages.

Introduction

In 1992 business received a wake-up call. The Rio Earth Summit high-lighted the potential risks to ecology and long-term economic and social development created by current patterns of industrialization, population growth, and social inequality. The message to companies doing nothing was the need for urgent action. The message to companies already taking the environment seriously was to do more—and to pay greater attention to the issue of sustainable development.

Those issues were set out in a blueprint—called Agenda 21—signed by over 150 heads of state and government. Agenda 21 stresses the need for fundamental political, social, economic, and industrial change in order to conserve natural and biological resources, limit pollution, and build strong and prosperous communities in all parts of the world.

The business inputs to Rio were summarized in two influential books. One, *Changing Course,* was a product of the Business Council for Sustainable Development.[1] The other, *From Ideas to Action,* was associated with the International Chamber of Commerce.[2] The books set out the views of progressive business leaders who recognized the challenge of sustainable development and were—as a number of case studies showed—already beginning to integrate it into their business strategies. *Changing Course* also coined a term—eco-efficiency—to describe activities that create economic value while continuously reducing ecological impact and the use of resources.

Since then, business—and its new representative body for environmental and sustainability issues, the World Business Council for Sustainable Development (WBCSD—see appendix)—has done a great deal to develop the principles and practices of eco-efficiency. It has also responded to a changing business and social climate. Corporations today are publicly accountable. People don't just complain if they do not like what business is doing: they stop buying, sue, and lobby for new laws. Industry—and its business customers—operates under constant scrutiny. This is an uncomfortable development, but it is positive because it encourages corporations to think strategically about the needs of society.

As so much has happened in the half decade since Rio it is time to take stock of where eco-efficiency is now and what the companies that are implementing it have learned. The overall message from doing this is that eco-efficiency works and builds value for customers and stakeholders. The secret is moving away from a compliance-focused, crisis-avoidance mentality and seeing good environmental and social performance as the essential foundation for the market and public reputation and the motivated and confident staff that creates success in today's business environment.

Chapter 1 develops this point and shows the environmental and business logic for change. It also demonstrates that eco-efficiency has much in common with other business ideas.

Chapter 2 shows how the issues of sustainable development already impinge on the business bottom line and influence competitive advantage. Taking them seriously can create such tangible benefits as enhanced resource productivity, reduced liability risks, preferential and/or cheaper access to capital, insurance and other resources, and new product and business opportunities.

Chapter 3 spells out in detail just what eco-efficiency is and describes guidelines for practical action.

Chapter 4 shows how companies can organize for and implement eco-efficiency. Many elements are involved, but underlying all of them is the importance of people. It is their ideas and commitment that make eco-efficiency happen in the real world.

Chapter 5 addresses the critical issue of partnership—with other companies, business associations, communities, regulators and environmental groups, and other nongovernmental organizations (NGOs)—as an essential prerequisite for achieving eco-efficiency.

Chapter 6 provides case studies of progress toward eco-efficiency in Colombia and at ABB, Andersen, Dow, EBARA, S.C. Johnson, Kvaerner,

Ontario Hydro, Philips, Roche, Statoil, Swiss Bank, and 3M. (Shorter case studies of other WBCSD members are found throughout the book).

The final chapter concludes that business can and will play a leadership role in achieving sustainable production and consumption. At the same time, governments and others can advance sustainable development by changing the "framework conditions" within which business operates—such as regulatory and tax regimes—to make them more conducive to eco-efficiency.

Of course, changing framework conditions does not mean "get the regulator off our backs"—we recognize that regulation has improved environmental conditions and will always be necessary to achieve baseline standards and control free riders. But, as we show, there is evidence that command and control regulatory approaches can hamper—and conversely that more flexible regulatory approaches can encourage—the innovation and proactive actions we need.

What we ask of governments and other stakeholders is no more than we ask of ourselves and our fellow business leaders. Recognize that sustainable development is the big issue of our time and that all of us—business included—must do much more to be sustainable. Recognize too that the journey toward it—and the full implementation of an eco-efficient business strategy—will take decades and require a great deal of learning and adaptation. In that spirit, we offer this book as work in progress in responding to Rio's wake-up call. We know that the concept of eco-efficiency needs further refinement. The process of developing this book, for example, has made us aware that we need more and better eco-efficiency metrics. But industry has done enough to show that eco-efficiency can deliver environmental, social, *and* business benefits and is a practical route toward sustainable development. The companies we are associated with—and fellow members of WBCSD—are committed to continue their journey along this route. We hope that this book provides them with encouragement and arguments to go further, faster. We hope too that it will persuade those who are not yet traveling to join us, and provide a useful map to guide them. Both of these actions are necessary if we are to create a better planet through better business.

Appendix—The World Business Council for Sustainable Development

The World Business Council for Sustainable Development (WBCSD) is a global organization that has been established to encourage these initiatives and further develop policy proposals and best practices including the concept of eco-efficiency. The Council has two broad aims. One is to develop closer cooperation among business, government, and all other organizations concerned with the environment and sustainable development. The other is to encourage high standards of environmental management in business itself. Its specific objectives are:

Business leadership—to be business's leading advocate on issues connected with the environment and sustainable development

Policy development—to participate in policy development to create a framework that allows business to contribute effectively to sustainable development

Best practice—to demonstrate progress in environmental and resource management in business and share leading-edge practices with members

Global outreach—to contribute to a sustainable future for developing nations and nations in transition.

The Council builds on the work of two predecessors, which merged in January 1995. One was the Business Council for Sustainable Development (BCSD) in Geneva, set up by Swiss industrialist Stephan Schmidheiny in response to a UN request for business inputs to Rio. The other was the Paris-based World Industry Council for the Environment (WICE), a post-Rio initiative of the International Chamber of Commerce (ICC) to provide business inputs to the implementation of Agenda 21.

The WBCSD now has over 120 individual members—drawn from 34 countries and more than 20 major industrial sectors—who are united by a shared commitment to the environment and to the principles of economic growth and sustainable development. The council also benefits from a thriving network of national and regional business councils and partner organizations in all continents. This incorporates 600 other companies, many in developing countries and those in transition from a former communist rule to market economies. Chapter 5 provides some examples of their work. The geographical and sectoral diversity of this grouping is a source of considerable strength to the WBCSD, and it allows the organization to speak for business with a credible voice on sustainable development matters.

The WBCSD also has two distinctive features—proactivity and CEO leadership. All members share a triple responsibility: to participate in the work program; to advocate publicly the sustainable development message; and, perhaps most important, to lead by example in the field of environmental protection. They are all committed to taking action now and in the future to make their own activities more sustainable.

This commitment is reinforced by WBCSD's CEO-based leadership. Its council comprises the chief executives of its member companies. Their support is vital in three ways. First, each WBCSD work group is led by one or more CEOs, which means that their wide business experience and personal authority can be brought to bear on the project's many, and sometimes divergent, threads. Second, as prominent members of the business community, they can act as advocates for the policy positions developed by the WBCSD. And third, they are able to enlist support from within their own organization, both for the WBCSD's work program itself and, more generally, for the adoption of sustainable environmental management practices by their companies.

This book draws heavily upon the publications and other outputs that have emerged from these processes. The box provides a summary of some of them.

Major WBCSD Projects

Policy Development and Business Leadership
Work in the policy development field aims to secure a political and regu-latory framework that allows business to operate profitably while safe-guarding the environment and contributing to a sustainable future.

Agenda 21 called for moves toward Sustainable Production and Con-sumption. In the follow-up deliberations among governments WBCSD was invited to formulate and forward the views of industry. It created a working group, chaired by Edwin G. Falkman, chairman of Waste Man-agement International. The group's report "Sustainable Production and Consumption" was published in 1996.[3] The report outlines criteria to be considered in the evaluation of legislative or regulatory initiatives. It underlines also that producing and consuming sustainably is a long-term venture and one that must be tackled through partnerships between var-ious stakeholders.

Parallel working groups of the WBCSD have explored other aspects of a sustainable industry sector:

The Working Group on Trade and Environment, chaired by Ludolf Plass of Lurgi and Keith Erlam of Rio Tinto Corporation, has looked into the interaction between environmental agreements and the open trading system.[4]

The Working Group on the Sustainable Paper Cycle, chaired by Erling Lorentzen of Aracruz, commissioned an international research team to consider the full life cycle of paper production and consumption, from forestry to final disposal. The WBCSD report "Towards a Sustainable Paper Cycle" was published in 1996 by the International Institute for Environment and Development (IIED).[5]

The Working Group on Environmental Shareholder Value, chaired by J. A. Blumberg (DuPont), Georg Blum (Swiss Bank Corp.), and A. Korsvold (UNI), identified the links between eco-efficiency and the eval-uation of a company's financial performance and long-term economic prospects, resulting in a WBCSD guide called "Environmental Perfor-mance and the Bottom Line: A New Competitive Advantage?"[6] Their work built on a previous study of the relationship between environment and capital markets.[7]

The Working Group on Eco-efficiency in the Electronics Industry, chaired by Sumio Sano of Sony, tries to take eco-efficiency one step further and evaluates its long-term impact on an industry as a whole.

A joint publication with the United Nations Environmental Programme (UNEP) also showed how two closely related concepts, eco-efficiency and cleaner production, can help in achieving sustainable production and consumption.[8]

Best Practice

WBCSD provides a forum for members to share their expertise and experience with others and in turn learn from them. The council's work groups consolidate and build on these interactions to develop short, best-practice guides for the wider business community—for example, on eco-efficient leadership and environmental assessment.[9]

Global Outreach

WBCSD has a strong network of regional and national business councils in all continents (see chapter 5). Several initiatives also encourage transfer of know-how, technology, and capital between countries. One brings together WBCSD; the European chemical association, CEFIC; Green Cross International; and UNEP to transfer experience on preventing and controlling chemical accidents to eastern Europe. Another involves WBCSD members and several Scandinavian governments in a $10 million educational initiative to inform future Russian business leaders about sustainable development and its business implications. A third involves WBCSD helping developed country members to partner with companies in developing countries to find joint projects that can reduce the global emissions of so-called greenhouse gases. These projects can become part of the joint implementation schemes being elaborated under the UN Convention on Climate Change. WBCSD also has a web site (www.wbcsd.ch).

1   Eco-efficiency and
Sustainable Development

In 1990 DuPont's then CEO, Edgar Woolard, anticipated many of the themes of this book when he said:

The green economies and lifestyles of the twenty-first century may be conceptualized by environmental thinkers, but they can only be actualized by industrial corporations. Industry has a next-century vision of integrated environmental performance. Not every company is there yet, but most are trying. Those that aren't trying won't be a problem long-term, simply because they won't be around long-term. That is the new competitive reality.[1]

Since then, many companies have developed and begun to implement this next-century vision. And, as the following chapters show, they have had considerable success. Emissions and wastes have been reduced, recycling has become common and many hazardous materials have been eliminated from products and processes. Source reduction approaches such as pollution prevention and design for environment are increasingly preferred to "end-of-pipe" methods that are expensive and simply transfer pollution from one medium to another.

These source reduction measures have contributed to real environmental improvements at the local level, such as cleaner air and water, in many parts of the world. Global problems have also been addressed. Industry has cooperated with policy makers and NGOs to first develop a global treaty (the Montreal Protocol) to phase out chlorofluorocarbons (CFCs) and then taken action to remove them from products and processes. This has been a significant technical challenge, both for the companies who had to develop alternative products and those who have had to change their equipment and products to use substitutes. But the environmental and health benefits should be seen in the next century as stratospheric ozone levels—which are lowered by CFCs—are expected to slowly return toward their normal level.

More and more companies—around the world and in a variety of industries—are also discovering opportunities to achieve environmental improvement and gain business benefit. Their efforts—as the following chapters show—are driving the new competitive reality, whether this be through sustained pollution prevention programs that create cost advantage or new products that create enhanced customer value and reduced environmental impact.

Minnesota Mining & Manufacturing Co. (3M), for example, began running its 3P (pollution prevention pays) program in 1975. Its aim is to prevent pollution at the source. The program alone has generated over $750 million in first-year savings over the last two decades. More important, however, is the quantity of pollution prevented:

Air pollutants	234,000 tons
Water pollutants	31,000 tons
Wastewater	3.7 billion gallons
Sludge and solid waste	474,000 tons.

This means less pollution per product or dollar of turnover. Energy consumption has also been cut by 58% per unit of product since 1973. Since the program began, 3M has continued to raise its environmental performance goals. The target for the year 2000 is to reduce process emissions by 90% and waste by 50% from the 1990 figures. It has also won new markets with products such as Never Rust soap pads. These are made from, and are packaged in, recycled materials and are more durable than competitive pads. Such attributes are key elements of sustainable products.

3M, Dow, and many other companies now use a new concept to describe and guide their activities. Called "eco-efficiency," it has been developed by business for business. The first word of the concept encompasses both *eco*logical and *eco*nomic resources—the second says we have to make optimal use of both. One important aspect of eco-efficiency in practice is resource productivity—doing more with less. Reducing waste and pollution, and using fewer energy and raw material resources, is obviously good for the environment. And making better use of inputs translates into bottom-line benefits. These benefits potentially will increase as governments implement plans to change market frameworks in order to make resources and pollution more expensive.

Eco-efficiency focuses as well on creating additional value by better meeting customer's needs while maintaining or reducing environmental impacts. And its implementation draws on the insights of other business and environmental approaches such as total quality management and pollution prevention.

The following chapters show that eco-efficiency is as valid for small businesses and developing countries as it is for large multinationals. Its essence, as chapter 3 explains, is contained in seven simple guidelines:

- Reduce the material intensity of goods and services.
- Reduce the energy intensity of goods and services.
- Reduce toxic dispersion.
- Enhance material recyclability.
- Maximize sustainable use of renewable resources.
- Extend product durability.
- Increase the service intensity of products.

Following these guidelines can give companies a competitive head start into the next century—but not if they are treated as an add-on to "business as usual." As chapter 4 shows, eco-efficiency does require a profound change in the theory and practice of core business activities such as procurement, production, product development, and marketing.

The Challenge of Unsustainable Development

Eco-efficiency has to be more than business as usual because there are still many challenges to be overcome to achieve sustainable development. *Sustainable development* has been defined by the Brundtland Commission as "development which meets the needs of the present without jeopardizing the needs of future generations."[2] This means economic growth that does not deplete irreplaceable resources, does not destroy ecological systems, and helps reduce some of the world's gross social inequalities. For all the progress we have made, we are still a long way from those goals. We still consume vast quantities of nonrenewable resources. Many environmental situations are at best stabilized and at

worst intensifying. Between a fifth and a quarter of the world's population live in poverty, without adequate food, clothing, and shelter.[3]
Ninety percent of these people are in developing countries. All of us—
including business—need to do even more to solve these problems.

Some examples of serious environmental problems are deforestation,
destruction of coral reefs, introduction of aggressive new predators,
and other human activities that are making many species extinct—as
many as seventy a day according to some estimates.[4] The paleontologist
Richard Leakey claims that this rate makes our time the sixth period of
"mass extinction" in the earth's history—comparable to that of the Cre-
taceous period when dinosaurs became extinct.[5] The same factors are
also reducing biodiversity by reducing the prevalence of many species.
As a result we may be losing potential sources of drugs, useful plant
genes, and other resources.

Marine ecosystems are already damaged. According to the UN's
Food and Agricultural Organization (FAO), more than two thirds of the
world's fish stocks are being fished at or beyond their level of maximum productivity.[6] The world's marine fish catch has been in decline
since 1990. With population growth, the result is a 10% fall in per capita
availability of fish protein—a vital part of the diet for billions of people.
The precise causes of declining fish stocks are unclear but overfishing is
clearly a major cause. Pollution and habitat destruction—for example,
of the mangrove swamps where many tropical fish lay their eggs—also
contribute.

These losses of biodiversity can be reduced by following such tenets
of eco-efficiency as recycling, maximizing use of sustainably produced
renewable materials, and reducing material intensity and increasing
durability—all of which mean that less resource destruction is necessary.

Human activity may also be affecting our climate through the
"greenhouse effect." This is the trapping of heat that would otherwise
be radiated to space as a result of rising concentrations of carbon dioxide, methane, and other gases in the atmosphere. The Intergovernmental Panel on Climate Change (IPCC) comprises independent scientists
with the task of assessing evidence as to the likelihood of climate
change. Their 1996 report concluded that "the balance of evidence suggests a discernible influence on global climate through emissions of
carbon dioxide and other greenhouse gases."[7] However, there are still
many disagreements among reputable scientists about key questions,

including the climatic significance of this influence, which is still highly debatable.

Eco-efficiency may help solve any problems created by global warming by emphasizing the need for more efficient use of energy and maximizing use of renewable resources—for example, by substituting solar energy for fossil fuels. It also reduces the need for more drastic—and potentially very costly—measures, at least until firmer evidence is available about the existence and implications of global warming.

Urban air quality, while improving in many areas, is still not good— and may be damaging to health—in a number of cities.[8] In many northern cities quality improved as clean air legislation in the 1960s and 1970s cut levels of smoke, sulfur dioxide, and carbon monoxide. But emissions of nitrogen oxides and volatile organic compounds (VOCs)— after atmospheric reactions—can create disturbing levels of ozone. Many cities in developing countries and transitional economies are experiencing the problems of ozone without yet having resolved first generation air pollution problems such as those of sulfur dioxide. In the Polish city of Katowice, for example, life expectancy is a year below the national average—a difference that is caused at least partially by air pollution and other environmental problems.[9]

Eco-efficiency can help here by improving energy efficiency (so that fewer pollutants are created per unit of fuel or material used) and by reducing the generation and dispersion of toxic substances.

As the problems of urban air quality demonstrate, the pressing environmental concerns for many developing countries are basic ones such as provision of clean water and adequate sewage disposal as well as improvement of choking air—the so-called brown agenda.[10] In 1994, at least 220 million people still had no source of potable water near their homes—and many more used supplies that would not be acceptable in developed countries. More than 440 million urban dwellers lack access to even a simple latrine—and only 8% of low-income families in developing countries have a house-sewer connection.

While business alone can not solve these deep-seated social problems, eco-efficiency is a practical approach to helping to resolve them. The service intensity guideline focuses on unmet or poorly serviced needs that can be provided in ways that both create business and customer value *and* reduce environmental impact. No needs are more unmet or poorly serviced than those of the world's poor. And, as they are often the worst affected by pollution or energy-inefficient equipment, the other six guidelines are also highly relevant to them.

Running to Stand Still

Two major causes of these continuing challenges are economic growth—of a kind that remains energy- and materials-intensive—and rising numbers of people on the planet. The rate of population growth is declining, but absolute numbers are likely to increase for many decades. It seems equally likely that most people will want higher living standards for the foreseeable future. Economic development, which leads to higher incomes and an improved standard of living, is absolutely essential to relieve the most basic environmental problems for the world's poor—such as providing safe drinking water, controlling sewage, and limiting emissions from primitive wood heating and cooking stoves. However, this economic development needs to be conducted in a manner that reflects the learning gained over the past century in the industrial world. Toxic pollution must be controlled in ways that comprehend essential economic growth and resources must be used wisely in ways that support both economic and environmental performance. The Factor 10 Club, a group of leading international figures in environment and development, have argued, for example, that a process of dematerialization requiring *a tenfold increase* in the average resource productivity of the industrialized countries is essential in the long term.[11] An interim target for the short–medium term is a "factor four" improvement.

Economic and population growth create rising demand for goods and services that, today, are often polluting. This rising demand frequently outweighs any improvements in their environmental performance. As societies, we are often running just to stand still. Hence, we need further improvement in all the dimensions of eco-efficiency. It is important to keep reducing energy and materials, and to recycle end-of-life products when environmentally and economically feasible. To provide the necessary technology breakthroughs to achieve progress in these areas, finite technical and economic resources must be used wisely. Improved coordination of industry and government research and development programs directed at environmental goals can help. Improved coordination of public policies can also contribute to enhanced eco-efficiency by recognizing that balance is needed, and by providing flexibility between policies addressing varying environmental goals.

Public Attitudes

But why should most businesses consider these kinds of subjects? Surely they have enough to worry about? One reason is high and continuing levels of public—and therefore employee and customer—concern about them around the world. Of course, environment and sustainable development jostle for attention in people's minds with jobs, crime, and other issues. Sometimes one is on top of their list of priorities and sometimes another. However, all the evidence is that most of the public consistently place high value on key aspects of sustainable development such as clean air and water and the preservation of their natural heritage for future generations. Not at the expense of economic development but as well as economic development. In short, they want eco-efficiency. Three very different countries—the United States, Mexico, and South Korea—illustrate the point.

In 1996 the household and institutional consumer products company S.C. Johnson & Son, Inc., published the latest in a series of opinion surveys of American attitudes to environment carried out by the pollster Roper Starch.[12] The survey finds that a great majority reject "tradeoffs" between different social needs, with two thirds (66%) saying that economic development, environmental protection, and the health and happiness of people can go hand in hand.

Roper Starch finds "considerable cause for optimism" for sustainable development from the survey. It identifies a sizable group—around 23% of the respondents, or the equivalent of 45 million adult Americans—of "New Dreamers" who not only endorse the key goals of sustainability but also take an active role in their communities and personal lives to achieve them. Interestingly, they cross conventional political boundaries—indeed, the survey finds that many are conservative, middle-aged, and relatively wealthy men or women from the Midwest.

An earlier, 1993, survey by S.C. Johnson and Roper Starch, examined environmental attitudes in Canada, Mexico, and the United States.[13] It found that "pollution of air and water is the most pressing issue for the

Mexican people today, with an impressive 56% majority calling it one of their top personal concerns—far higher than the 38% of Canadians or 16% of Americans worried about pollution." A large majority of Mexicans also believed that economic growth should not occur at the expense of environmental protection. Although the country's current economic difficulties might lead to different results if the survey were repeated now, the results show that, as citizens and consumers, Mexicans will be appreciative of eco-efficiency.

A recent survey by the Korea Environmental Technology Institute also found that 85% of the South Koreans it polled said that environmental protection is as or more important than economic development.[14]

A Competitive Issue

These issues and trends are already affecting many businesses. Environmental performance is increasingly a determinant of a company's reputation, among employees, customers, and stakeholders alike. A poor environmental reputation can harm recruitment, retention, and morale, damage sales, and threaten a company's "license to operate." Good performance can have the opposite effect. And the visibility of both is increasing as legislation, stakeholder, and peer pressures require more and more external reporting on the topic and media coverage becomes ever more global and instantaneous.

Companies with an eye on long-term markets and profits also know how important it is to build a good reputation with, and understanding of, today's children and young people. Those intent on a global presence know too that the majority of tomorrow's consumers will be in developing countries, and that they will have growing influence on the design and marketing of many products. As a *Financial Times* survey of international youth points out:

With currencies, commodities, capital and a variety of consumer and industrial products flowing freely around the world, corporations are becoming increasingly aware that they have a stake in the economic health and development of all the societies where they do business. . . .

The reasons are simple. For any global company, the 1.5 billion children that will be born in this decade—four-fifths of them in developing countries—represent the markets, creativity and labour force of the future.[15]

With its emphasis on the things that today's children will want as adults —affordable products and services that create customer value *and* minimize environmental impact—eco-efficiency will be an important element in aligning any business with long-term social needs.

As chapter 2 discusses, environment is also an important bottom line issue for many companies and will become so for more. Pollution control equipment can account for up to 20% of the cost of capital projects while the full costs of waste can sometimes be as much as 5% to 10% of sales.[16] For some companies these are a continuing drain on resources. But their eco-efficient competitors see them as an opportunity to prevent the pollution at source and thereby reduce costs *and* environmental impact.

Many businesses, especially in the United States, are well aware of environmental liabilities generated by past contamination of land or accidents. Recent court settlements mean that Exxon's out-of-pocket expenses as a result of the *Exxon Valdez* oil spill are approaching $10 billion (although it is appealing some court judgments). And the costs of cleaning up contaminated land in the United States will be many billions of dollars, even if a more flexible regulatory approach is introduced. What is less well understood is that today's actions in other areas might be judged ultimately against the standards of tomorrow and thereby generate large future liabilities.

If companies respond to these pressures only when forced to do so, they will miss important opportunities to gain the competitive advantage that accrues to early movers. Introducing new technology ahead of regulatory requirements can avoid delays and higher costs later. Similarly, firms that give priority to resource productivity, process change, and product innovation will achieve significant performance gains at lower cost. And there will also be huge new business opportunities from meeting the continuing need for added-value products and services.

What Is Special about Eco-efficiency?

Of course, many environmental concepts and initiatives emphasize the importance of resource productivity or doing more with less. It is central, for example, to the United Nations Environmental Programme's concept of cleaner production.[17] There are also many proven approaches

to achieving it, such as design for environment (DFE), pollution prevention, and product stewardship.

While eco-efficiency draws upon and has much in common with
these and other approaches it has several distinctive features. These can
be summarized as: an emphasis on value creation; an emphasis on
stretching, long-term, targets for improvement; linking environmental
excellence to business excellence; and considering sustainable consumption as well as sustainable production.[18]

Value Creation

Eco-efficiency harnesses the business concept of creating value and links
it with environmental concerns. The goal is to create value for society,
and for the company, by doing more with less over the entire life cycle,
that is, from creation of raw materials to disposal of products at the end
of their life. The idea is captured in Procter & Gamble's statement: "Our
goal is to provide more consumer performance and value with the use
of less resources, including energy, and the creation of less waste."

By promoting change toward *sustainable* growth, eco-efficiency enables
a company's business to grow in a qualitative way (by adding value),
while reducing adverse effects on the earth. It also signals a significant
shift in focus to concentrate on real customer needs.

This emphasis on creating and adding value is clearly to society's
benefit. Further, it's often in line with the changing dynamics of the
marketplace. Consumers everywhere want higher performance and
increased value, at lower cost.

Setting—and Meeting—Stretch Targets

Eco-efficiency asks companies to consider long-term trends and make
ambitious long-term commitments in response. One way of making this
concrete is by emulating the quality concept of "zero defects." Although
this was often not a practical target, it provided a concrete goal that
created a constant dissatisfaction with the present. Over time, that dissatisfaction resulted in more and more improvements that were previously thought impossible.

The environmental equivalent of zero defects is zero emissions of hazardous or potentially hazardous substances from a facility or product. Although strictly speaking this is impossible—the laws of thermodynamics state that there must be some wastes from every process—in practice it provides a clear sense of direction, so we use the term for the remainder of the book. Monsanto and 3M are two companies that have introduced zero emissions as a long-term aspiration—and introduced medium-term stretch targets to move a long way toward it. Xerox Corporation too has set the goal of waste-free products from waste-free factories and introduced clear targets for reducing solid wastes, air emissions, hazardous wastes, wastewater discharges, lower energy usage, and the inclusion of 25% postconsumer recycled materials in parts and packaging. And Dow has recently announced aggressive 10-year reduction goals for environmental performance and resource conservation.

Environmental Excellence Is Business Excellence

Eco-efficiency is a *management philosophy* that links environmental excellence to business excellence and is synergistic with general trends in leading edge businesses. For example:

• More and more companies are seeing shared values and a common sense of purpose among their staff as a key success factor. Making an environmental and social contribution can be an important element of these.

• Eco-efficiency has close affinities with total quality management—"zero defects," as we have seen can be translated into "zero emissions."

• Eco-efficiency's emphasis on collaboration with suppliers, customers, and stakeholder organizations provides a practical example of the strategic collaboration that many management theorists are now advocating (see below).

A Sense of Purpose

Almost all social forecasters agree that more and more people, especially in the developed world, are searching for meaning in their lives—something traditionally provided by established religion or traditional communities and families. For a growing number, helping to protect the environment for future generations is an important part of their "sense of purpose." This will drive their purchases—and favor the businesses whose own behavior and values resonates with their own.

More and more companies too are realizing that the best performance comes from staff or associates who share and commit to common values. 3M, for example, bases its success on consistent application of four key values:

• Satisfying customers with innovative products, superior quality, and value,
• Providing investors with an attractive return,
• Respecting the social and physical environment,
• Being a company employees are proud to be part of.

These values provide employees with a sense of business purpose, based on meeting the requirements of stakeholders *and* making a broader contribution to the communities and countries they operate in.

Eco-efficiency contributes to this sense of purpose by providing a transcendent goal—respecting nature and helping to create a fairer world—that is in harmony rather than in conflict with business objectives. This same combination of long-term purpose and practical focus on current requirements is also attuned to the needs of customers, who will increasingly want both rather than one or the other.

Of course, to be effective, the everyday manifestations of core values must stand up to the test of reality. If an organization professes and emphasizes sustainable business practices, it must conduct its business accordingly or risk a loss of credibility and stature with regard to all its values from internal and external constituencies alike. Eco-efficiency does not require organizations to be environmentally perfect—but it does require them to be honest about their achievements and aim for continuous improvement.

Total Quality Management

Eco-efficiency has many affinities with total quality management (TQM). We have previously discussed how the idea of zero defects can easily be converted into one of zero emissions—a concept that, although impossible to achieve in practice, can provide a clear sense of direction. An emphasis on pollution prevention is also an environmental application of the central total quality tenet of dealing with causes rather than symptoms of defects. Both approaches also place great emphasis on continuous improvement and the value of measurement and targeting as means of achieving this. Eco-efficiency's stress on the importance of stakeholders too can be seen as an application of the TQM view that every process has a customer whose needs must be satisfied. In this perspective, regulators, NGOs, and others are "customers" for a company's environmental management and innovation processes. Finally, both approaches place great emphasis on the importance of cross-functional collaboration. This can identify opportunities for improvement and build information and commitment for effective implementation.

There are many examples of the successful application of quality approaches to the environment.[19] Take, for example, Thomson Crown Wood Products, a small manufacturer of wood and wood-finished audio and television cabinets and storage units. The company employs about 700 people at its Mocksville, North Carolina, plant. In the early 1990s a number of teams within its overall quality initiative focused on environmental issues—and achieved considerable success.[20] As is often the case these teams had frivolous nicknames but serious intent.

• The "Hazardous Five" team analyzed the quantity and origin of liquid hazardous waste streams. They realized that the hazards were created by a relatively small amount of material that could be separated out. Doing this meant that 5.7 million liters of water a year was no longer contaminated and could be used for recycling. It also created annual savings of $100,000 a year at a cost of only $26,000.

• The "Millroom Madness" team made a small process change so that a piece of fiberboard cut out of a speaker panel could be used as a shelf for the same cabinet, saving $15,000 a year at no cost.

• The "OOC/Fineliners" team addressed and resolved the gluing problems that were resulting in about twenty-one finished end panels being sent to landfill. This saved around $250,000 a year.

• The "Mix-Ups" team researched coating guns and identified one that would meet its specifications and reduce waste. This reduced wastage of coatings by over 50,000 liters a year and had a two-month payback.

Strategic Collaboration

Total quality management has brought many benefits. But business academic Richard Schonberger believes that there are many more still to be achieved.[21] The barriers are continuing divides between internal functions and departments, and between companies and their suppliers and customers. He calls for much greater "strategic collaboration" within and between companies to reduce these barriers and achieve even better customer service.

Once again eco-efficiency is synergistic with this goal. It too seeks to reduce functional barriers by extending environmental initiatives into all areas of a company and to better integrate supply chains through life cycle management and design for environment. Indeed, as many examples in later chapters show, environment initiatives to achieve these ends often can be a vehicle for achieving the broader business benefits that Schonberger wants.

Sustainable Production and Consumption

Agenda 21—the blueprint for sustainable development that emerged from the 1992 Rio Earth Summit—states:

Achieving the goals of environmental quality and sustainable development will require efficiencies in production and changes in consumption patterns in order to emphasize optimization of resource use and minimization of wastes.

Dealing with the unresolved challenges of sustainability now means shifting the emphasis beyond sites to industrial systems and society as a whole. This involves a transition from the site-based approaches of pollution control, process integration, and whole facility (multimedia) planning. The emphasis is shifting to integrating environment throughout product chains—through ideas such as life cycle management and industrial ecology (in which one company's wastes are used as inputs by others)—and the development of sustainable communities, cities, and regions (see figure 1.1). This means environment is not just a challenge for producers but for consumers, too.

A recent report by the WBCSD argues that business can best respond to the challenges of sustainable production and consumption by:

Moving Toward Sustainable Solutions

- LESS ENERGY INTENSITY PER UNIT OF PRODUCT OR SERVICE
- LOWER MATERIAL INTENSITY PER UNIT OF PRODUCT OR SERVICE
- LOWER LEVELS OF ENVIRONMENTAL TOXICITY AND RISK

| POLLUTION CONTROL | PROCESS INTEGRATION | WHOLE FACILITY PLANNING | INDUSTRIAL ECOLOGY | SUSTAINABLE COMMUNITIES/ CITIES/REGIONS |

TIME

Figure 1.1
The shift to more sustainable technologies will mean significantly reducing the amount of energy and materials we use in producing our goods and services while decreasing risks to humans and the environment.
Source: National Science and Technology Council, *Bridge to a Sustainable Future,* Washington D.C., 1995, p. 20.

- Taking account of the entire life cycle of goods and services—design and engineering, purchasing and materials management, production, marketing, distribution, use, and waste management
- Applying the principles of eco-efficiency to create increased value for customers through the sustainable use of resources
- In its role as consumer, procuring and requesting products and services that have less environmental impact

• Making accurate, scientifically sound environmental information available to customers and the public so that they can make informed decisions about purchasing, use, and disposal.[22]

The examples throughout this book illustrate the progress some members of the business community have already made in these areas. However, much work still lies ahead.

We recognize there is one key issue that is not fully addressed at this interim stage of our ongoing work on eco-efficiency, and that is the issue of consumer needs and its relation to consumption in the context of sustainable development. We do believe the widespread practice of eco-efficiency coupled with marketplace forces will make a significant contribution to the issue of consumption. We also are aware that some stakeholders will say it does not fully address the issue of what products we should make. As these discussions on consumption continue, it will be important for the business community to develop their ideas and positions on this subject by participating in the debate.

Framework Conditions

Eco-efficiency starts in the workplace, and it is up to business to maintain and strengthen its existing initiatives and begin new ones. However, these steps need to be matched by changes in the behavior and consumption patterns of individuals, households, and institutions. These players—and government in particular—also have a key role in accelerating this process by creating favorable "framework conditions."[23]

The existing framework conditions in which business operates do not, generally speaking, encourage the wiser use of resources, a shift from labor to resource productivity, or the search for new, innovative, and eco-efficient methods of production, products, or services. Indeed, some (e.g., agricultural and energy subsidies) encourage the misuse of resources, while others penalize eco-efficiency initiatives.

Environmental regulation is a case in point. It has achieved a great deal and is necessary to prevent environmental "free riders" who will not commit to voluntary improvements. But it has often carried an unnecessarily high price and given companies no incentives to move beyond compliance (see box and discussion in chapter 5).

The U.S. President's Council on Sustainable Development includes members from a wide spectrum of American society, including federal and state government, business, NGOs, unions, and minorities and was co-chaired by a business leader and an environmentalist. Its consensus view on traditional "command-and-control" regulation—which was endorsed by its environmentalist members as much as by others—was that

there is no doubt that some regulations have encouraged innovation and compliance with environmental laws, resulting in substantial improvements in the protection of public health and the environment. But at other times, regulation has imposed unnecessary—and sometimes costly—administrative and technological burdens and discouraged technological innovations that can reduce costs while achieving environmental benefits beyond those realized by compliance. Moreover, it has frequently focused attention on cleanup and control remedies rather than on product or process redesign to prevent pollution.[24]

There is a continuing need for environmental policies and regulations to establish minimum standards and to set broad performance-based targets. But we believe that tomorrow's policies and regulations can be more inspiring and less prescriptive than those on the books today. Their key characteristics include:

• Addressing environmental issues that have been defined and given priority by a broad base of society

• Encouraging solutions that are effective in dealing with environmental issues but do so in the most economical means possible

• Maximizing freedom of choice for business and consumers to determine the best ways to reduce pollution and environmental impact

• Maximizing economic benefit to companies that exceed baseline requirements

Chapter 5 discusses regulatory innovations, such as the U.S. Environmental Protection Agency's Common Sense initiative or the Dutch covenants between government and industry sectors, which may support the achievement of these goals.

Changes in other areas of government policy, such as taxation and trade, would foster additional movement toward eco-efficiency in business (see chapter 7).

If these changes occur, then companies who are not responding to the challenge of sustainable development may face an increasing competitive disadvantage and suffer where it hurts them most—on the bottom line. The next chapter shows just how this can happen.

The Case for Regulatory Reform

The general construction of command- and control-type regulatory programs relies heavily on standardization of technologies and practices to achieve environmental improvements. While in some instances standardization can be a valuable tool, in a prescriptive regulatory template it can also require the use of technologies or practices that:

do not fit the application well

are less eco-efficient in the long run because other innovative options can achieve comparable overall results with less resources and energy

once installed, are unlikely to be improved upon because of the initial high investment.

The following paragraphs elaborate on these points. We focus on the United States—both because there is an extensive debate and because our companies and their staff have been involved in practical reform initiatives in partnership with regulators, communities, and others—but believe that the points have relevance to other countries.

To control air and water emissions, the U.S. federal and state regulatory systems often require the installation of "best available control technology" (BACT) or maximum available control technology (MACT) at the end of process or waste management equipment. In some cases this is interpreted to require the installation of specific equipment, irrespective of whether other options are available or the pollutant of concern has already been significantly reduced using process change. This can result in an extremely high cost on a dollars per ton removed basis. In other situations these regulations are applied on a source specific basis even when a greater reduction could be achieved by controlling other sources at the facility.

From a pollution prevention perspective, prescriptive command and control approaches impose strict statutory or regulatory compliance deadlines that, if exceeded, can result in significant penalties against the company. This creates the situation where the company must install the off-the-shelf pollution control device because there is insufficient time to conduct the work needed to determine how to eliminate the pollution at its source. Thus, the most preferable option is never evaluated at all, or not until after significant dollars have been spent on end-of-pipe solutions.

Some more specific difficulties were also identified by the task force that undertook a case study of the automobile industry for the U.S. President's Council on Sustainable Development.[25] Their conclusions—

which have special weight because the team contained representatives of the Environment Protection Agency (EPA) as well as auto manufacturers—identified the following potential regulatory barriers to continued environmental improvement:

Delays and uncertainties in receiving federal agency approval for permit applications, State Implementation Plan (SIP) revisions under the Clean Air Act (CAA), and delisting of hazardous waste under the Resource Conservation and Recovery Act (RCRA) may discourage technological innovation and hinder industry's ability to respond quickly to market changes.

There is currently a lack of clarity over state authority to implement regulatory programs versus oversight responsibilities of EPA. This can result in inconsistencies in regulatory interpretation and time lags in both state submittal of permit or SIP modifications and federal approval of these submissions. Existing reporting requirements are complex and time consuming and may require collection of redundant information. The information assembled is often not as effective as it could be at identifying pollution opportunities. The information assembled is often oriented toward controlling pollution, not prevention. The information obtained does not easily lend itself to providing the public with meaningful opportunities to participate in environmental decision making.

The method to determine whether manufacturing process changes cause significant emission increases is often rigid. This rigidity is most apparent for cyclical industries complying with the New Source Review requirements under the Clean Air Act.

Required disclosure of environmental audits may discourage preventive measures. Federal and state policies on disclosure of the contents of environmental audits are ambiguous and may discourage companies from undertaking self-audits. Failure to undertake self-audits hinders early detection of environmental problems and identification of pollution prevention opportunities.

The Council developed a detailed model of an Alternative Regulatory System for companies that exhibit environmental leadership potential with the aims of fostering continuous improvement in environmental protection as well as continuous improvement in the system of environmental regulation.

Their proposed system has ten main points (which we summarize as far as possible in their words):

Sustainability Vision—setting long-term goals to assure protection of human health and ecosystem integrity and achieve better environmental protection than would be achieved by full compliance with the standard regulatory system.

Continuous Improvement—removing disincentives to go beyond compliance such as inflexible regulatory timetables, tempered by at least annual checking of performance against key environmental parameters to ensure progress beyond compliance requirements.

Multimedia Approach—to foster whole facility pollution prevention.

Measuring and Reporting Progress—in ways that minimize the generation of redundant or useless information and helps emphasize pollution prevention opportunities (probably involving collection of material flows data as well as emissions).

Enforcement and Incentives to Perform—providing incentives to excel as well as deterrents if goals aren't met.

Public Participation—providing greater opportunities for constructive stakeholder involvement in areas such as long-term sustainability goal-setting, facility goal-setting, and review of progress toward goals.

Life-Cycle Perspective—developing regulatory approaches that go beyond individual companies or sites.

Flexibility and Incentives to Participate—avoiding the problems of the current system that sometimes unnecessarily dictates the means of protection rather than emphasizing achievement of the ends.

Eligibility to Participate—encouraging select companies to be pollution prevention leaders.

Implementation—pilot projects to develop the practical details of the system.

One such pilot initiative was that carried out at 3M's St. Paul plant.[26] Because of the nature of its processes, the plant emitted solvents. In the early 1990s the Minnesota Pollution Control Agency (MCPA) regulators were seeking to reduce these. At the same time 3M could see that, for business development reasons, it would be making a number of process changes that it did not want to be delayed by permitting procedures. Hence, it agreed to make deep cuts in solvent emissions—from around 10,000 tons a year to a maximum of 4,600 tons—in exchange for preauthorization from the MPCA for it to change specified processes within the plant. The result was environmental benefit from a rapid reduction in emissions and the ability to make the reductions in the most cost-effective manner for 3M.

Summary

Eco-efficiency is the business response to the challenge of sustainable development—that is, meeting "the needs of the present without jeopardizing the needs of future generations." It stresses:

- increasing resource productivity so that more is obtained from less energy and raw material input
- creating new goods and services that increase customer value while maintaining or reducing environmental impacts.

Economic development is the best response to this challenge—but we need a new kind of development that follows the seven guidelines of eco-efficiency:

- reduce the material intensity of goods and services
- reduce the energy intensity of goods and services
- reduce toxic dispersion
- enhance material recyclability
- maximize sustainable use of renewable resources
- extend product durability
- increase the service intensity of products.

Businesses that do this will create bottom line benefits from:

- creating new products and services that meet the aspirations of most of the world's consumers for prosperity and a clean and healthy environment.
- reducing the costs and liabilities associated with resource consumption, waste, and end of pipe pollution control (which are likely to rise as a result of environmental taxes and other measures).

Eco-efficiency is the most practical means of achieving these benefits because:

- it is a management philosophy that links with other business ideas such as total quality management and strategic collaboration
- it contributes to the sense of purpose and shared values that are central to achieving business excellence.

Eco-efficiency is already creating great benefit to business and society but there is more to be done if its full potential is to be unleashed:

- business needs to develop better ways of measuring eco-efficiency and pay greater attention to the issues of sustainable consumption

- governments and society can develop more incentives—and removing disincentives—for eco-efficient action
- capital markets can become more aware of the links between eco-efficiency and long-term shareholder value.

2   Eco-efficiency and the Bottom Line

Is eco-efficiency really possible? Can companies really find opportunities to make environmental improvements and create business benefits? Many managers do not think so. Nor do McKinsey consultants Noah Walley and Bradley Whitehead, who have written:

Questioning today's win-win rhetoric is akin to arguing against motherhood and apple pie. After all, the idea that environmental initiatives will systematically increase profitability has tremendous appeal. Unfortunately, this popular idea is also unrealistic. Responding to environmental challenges has always been a costly and complicated problem for managers. In fact, environmental costs at most companies are skyrocketing, with little economic payback in sight. . . . To achieve truly sustainable environmental solutions, managers must concentrate on finding smarter and finer tradeoffs between business and environmental concerns, acknowledging that, in almost all cases, it is impossible to get something for nothing.[1]

Of course, their point is true in many instances. However, eco-efficiency is a dynamic strategy that presupposes that social expectations of corporate environmental performance are constantly rising. This is often expressed as more stringent legislative or regulatory measures—or it can be satisfied by proactive business action. The former will inevitably raise costs—so that preventive measures now are real savings.

This is certainly the view of business strategist Michael Porter. His study—with German colleague Claas van der Linde—of environmental influences on business performance and innovation also suggests that external pressures can enhance resource productivity and innovation. They believe that companies

are constantly finding innovative solutions to pressures of all sorts—from competitors, customers, and regulators.

Properly designed environmental standards can trigger innovations that lower the total cost of a product or improve its value. Such innovations allow companies to use a range of inputs more productively—from raw materials to energy to labor—thus offsetting the costs of improving environmental impact and ending the stalemate. Ultimately, this enhanced resource productivity makes companies more competitive, not less.[2]

They point to the Dutch flower industry as an example. This industry faced stringent restrictions on the use of pesticides, herbicides, and fertilizers, which were contaminating soil and groundwater. The industry's innovation was to replace soil as the growing medium with water and rock wool. This allows the flowers to be grown in a sealed environment, with complete recycling of water and the unused chemicals it contains. Hence input requirements are reduced. The sealing also means less risk of infestation so that less pesticide is needed. In addition, the continuous monitoring of the system means more uniform and improved product quality while the design used has reduced handling costs. The result is more revenues from better-quality products and reduced operating costs.

Of course, many of these benefits can be achieved independently of regulation. They have been in the past and will be to an even greater extent in the future as more and more companies adopt an eco-efficient approach. As chapters 5 and 7 discuss, they have sometimes been offset by a number of unnecessary costs created by overly bureaucratic and inflexible ways of regulating. The innovations may have been greater if proper, or even no, regulation had been in place.

Financial Benefits of Eco-efficiency

The case for eco-efficiency can also be difficult to make because the financial benefits of environmental action are not always easy to demonstrate and calculate. They sometimes take years to materialize, often stem from intangible factors—such as an enhanced company image—and frequently take the form of avoided costs rather than actual cash flows. However, experience shows that the benefits are both real and significant—and will become even more so in coming years.

The following pages discuss five broad categories of benefit arising from eco-efficiency, with examples of companies that have enhanced their competitive position by exploiting them. The five categories are:

1. Benefits from reducing the current costs of poor environmental performance,

2. Benefits from reducing potential future costs of poor environmental performance,

3. Reduced costs of capital,

4. Benefits from increased market share and improved or protected market opportunities,

5. Benefits from enhanced image.

Reducing Current Environmental Costs

The U.S. Environmental Protection Agency (EPA) has produced a list of environmental costs that runs to more than seventy categories (see figure 2.1). Only a small proportion of these categories are what it calls "conventional costs"—the costs that are normally identified by accounting systems and usually (although not invariably) allocated to departments, processes, or products. This means that most potential environmental costs are "potentially hidden," and therefore do not impinge on decisionmakers. The costs of obtaining and maintaining regulatory permits, for example, are usually treated as a site overhead rather than related to the processes that create them.

The EPA also distinguishes two other cost categories, which are considered in following sections. Contingent costs are ones that may possibly be incurred in future. Land remediation and associated legal expenses provide one example. Image and relationship costs are intangible but very important to companies that must spend heavily to ensure positive stakeholder opinions about their environmental performance.

Research is showing that even the first two of the EPA's categories—conventional and hidden costs that are currently being incurred in a business—can be considerable in all parts of the world. In the United States researchers from the World Resources Institute (WRI) worked with nine companies to quantify how environment affected the costs of particular products or processes. Some of their findings—contained in a report entitled *Green Ledgers*—are startling.[3]

- Environmental costs made up at least 22% of the nonfeedstock operating costs of Amoco's Yorktown oil refinery. This compared to Amoco's

Potentially Hidden Costs

Regulatory	Upfront	Voluntary (Beyond Compliance)
• Notification • Reporting • Monitoring/testing • Studies/modeling • Remediation • Recordkeeping • Plans • Training • Inspections • Manifesting • Labeling • Preparedness • Protective equipment • Medical surveillance • Environmental insurance • Financial assurance • Pollution control • Spill response • Stormwater management • Waste management • Taxes/fees	• Site studies • Site preparation • Permitting • R&D • Engineering and procurement • Installation **Conventional Costs** Capital equipment Materials Labor Supplies Utilities Structures Salvage value **Back-End** • Closure/ decommissioning • Disposal of inventory • Post-closure care • Site survey	• Community relations/ outreach • Monitoring/testing • Training • Audits • Qualifying suppliers • Reports (e.g., annual environmental reports) • Insurance • Planning • Feasibility studies • Remediation • Recycling • Environmental studies • R&D • Habitat and wetland protection • Landscaping • Other environmental projects • Financial support to environmental groups and/or researchers

Contingent Costs

• Future compliance costs • Penalties/fines • Response to future releases	• Remediation • Property damage • Personal injury damage	• Legal expenses • Natural resource damages • Economic loss damages

Image and Relationship Costs

• Corporate image • Relationships with customers • Relationships with Investors • Relationships with Insurers	• Relationships with professional staff • Relationships with workers • Relationships with suppliers	• Relationships with lenders • Relationships with host communities • Relationships with regulators

Figure 2.1
Examples of environmental costs incurred by firms.
Source: Environmental Protection Agency, *An Introduction to Environmental Accounting as a Business Tool: Key Concepts and Terms,* Washington D.C., 1995, p. 9.

preinvestigation estimate of 3%. The largest components were costs of waste treatment, maintenance of environment-related equipment, and meeting environment-related product specifications (which add no value but are required by law).

• For one DuPont pesticide, environmental costs represented 19% of the total manufacturing cost. The largest components were general overhead (including taxes and training and legal fees) and depreciation and operation of pollution control equipment.

• Environmental costs of one Novartis additive were a minimum of 19% and possibly a higher proportion of manufacturing costs (excluding raw material). The most obvious costs were operation and depreciation of wastewater treatment and solvent recovery equipment, which alone totaled 15% of non-raw material manufacturing costs. Others were hidden but no less significant—some line managers estimated that up to 25% of their time was spent on environmental considerations.

Other projects have revealed cost saving opportunities. The U.S. drug manufacturer Bristol-Myers Squibb conducted life cycle reviews of its products between 1992 and 1997. In each review, an employee team representing a range of business areas and skills used product life cycle analysis tools to identify opportunities for environmental improvement and cost savings. Average savings of $300,000 were identified for each product.[4]

The costs can be no less great for small companies—as the WRI researchers found when they studied four based in Washington state.[5] They have taken action because the state requires manufacturers to prepare a pollution prevention plan, which must include some estimate of environmental costs.

Cascade Cabinet, a furniture manufacturer, used a nitro-cellulose lacquer to coat components. But it created volatile organic compounds (VOC) emissions—which new legislation was making costly to control—and was also a fire hazard. Residual dust triggered one blaze that caused $1 million damage. Understanding the full costs of using the lacquer—which included controlling emissions, gaining and maintaining permits, and higher insurance premiums—made clear that the higher purchase costs of an alternative product were more than outweighed by benefits. The result was financial gain and a reduction in toxic emissions.

Individual assessments by several North American companies have reached similar conclusions. A pilot study at Ontario Hydro Retail found that environmental expenditures amounted to 8% of overall spending. It also identified a number of opportunities for improving the efficiency of environmental spending through reduced landfill and other costs, revenue opportunities, or enhanced environmental protection for the same level of spending. The improvements allowed for a reduction in spending of 10% to 30% without compromising, and in

BAXTER ENVIRONMENTAL FINANCIAL STATEMENT

ENVIRONMENTAL COSTS	1995	1994	1993
Costs of Basic Program			
Corporate Environmental Affairs and Shared Multidivisional Costs	1.5	1.4	1.6
Auditors' and Attorneys' Fees	0.4	0.6	0.3
Corporate Environmental Engineering/ Facilities Engineering	0.7	0.8	0.9
Division/Regional/Facility Environmental Professionals, and Programs	7.0	7.0	6.5
Packaging Professionals and Programs for Packaging Reductions	2.8	2.1	2.0
Pollution Controls-Operations and Maintenance	5.0	4.7	4.0
Pollution Controls-Depreciation	1.9	2.5	2.7
Total Costs Of Basic Program	19.3	19.1	18.0
Remediation, Waste, and Other Response Costs **(Proactive environmental action will minimize these costs)**			
Attorneys' Fees for Cleanup Claims, NOVs	0.4	0.3	0.2
Waste Disposal	3.2	2.8	3.4
Environmental Taxes for Packaging	0.3	0	0
Remediation/Cleanup-On-site	1.0	1.2	0.8
Remediation/Cleanup-Off-site	1.0	1.1	0.3
Total Remediation and Waste, and Other Response Costs	5.9	5.4	4.7
TOTAL ENVIRONMENTAL COSTS	25.2	24.5	22.7

ENVIRONMENTAL INCOME, SAVINGS, AND COST AVOIDANCE ASSOCIATED WITH ENVIRONMENTAL INITIATIVES IN 1995 ($)	1995	1994	1993
Ozone-Depleting Substances Cost Reductions	0.5	1.8	1.2
Hazardous Waste-Disposal Cost Reductions	0.6	0.8	0.6
Hazardous Waste-Material Cost Reductions	0.6	0.4	0.4
Nonhazardous Waste-Disposal Cost Reductions	0.4	0.5	0.5
Nonhazardous Waste-Material Cost Reductions	0.2	5.2	1.1
Recycling Income	5.9	3.5	2.7
Green Lights Energy Conservation-Cost Savings	0.4	0.3	1.1
Packaging Cost Reductions	6.6	7.2	7.2
TOTAL INCOME, SAVINGS, AND COST AVOIDANCE FOR 1995 INITIATIVES	15.2	19.7	14.8
— As A Percentage of the Costs of Basic Program	79%	103%	82%
Total Income, Savings and Cost Avoidance from 1995 Initiatives	15.2	19.7	14.8
Cost Avoidance In 1995 from Efforts Initiated in Prior Years back to 1989	72.2	65.8	52.2
TOTAL INCOME, SAVINGS AND COST AVOIDANCE IN 1995	87.4	85.5	67.0

some cases, enhancing environmental protection. These savings represent as much as a 5% to 15% additional contribution to the utility's bottom line.

Baxter International, a producer, developer, and distributor of healthcare products and services, also compiles an annual environmental "balance sheet" to assess its environmental costs and savings (see box). The 1995 version demonstrated that savings greatly exceed costs. In that year Baxter calculated that income, savings, and cost avoidance from current-year initiatives totaled $15.2 million, while continuing savings from previous initiatives amounted to $72.2 million. The total savings of $87.4 million was almost three times greater than the 1995 costs of $25.2 million. According to Baxter's vice president for environmental health and safety, Bill Blackburn, doing the calculations has been invaluable by "bringing together our environmental and business professionals. It enables these professionals to focus on common opportunities using a common language—the language of business—money. It has been the ultimate tool for integrating our environmental program into our business."[6]

Similar stories are repeated in other parts of the world. The Dutch Prisma project, for example, examined opportunities for waste minimization at ten chemical, plating, and printing companies in Amsterdam and Rotterdam.[7] They found a total of 164 waste reduction opportunities, of which forty-five were implemented during the project's first 2 years. Over 40% of the implemented projects involved no capital expenditure and a further 25% had a payback period of less than a year.

Across the North Sea a project in Yorkshire's Aire and Calder valley examined waste minimization opportunities at eleven industrial sites (ranging from Coca-Cola and British Rail to small chemical companies). Potential savings of $2 million per annum were identified, with 72% of the individual proposals having paybacks of less than a year. One bottling plant found that it could save $60,000 per annum in raw material costs alone by using less shrinkwrap film on products—with further savings for customers who had less waste to dispose of.[8]

Another project by the U.K. Environment Agency (and its predecessor body Her Majesty's Inspectorate of Pollution) and a chemical company, Allied Colloids, was similarly successful. It examined two licensed processes and an effluent treatment plant for opportunities to create economic and environmental benefit. The study found potential savings of almost $7 million per annum and, within the first six months, resulted in annual savings of over $600,000 being achieved from an expenditure of only $105,000. The biggest savings were from preventive maintenance and discontinuing manufacture of a low volume chemical that was responsible for a large amount of both emissions and plant downtime. Allied Colloids production director Alan Whitehead believes that what the exercise "clearly demonstrates, not just to Allied Colloids, but to many companies involved in process industries, is that cost savings and productivity gains—bottom line benefits—run in parallel with environmental benefits."[9] The lessons of this and five other pilot projects have been summarized in a 3Es (emissions, efficiency, and economics) workbook.[10]

Environmental costs and benefits are not confined to the developed world. The United Nations Environment Programme (UNEP) cleaner production program has found many instances of high waste and regulatory compliance costs in companies in developing countries—and helped to reduce them, as the following examples show.[11]

In India, for example, the UN Industrial Development Organization and the National Productivity Council established DESIRE (Demonstrations in Small Industries for Reducing Waste). Four to six small companies in three sectors—agro-based pulp and paper, pesticides formulation, and textile dyeing and printing—examined opportunities for waste minimization. Ashoka Pulp and Paper Mills was one. It was generating substantial waste—and incurring substantial costs—because of paper breakage during manufacturing. A combination of process and equipment modification and new technology solved the problem, creating net annual savings of $118,000 for only $25,000 of capital expenditure. The environmental consequence was a reduction not only in wastes but also in pollution to a local river.

Industrias Fronterizas is a small Mexican manufacturer of car engine manifolds. It was spending over $3000 a day in disposing of oily wastewater and oil-contaminated aqueous machine coolant. The coolant contamination was also creating regular—and expensive—machine downtime. A cleaner production audit led to a process change to eliminate the contamination and installation of an ultrafiltration unit. This now separates clean water from an oil waste that can be used in a fuel-blending operation. The measures had a payback of 4 months and are now saving the company over $1 million per annum.

The financial savings were smaller—but relatively just as important—at Galco, a Tanzanian manufacturer of corrugated iron sheets and galvanized products. This took part in a national cleaner production initiative, CEPITA (Cleaner Environmental Protection in Industry Tanzania). It found that a mix of good housekeeping and process modification reduced ammonia emissions by 40%—to the benefit of both workers and nearby residents—and reduced waste. The result was tangible savings of $700 a year for a capital investment of $1,547. An equally important, but uncosted, benefit was an improvement in product quality, due to less blackening of galvanized sheets by smoke.

Environmental Liabilities

Companies with long experience of dealing with environmental issues have learned that "out of sight, out of mind" is no longer a valid statement—past environmental actions can return with a vengeance to cause current environmental costs through the mechanism of environmental liabilities. While many believe that such retrospective liability is unfair, the principle is becoming a fact of business life that has to be taken into account. These liabilities may be generated by legal requirements to clean up contaminated land. Or they can arise from lawsuits about damage created by processes or products to employees, neighbors, consumers, and others. Although liability costs have been greatest in the United States, they are becoming significant in many other countries around the world.

In the United Kingdom the possible cost to industry of remediating land contamination is—even within a relatively liberal regime—tens of billions of pounds. Impending European Union legislation may also introduce additional costs both for British and other European companies.

Liabilities are also becoming a potential business risk in developing countries. In 1996, for example, the Australian mining company BHP agreed to a settlement of over A$500 million with Papua New Guinea villagers in compensation for environmental damage associated with the OK Tedi gold and copper mine that it manages and has a majority stake in. (The Papua New Guinea government has a 30% minority shareholding.) The largest part of the settlement is to clean up copper- and cadmium-containing sediments that have flowed into local rivers after torrential rain and seismic activity caused the collapse of a dam containing a mine slurry pond in 1984. The remainder is compensation for villagers, relocation of ten villages that have been severely affected, and payment of legal costs. According to Jerry Ellis, BHP executive manager, the affair has demonstrated "the absolutely paramount importance of getting our relationships right with the communities in which we work."[12]

Reducing Potential Future Costs

The liabilities from past actions are today's bottom-line impact. But it is possible that many companies are creating future liabilities by their present actions. Insurers and environmentalists have suggested that there may be legal action against fossil fuel producers to recover the costs of storm, flood, and other kinds of damage created or exacerbated by global warming, as and when it is proved to be a real phenomenon. Of course, fossil fuel producers have strong arguments on their side and may be proved right in court. But the underlying point is that such legal action will be a risk for many products and industries in the future. And experience suggests that the criteria by which liability will be judged will become more, rather than less, exacting—and that merely complying with legislation at the time of the actions may well be an ineffective defense. The outcome could be substantial liabilities for a number of companies.

Fortunately, companies adopting a policy of eco-efficiency greatly reduce the risks of such future liabilities by, for example, reducing dispersion of toxic materials as a result of their activities.

As previously discussed, the dynamic view of environmental regulation—which believes that new measures will constantly be introduced and impose additional costs—also suggests that there will always be opportunities for cost-effective pollution prevention, waste minimization and similar initiatives. Dow's WRAP (waste reduction always pays) and 3M's 3P (pollution prevention pays) have been running for decades and still have no difficulty in finding cost-effective opportunities (see cases in Chapter 6). In 1996, for example, Dow announced plans to spend $1 billion to achieve new environmental, health and safety targets over the next decade—including further waste reduction initiatives—and that it expects to generate a return on that investment of 30% to 40%.

Ever increasing environmental expectations—and the constant development of new environmental issues requiring business actions— also provide continuing opportunities to avoid future costs by taking proactive action today.

For example, one future cost that is likely to rise for poor environmental performers is that of insurance. Insurers are paying to remedy many past environmental problems and are determined not to incur losses from potential future liabilities. The result is much more restricted and costly policies for environment-related problems and more stringent criteria for accepting clients. And in the future many insurers probably will require that a certified management system be in place as well as making an independent "environmental risk rating" of the company's activities before providing coverage.

Procter & Gamble demonstrates that the reduced insurance costs deriving from good environmental management and eco-efficient policies can be substantial. The company's insurance and self-insurance costs are estimated to be $113 million per annum lower than companies of comparable size and risk profile.[13]

Cost of Capital

Investors and banks are deeply concerned about any threat to the returns from, and repayments of, their investments and loans. As a last resort, they will refuse to lend to or invest in risky ventures. If risks are worrying but manageable they will demand higher returns or interest rates to compensate. Both of these can affect the cost of a business's capital. When these concerns are publicly signaled they can have other effects such as damaging a reputation.

Of course, many believe that financial markets encourage a short-term, profit first-and-last mentality, are unconcerned about the long-term risks that can result from poor environmental performance, and fail to reward companies that behave responsibly. However, a recent WBCSD study, *Financing Change*, concludes that there are sufficient encouraging signs to refute, at least partly, the perceived wisdom that the financial world is ignorant of the idea of sustainable development or dismisses it.[14] While mainstream investors often regard environmental concerns as moral issues outside their remit, and fund managers point to their legal duty to maximize returns on investments, there is evidence of change. Investors are beginning to look at the environmental costs and liabilities of companies and at how these affect profits and therefore share performance.

One aspect of this is the growing presence of green investment funds. For example, the Norwegian insurer Storebrand and a leading American fund manager, Scudder, Stevens and Clark, have established an Environmental Value Fund. The fund's investment portfolio is drawn from Scudder's constantly updated list of about 200 companies around the world that it recommends as good investments. These companies are then rated on a "sustainability index" devised by Storebrand. This takes eight criteria (all relevant to eco-efficiency) into account—impact on global warming; contribution to ozone depletion; material intensity; toxic releases; energy efficiency; water use; environmental liabilities and quality of environmental management. At any one time about seventy to eighty companies from the shortlist are sufficiently highly rated to qualify for the fund and twenty to thirty are actually invested in.

According to Carlos Joly, senior vice-president for environmental policy at Storebrand:

From the investor's point of view, the important thing about the fund is that it begins with financially sound and well managed companies. So they can help the environment without taking major risks. From our point of view, we not only create good business but also help achieve our corporate goal of environmental improvement. By sending signals about good corporate behaviour and supporting companies which are environmentally responsible we also help reduce the long-term risks of claims for environmental damage under the policies we write.

Prior to the fund's launch the Storebrand screening procedure was backtested on Scudder's investment recommendations for 1991. If the stocks that passed the sustainability screen had been invested in then, they would have had an annual return of 22% over the period 1991–96. This compares to 17% for all the recommendations and 12% for the Morgan Stanley World Index.

Storebrand's actions reflect growing concern among insurers about the potential risks of climate change, which encompasses both increased claims for flooding and storm damage and possible reductions in the value of their investment. The research arm of the German insurance company, Gerling-Konzern Globale, financed a study of these risks by Greenpeace scientist Jeremy Leggett.[15] Carlos Joly of Storebrand also believes that

The investment side of the insurance business hasn't focused on climate-change issues, and those risks are not discounted in the valuation of the stock price of oil companies.

A study by Mark Mansley of the Delphi Group of long-term environment-related risks for the carbon fuel industry supports his view—and provides an interesting foretaste of the kinds of analysis that might be more frequent in future. Mansley first notes that

An oil stock yielding 4% (close to the sector average), with dividend growth of 15% (very high given the track record of the industry) will repay only half of the original investment within ten years, discounting back at a (low) discount rate of 10%. Therefore, fundamentally, the current price of the stock depends significantly on events beyond that ten year horizon.[16]

He then considers the financial implications for oil, coal, gas, and power companies if the linkage between carbon dioxide emissions and climate change is proved and policy measures to reduce emissions—such as a carbon tax—are introduced. The report identifies three main business risks for carbon fuel producers in such a scenario:

1. reduced demand owing to energy efficiency measures,

2. increased competition from non-fossil fuel sources, which would both take market share and cap any rise in overall energy prices,

3. a reduction in long-term producer surplus owing to introduction of a carbon tax.

The study also noted that insurance companies such as Swiss Re have suggested that carbon fuel producers might face liability claims in the next century from parties suffering serious losses from climate change.

The study concludes that the potential risks are being underestimated by investors, especially with regard to the most vulnerable sectors—which it identifies as high-cost coal producers and nonintegrated oil exploration companies. Of course, there is much scope for discussing the precise findings of such a preliminary study. But it nonetheless demonstrates the possible risks created by environment and the way these may increasingly be taken into account by investors.

Improved or Protected Market Opportunities

Environmental regulations, potential liability claims, and customer sensitivity to environmental performance means that many products are "sunsetting," that is, no longer being sold. CFCs provide an obvious example. The developed world market for these high margin chemicals was over 600,000 tons per annum in the mid 1980s—but has now been reduced to a fraction of this by customer resistance and new regulations. Adopting an eco-efficiency approach, and systematically assessing products against the seven guidelines outlined in chapter 1 (and examined in more detail in chapter 3), can provide valuable early warnings about those at risk of sunsetting.

Every sunsetting product creates an opportunity for a replacement. New products that provide both customer value and respond to the needs of sustainable development will also be favored. In the past, for example, Dow's businesses focused on environment from a defensive, product stewardship standpoint. During the 1990s the company has looked hard at the actual and potential environmental attributes of its products and asked whether there are opportunities to create additional value from them.

Dow believes that it is a highly efficient chlorinated solvents producer, with low discharge from its plants. However, with traditional industrial cleaning solvents being phased out under the terms of the Montreal Protocol and the U.S. Clean Air Act, customers are seeking alternatives for existing solvents and ways to reduce volatile organic compounds (VOCs) in their work processes. So the next step was to develop INVERT solvents, a new generation of aqueous-based solvents with no ozone-depleting chemicals and half the VOC levels of conventional solvents.

Another example of responsible product stewardship is the Sentricon Termite Colony Elimination System from DowElanco. In contrast with conventional treatments that use insecticides to keep termites away from structures, the Sentricon system eliminates entire termite colonies with only 100 grams of product placed in small stations around the home. The bait has extremely low toxicity to mammals and is used only where termites are actively feeding.

In Brazil, Dow developed new technology for making polystyrene foam cups and other products. Carbon dioxide replaced CFCs as the blowing agent. The technique has proved so successful that Dow gains considerable income from licensing the technology.

The demise of CFCs—and the time limits on use of "first generation" substitutes such as hydrochlorofluocarbons (HCFCs)—has created great opportunities for completely new refrigerants and propellants. One class of these are the chlorine-free hydrofluoroethers (HFEs) that have been developed by 3M and whose sales are growing rapidly. These are not ozone-depleting, have low global warming potential, and reside in the atmosphere for only a few years. They are also of low toxicity and flammability and do not contribute to urban smog formation.

Access to Markets

Environmental performance can also be a significant determinant of whether a company can bid for commercial or public contracts. More and more companies and public agencies are making an environmental policy or good environmental performance a criterion for making bids for new business or continuing with existing business. In the United States, for example, the environmental safety and energy performance goals for federal government agencies oblige many American public agencies to take these factors into account when making purchasing decisions. And British DIY retailer B&Q is just one of a growing number of companies that require their suppliers to demonstrate environmental concern and, in extremis, delists those who cannot.

As chapter 7 discusses, there can also be trade barriers to companies with poor environmental performance.

Enhanced Image

Although intangible and difficult to value, the image of a product or corporation generally makes a vital contribution to corporate success. It gives customers confidence in making purchases, improves employee morale, and aids recruitment and retention.

Environmental reputation is an increasingly important element in determining image. It is, for example, usually a component in the surveys by the *Financial Times* and other newspapers that assess corporate reputation. It can also directly affect the reputation and positioning of products. The advertising of upmarket German and Swedish car brands such as Audi, BMW, Saab, and Volkswagen stresses their environmental strengths not only from a sense of corporate responsibility— although that is important—but also because their reputation is built on excellence in every area.

The employment choices of young people and graduates in particular are also influenced by companies' reputations for environmental and social responsibility.

Competitive Advantage in the Long Term

The factors described make it unlikely that long-term competitive advantage can be obtained through noncompliance or minimal compliance. Some companies will try to reduce costs this way. But it is deadly. Sooner or later mandates will come into place to prevent such an approach, and put the company—or the whole industry—at an enormous competitive disadvantage. Long-term success almost certainly belongs to those companies that not only comply with environmental standards, whether mandated or self-imposed, but do it more efficiently and effectively than others. If they conserve energy more effectively, for example, they will have lower costs. And if they develop products that deliver superior customer value and reduce environmental impacts compared to alternatives, they will win a higher market share than from either alone. The business benefits of this could well exceed all the other benefits put together.

So there is a growing link between environmental performance and the bottom line.[17] Strengthening this link requires that the capacity to generate and implement eco-efficient innovations is seen as a core business competence. There are two means of accomplishing it. The defensive means is to reduce current and future environmental costs through measures such as waste minimization initiatives and screening of capital investments and products. The creative means is to see every environmental problem as an unmet need for more effective processes and innovative products and to fill it. Both means are necessary to achieve eco-efficiency, although in the long-run the balance is likely to shift from the former to the latter.

3M

3M's Reusable Packaging Systems business unit—established in early 1997—is one example of a creative approach. It is part of a newly formed Corporate Enterprise Development organization, whose aim is to build new businesses based on the many 3M technologies and know-how that have applications beyond the divisions that first developed them.

The unit's history began in 1992 when bulk customers for 3M's audio and video tapes became concerned about the costs and environmental impacts of dealing with the waste cardboard, foam, and shrink wrap packaging of their orders. Working through the Audio Video Duplicating Association they began discussions about alternatives. The outcome was a new bulk videotape shipping container, the 3M Reusable Pak. This is made from recycled high density polyethylene (HDPE). It has two substantially identical rectangular pieces that provides flexibility and makes stacking easy. Each container has a minimum usage of 40 return cycles. And it not only eliminates conventional packaging materials—with consequent procurement and process savings for packers and reduced materials and waste handling costs for customers—but also provides superior protection against dust.

Since its introduction the system has reduced packaging waste by over 45,000 cubic yards at a cost saving of over 4 million dollars to 3M alone. Other industry leaders such as Sony and JVC have also adopted the design.

Despite this success—and strong patent protection for the product— the reusable packaging system wasn't marketed outside the audiovisual industry for some years. It was only the creation of the Corporate Enterprise Development organization that led its vice president, Dr. Harry Andrews, to examine its broader potential and to establish an autonomous business team to develop and market it further. According to the unit's leader, Richard Salomone, the Reusable Packaging System demonstrates that:

the idea of eco-efficiency can generate new markets. Customers are very interested in it—but customer interest alone isn't sufficient. You also need an organizational commitment to push the ideas. Our vision is to take something that in a way was a by-product of other activities and turn it into a new business with eco-efficiency as a central part of its strategy. We think we can sell a competitively priced packaging system to many additional internal and external customers in a wide range of industries—thereby helping customers, the environment, and 3M.

Dow

Dow is another organization that is convinced that it can obtain long-term competitive advantage from eco-efficiency and developing its environmental core competence. In 1996, the company announced a new set of environmental, health, and safety performance targets for the year 2005 that call for incorporating the principles of eco-efficiency into its business strategies.

As the case shows (see chapter 6) Dow has done, and continues to do, much in the way of waste minimization initiatives, product screening, and other prevention initiatives. However it is also doing much to build a range of products and services to provide eco-efficient solutions to the needs of sustainable development.

One example of this is a rental plan for chlorinated hydrocarbon-based solvents. These are highly effective for many applications such as dry cleaning and metal finishing. They are also chemically very stable, nonflammable, and insoluble in water. However, the very properties that make CHCs so useful also make them potentially dangerous to health and the environment. Because of their high fat solubility, they penetrate easily into the fatty tissues of humans and animals. There they can cause significant health issues. Yet in 1992 over 80% of the 600,000 tons of CHC solvents sold in Europe evaporated into the atmosphere or soaked into groundwater. Only 90,000 tons was recycled.

Faced with growing regulatory pressures, and wanting to be proactive, Dow now has a plan to recycle the chemicals. The idea was developed by Dow Germany in a joint venture, SafeChem, with a local recycling company, RCN.

SafeChem takes care of the storage and transportation of the solvents and has designed airtight containers specially for this purpose. In this way the solvents can be transported safely, used with no sacrifice of function, and then reused by other customers. Toxic dispersion is greatly reduced, the same molecules are now used a hundred times over, and the energy and material intensity of the solvent life cycle is much lower. Customers have less anxiety and lower costs than in managing new regulatory requirements themselves while Dow saves money on raw materials and forms a close relationship with its customers.

After initial skepticism, the system has proved extremely popular in Germany and in 1996 Dow and SafeChem extended it throughout Europe. The system may also be applied to other chemicals in future.

Dow Europe is building further on such schemes and a vice president, Claude Fussler, recently authored a book on using the ideas of eco-efficiency to create new products called *Driving Eco-Innovation*.[18]

One output of Dow Europe's eco-innovation processes is a housing system known as *Azurel*. The original vision for this came from a Dow employee and architect, Jean-Phillipe Deblander, who wanted to design—both for himself and because he felt there would be a market—a house that was more energy efficient and comfortable than traditional designs and made from lighter materials. After experimentation, he found that—when made to a slightly different formulation and put in a timber frame—Dow's existing polystyrene insulation boards could be made strong enough to replace conventional roofs and walls. The resulting savings in masonry and timber means that Azurel houses use 40% to 50% less material over the life cycle, and 6% to 11% less energy, than conventional homes.[19] They are also less costly to build. Dow Europe markets the concept of the house and provides the boards but allows licensed contractors to build them. The system has already been commercialized in France and thousands of units are likely to be built in Europe and throughout the world in coming years.

Volkswagen

Volkswagen also sees environment as a critical determinant of its long-term business health—and a means of long-term competitive advantage. The company has done much to meet German environmental legislation—but even more to meet its environmental policy. This states:

The company accepts responsibility for the environmental compatibility of its products and for the increasingly conservative use of natural resources, with due regard to economic aspects. Accordingly, the company makes environmentally efficient, advanced technology available worldwide and brings this technology to bear over the full cycle of its products.[20]

There are many examples of this proactivity in practice.

• Development of the world's most fuel-efficient car engines, the direct-injection turbocharged diesel (TDI) designs that not only drive Audis and Volkswagens but also those of other manufacturers such as Ford and Volvo. This greatly reduces carbon dioxide emissions per mile traveled and—through exhaust gas recirculation and an oxidation catalyst—cuts emissions of the nitrogen oxides and particulates that give diesel a bad name in some quarters.

- Construction of a pioneering semiautomated car disassembly plant, with a German-wide network to handle all end-of-life Volkswagen and Audi cars, scheduled to be in place by 1997.

- Encouraging rail rather than road transport. For example, 81% of the material outputs and 46% of the material inputs at the company's flagship Wolfsburg plant were transported by rail in 1993.

Many of these environmental improvements have cost money. The company estimates, conservatively, that environmental protection involved DM50 million ($30 million) expenditures and DM175 million ($105 million) of operating expenditure in 1994 alone. But they have also created competitive advantage by positioning the company as one of the most ecologically conscious car manufacturers and enhancing the image of its high prestige and high-value products.

Volkswagen wants to maintain this reputation and ensure that it anticipates emerging trends. Its 1995 annual report carried two pages of comments by opinion-makers such as Heinz Dürr, chairman of the board of management of Deutsche Bank, and Prof. Dr. Ernst von Weizsäcker, president of Wuppertal Institut, on the future of mobility. The overall message is that cars have to become less environmentally damaging and be seen as only one part of an overall system for delivering mobility.

One implication Volkswagen draws from such thinking is that fuel efficiency will become even more important. Hence it has set a target of a "three-liter" mass market Volkswagen—that is, a car that uses only 3 liters (under one gallon) of fuel to cover 60 miles (compared to a current best of around 5 liters and an average for all cars far worse than this), with no sacrifice of performance.

Another conclusion is that the company's competitive future is in providing "mobility services" rather than just cars. Hence, it is developing traffic management systems, designing small, flexible, urban minibuses, and working with local authorities to develop "next generation" public transportation systems that provide people with attractive alternatives to using cars for short journeys. These include ideas such as scheduled taxi services, shared taxis, and telephone minibus services, all supported by advanced scheduling and traffic management systems.

American Reinsurance

Creative ways of turning costly environmental pressures into eco-efficient business are not confined to manufacturing. Take American Reinsurance Corporation (AmRe), the third largest reinsurer in the United States. Like all reinsurers, its payouts on environmental claims rose dramatically during the 1980s and 1990s. Unlike most other reinsurers it took the risk of hiring staff with environmental rather than insurance expertise to try and find solutions and limit future liability for itself and its clients.

The outcome is a Technology Transfer division that invests in, and provides business assistance to, new ventures with promising environmental technologies. AmRe then recommends their products to its clients, with the incentive of reduced insurance costs if they prevent or resolve potentially costly environmental problems.

The division's first investment was in Molten Metals Technology (MMT). The company's molten metal bath breaks down many hazardous and non-hazardous wastes into simpler components that can be used as raw materials. AmRe invested $5 million and introduced it to top management of its leading clients—assistance that resulted in a number of large orders. One of these was from Hoechst Celanese, which substituted the bath for landfill and incineration of many of its wastes. MMT operates the facility and sells the products back to Hoechst for use in its chemical processes. Jeff Reynolds, Hoechst Celanese's environmental manager, is delighted that "Waste disposal goes from being a negative cost to a positive saving."[21] He also hopes that this and other initiatives may eventually result in reduced insurance costs.

For AmRe, the Technology Transfer division now allows it to offer an integrated service of insurance and preventive technology to provide a complete solution to client's environmental problems rather than just a single product. It also benefits from the returns on its investment in the technology providers.

The Eco-efficient Mindset

3M, Dow, Volkswagen, and American Reinsurance demonstrate the key features of an eco-efficient business strategy mindset. These can be summarized as:

- An emphasis on performance that meets genuine needs rather than on products alone,
- Deriving competitive advantage from consideration of the entire product life cycle,
- A recognition that eco-efficiency is more a process than a once-and-for-all objective,
- Integrating sustainability into the overall business so that it forms a core competence,
- External collaboration to gain information, influence debates, and identify business opportunities.

The following chapters explore all of these points in greater detail.

Summary

Social expectations of corporate environmental performance—and the costs of poor performance—are constantly rising. So any bottom line benefits have to be judged against tomorrow's as well as today's standards. These benefits fall into five main categories:

Reducing the current costs of poor environmental performance through waste minimization and other measures.

Reducing potential future costs of poor environmental performance.

Reduced costs of capital.

Increased market share and improved or protected market opportunities.

Enhanced image.

There are two, complementary, means of achieving these benefits:

the defensive means is to reduce current and future environmental costs through measures such as waste minimization initiatives and screening of capital investments and products.

the creative means is to develop an "eco-efficient mindset" and see every environmental problem as an unmet need for more effective processes and innovative products and fill it.

The key features of such a mindset are:

an emphasis on performance that meets genuine needs rather than products alone

deriving competitive advantage from consideration of the entire product life cycle

a recognition that eco-efficiency is more a process than a once-and-for-all objective

integrating sustainability into their overall business so that it forms a core competence

external collaboration to gain information, influence debates, and identify business opportunities.

3   Defining and Measuring Eco-efficiency

The World Business Council for Sustainable Development (WBCSD) and its predecessors (the Business Council for Sustainable Development and the World Industry Council for the Environment) have held three major workshops in Antwerp and Washington to define the concept of eco-efficiency and identify ways of operationalizing it within business. The full definition that has emerged is:

Eco-efficiency is reached by the delivery of competitively-priced goods and services that satisfy human needs and bring quality of life, while progressively reducing environmental impacts and resource intensity throughout the life cycle, to a level at least in line with the earth's estimated carrying capacity.[1]

This definition has five core themes: (1) an emphasis on service, (2) a focus on needs and quality of life, (3) consideration of the entire product life cycle, (4) a recognition of limits to eco-capacity, and (5) a process view.

The first section of this chapter examines each of these themes in detail. A second section outlines and discusses seven guidelines that can help business to become eco-efficient. (An appendix to the chapter also provides a checklist for each guideline). The final section provides examples of how companies are beginning to address the important issue of measuring eco-efficiency.

Emphasis on Service

Until recently, industrial success was based on increasing quantities of material throughput. From coal to petrochemicals, textiles to computers, the volume or mass of output was one of the main measures of success.

Today there is a growing realization that customers do not value physical goods—or ownership of them—for their own sake. The goods are merely a means to an end—satisfying customers' needs. The implication is that the best marketing approach will be one that provides a complete service to meet those needs. Taking ownership of physical goods might be a part of this service, but it might not—renting rather than buying can often be less of a hassle. The consequence, in the words of Amos Tuck Business School professor Frederick Webster, is that

all business, even manufacturers, should define themselves as service businesses; customers buy benefits not products. For example, a package of Crest toothpaste offers a toll-free telephone number that a customer can call with questions or comments or to request information about dental care. The purchase exchange has become a two-way relationship and the customer is buying improved dental health, not just a physical product.[2]

Adopting such a definition means a rethink of what a company's core competencies and competitive advantage are. It also provides another instance where business trends are in alignment with eco-efficiency. By focusing on what services to provide, not just what products to supply, companies open up opportunities to deliver less eco-intensive, higher-value applications.

Computing provides an example of this synergy—and of the move from product to service. Computer users want ever greater processing power to meet their service needs—and electronics companies have provided it from ever-smaller chips. Energy consumption and material inputs per unit of computing power have therefore fallen rapidly. But meeting customers' needs is not just about hardware—it is about software. Advances in this field have reduced the costs of many basic business tasks and created previously undreamt of opportunities. Indeed, so critical is software to satisfying customer needs that companies focusing on this aspect of the overall "service package" are valued at much higher multiples of turnover and earnings than hardware manufacturers.

Electricity supply is also moving from a product to a service mentality—a move that has been substantially driven by eco-efficiency considerations in the United States and some other countries. Faced with regulatory pressures to reduce emissions—and market pressures that made it difficult to obtain financing for large investments in new physical capacity—innovative utilities have begun to see themselves as providers of energy services rather than simply electricity suppliers.

They now offer domestic customers options such as lower tariffs in exchange for occasional short-term interruptions to the supply of certain uses such as air conditioning where constant power is not required. Consumers save money. And utilities both avoid the need to build expensive capacity just to meet occasional electricity peaks and gain better long-term knowledge of their customers' needs and pattern of electricity use.

Hoechst's antifreeze business provides another example. In the past, the company had simply supplied the glycol to airports and airlines. But a prototype system at Munich airport now offers a complete service to airlines. Hoechst deices the planes and then collects the glycol for reprocessing and reuse. The service cuts the overall cost of the operation, eliminates disposal problems for the airlines and brings Hoechst closer to its customers. According to research and development staffer Hartmut Vennen, "Before, we were just the dumb suppliers of a material. Now, we're helping clients solve problems."[3]

The U.K. waste disposal industry is moving in the same direction. Historically, their core activity was collecting and transporting waste to landfill sites. But rising costs and levies in many counties have raised customers' waste disposal costs to the point where they're looking for alternatives. Hence companies such as UK Waste are beginning to provide an integrated waste service that includes advice on waste minimization and recycling, as well as disposal.

As these examples show, the business opportunity is to rethink the service that is currently being provided to customers—and devise a new one that creates additional value both by meeting customers' needs better and reducing environmental impacts.

Focus on Needs and Quality of Life

The key to improved service is understanding customers' real needs. Increasingly, these needs are not for the shining gadgets so prominent in recent decades but rather for more intangible sources of value— goods and services that contribute to quality of life. No one needs—and quality of life is not directly provided by—heavy, energy-intensive, and polluting products. Businesses that can address real or unarticulated needs and develop less eco-intensive product applications have an immediate opportunity for competitive advantage.

How can they do this? By understanding the basic function provided by products—and asking whether there are alternative ways of meeting it that can enhance customer value and reduce environmental impacts. In cities, most people's need is not for a car but for a service, that is, timely, convenient, and safe mobility. Although large cars have many advantages when roads are uncongested they are less attractive when stuck in traffic jams. Most forecasts suggest that congestion and pollution—and legislation to deal with them—will make using such cars in towns and cities more difficult and expensive in future. So there is an emerging need for an alternative. In some cases, this will be public transportation. But leading car manufacturers such as Mercedes and Renault see an unmet need for light, small "urban cars"—perhaps using electricity, fuel cells, or other, cleaner, alternatives to the internal combustion engine.

Meeting Basic Needs

The needs of the reasonably well off are rather different to those of the billions of people who lack adequate nutrition, medical care, clothing and shelter. While much of the solution lies in social and economic reforms to build their purchasing power business can help by developing affordable goods and services that meet their basic needs.

One unmet need now attracting attention is that of the 2 billion people who lack access to electric power and the further 1 billion who have limited access.[4] While some of these people will eventually gain access to conventional power sources delivered over long-distance power lines, financial and geographic constraints will remain barriers for many. Hence, there is an emerging market for low cost, decentralized technologies utilizing renewable energy. And such technologies often have less environmental impact over the life cycle than their fossil fuel equivalents.

Amoco/Enron Solar—a joint venture between the U.S. oil major, Amoco, and North America's largest gas supplier, Enron—is one company developing innovative products for this market. During 1996 the company signed a twenty-five-year supply agreement with India's Rajasthan State Electricity Board, based on a 50MW solar array in the

Energy Efficiency as a Business Opportunity

Energy is not used efficiently in central and eastern Europe. The electrical and heat energy distribution systems are anywhere between 10% and 30% less efficient than their western equivalents, and consumers are living and working in buildings consuming 20% to 30% more energy than should be needed. This wastes resources and increases power bills.

The potential savings from more efficient use of energy in the region are enormous—between $50 and $150 billion a year by some estimates. However, filling this unmet need for energy efficiency requires investment—which is always difficult and sometimes impossible for central and eastern European utilities. They are undercapitalized themselves and lack access to low-cost financing. This is a consequence both of political risk and lack of knowledge about energy efficiency opportunities among capital providers.

In the early 1990s the Swiss engineering company Landis & Gyr saw opportunities for its technologies to meet this need. It also believed that the political risk was overstated. Hence, it began to identify promising projects. Three emerged from its initial search—two large hospitals in the Czech Republic and a 50MW district heating scheme in Poland. Contracts were then negotiated between these organizations to purchase Landis & Gyr's technology to upgrade their heating systems. Landis & Gyr guaranteed a level of energy savings over a 7 to 10-year period that gives the operators a healthy return on their investments. Its systems also have low emissions and provide a more reliable service that better meets users' requirements. The hospitals and district heating company were able to obtain loans on the basis of Landis & Gyr's guarantees. These loans were arranged on a completely commercial basis, with no subsidies of any kind.

Landis & Gyr faced both internal and external skepticism about its idea. But now it is creating benefits for all parties. Its customers have lower fuel bills and more effective heating. The communities they operate in have cleaner air and job opportunities arising from the refurbishment work. And last, but not least, Landis & Gyr has created a new, profitable, business and a strong foothold in a potentially vast market.

Thar Desert. The company hopes that large-scale manufacturing will make its photovoltaics the most cost-effective option for all sunny areas without easy access to fossil fuels.

A Life Cycle Approach

Every business forms part of a product chain that transforms raw materials into goods and services for consumption and eventual disposal. A life cycle approach implies that companies have a responsibility to consider the upstream and downstream implications of their activities and take action to mitigate them—for example, by redesigning processes and products to minimize impact, maximize efficiency, and create additional value.

Many companies are developing such a life cycle perspective. The Danish textile producer Novotex—best known for its use of "green cotton"—focuses much of its environmental report on the entire textile life cycle and the actions it is taking to help its suppliers and licensees improve their environmental performance.

Fiat's CEO Paolo Cantarella also believes that:

As we stand on the threshold of the twenty-first century, automobile manufacturers must assume new social responsibilities. Our commitment now covers the car's entire life cycle. It is already present when the idea is conceived by the designer, it is embodied in the manufacturing processes and lives on while the product is being used by consumers, ending only at the completion of the cycle with the vehicle's dismantling and recycling. The materials are reutilized, the cycle starts again and a new, even more environmentally friendly car is born.[5]

A life cycle approach can produce surprising results. The German appliance manufacturer Bosch-Siemens Hausergäte conducted a life cycle assessment (LCA) of its dishwashers, in collaboration with the Munich Technical University. It found that manufacture accounted for only 2% of lifetime energy and material utilization, whereas use of the product was a staggering 96%. Designing products to use less energy and water is clearly the greatest eco-efficiency opportunity for dishwasher manufacturers. The company was also astonished to find that the daily car journeys to work by employees at its dishwasher plant (17,000 miles) actually create 10% greater emissions of carbon dioxide than that from the lifetime energy consumption of a single dishwasher.

Industrial Ecology

Some companies are beginning to use the term "industrial ecology" to define their ultimate life cycle goal.[6] Their vision is of an interconnected industrial system in which new products evolve out of, or consume, available waste streams, and where processes are in turn developed to produce usable "waste." In such a system waste is defined as those byproducts that had no useful application within the entire industrial system, rather than, as now, simply the discarded byproducts or emissions from individual products, processes, or service operations.

This idea is not new, nor is it contrary to business practice. For example, natural gas was originally, and in some parts of the world still is, an unwanted by-product of oil production. It was either flared or vented to the atmosphere. Today, however, for economic and environmental reasons, the gas is collected almost everywhere for use as a fuel or reinjected into oil wells to maintain pressures.

In the closed industrial ecosystem, consumers are also an integral part of the cycle, rather than just being the endpoint for the delivery of goods and services. They use products and energy resources, then return them to the industrial ecosystem for reprocessing and reuse.

Of course, translating the concept of industrial ecology into practice and into effective government policies is a challenge. But examples are beginning to emerge—such as Kalundborg in Denmark. In this community, the outputs ("wastes," water, and excess energy) from several industrial processes serve as the inputs to other industrial facilities, agricultural businesses, and the municipality. Statoil, the Norwegian state oil company, and Novo Nordisk, a pharmaceuticals and biotechnology company, are participants in this project, which is represented schematically in figure 3.1.

Kalundborg was not a planned industrial park. Instead the relationships between the existing entities were at first forged for economic reasons, but more recent initiatives have been made largely for environmental reasons. New industrial parks across the globe are looking toward Kalundborg as a model of how to attract businesses that can "feed" off one another. In the United States, for example, several development projects are under way to cluster businesses involved in recycling around materials-recovery facilities that process municipal solid waste.[7]

While these examples involve multiple exchanges of byproducts between companies within one geographic area, the same principle can

Kalundborg's "Industrial Symbiosis"

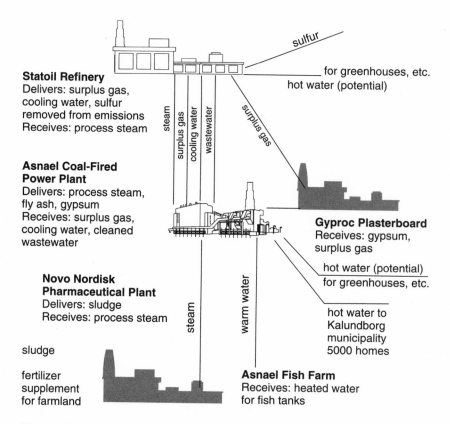

Figure 3.1
Kalundborg's (Denmark) industrial symbiosis.
Source: World Business Council for Sustainable Development, *Sustainable Production and Consumption* (Geneva: WBCSD, 1996), p. 22.

be applied on a smaller scale within one company. The pharmaceutical company Roche pretreats and recycles byproducts from its citric acid production facility in Belgium. The natural fermentation process of molasses results in cell fragments that are then concentrated and sold as animal feed and soil conditioner. Similarly, gypsum, another of its byproducts, is used by the cement industry; while waste sulfuric acid from a vitamin manufacturing process is used to neutralize alkaline wastewater in third-party treatment plants.

Eco-capacity

The eco-efficiency bottom line is to make profits within the earth's carrying capacity (eco-capacity). Eco-capacity is difficult to calculate but it is clear that limits are being reached in many places. It seems increasingly probable, for example, that the planet's capacity to soak up emissions of carbon dioxide and other greenhouse gases without any effects has been exceeded and that global warming may be occurring and could continue throughout the next century. Over much of northern Europe deposition of the acid products of emissions of sulfur dioxide and nitrogen oxides are exceeding the capacity of soils and watercourses to neutralize them, with possibly damaging effects on flora and fauna.

These examples show that eco-capacity is a moving target. There is often a threshold below which effects are easily assimilated but above which serious damage starts to take place. The nearer emissions are to this threshold the more urgent the need for action.

The constraints of eco-capacity have been summarized by the Swedish oncologist Dr. Karl-Henrik Robert, and the Natural Step organization he founded. The Natural Step approach is unique because it is based on large-scale expert and public discussions and marries scientific credibility with simplicity. While some regard the approach as too simplistic—or little more than a restatement of the laws of thermodynamics—it is being utilized by a number of companies, such as Ericsson and Ontario Hydro.[8] Its essence is three "system rules" that human activities need to respect:

1. Substances from the earth's crust must not systematically increase in nature.

2. Substances produced by society must not systematically increase in nature.

3. The physical basis for the productivity and diversity of nature must not be systematically diminished.

(There is also a fourth, social, rule—make fair and efficient use of resources with respect to meeting basic needs.)

Of course, it is difficult if not impossible for individual businesses to define the precise relationship between their activities and the earth's carrying capacity. The definition does not imply that it is feasible for companies to have a precise definition of such a macroissue for the foreseeable future. Nonetheless, understanding that some kind of limits exist—and that the targets are moving ones—can be a valuable spur to action. It creates a sense of urgency and an acceptance of the need for radical objectives. Indeed, just as the radical goal of zero defects in the context of TQM has stimulated companies to continuous improvement, so eco-efficient companies will have to adopt a parallel radical target of reduced use of eco-capacity per unit of production. These can be operationalized through means such as tough pollution and waste reduction goals for production facilities and product lines.

A Process View

Customer needs are always changing. So too is our understanding of the environment and the extent of eco-capacity. New risks emerge and existing ones become better characterized. And the continuing pressures of economic and population growth mean that some challenges—such as availability of clean water—become increasingly serious.

This means that eco-efficiency is more of a journey than a destination, as much a process as a set of techniques and "once-and-for-all-solutions." No company—either today or in the foreseeable future—can truly say that it is eco-efficient. What it can say is that it is moving toward eco-efficiency by constantly creating more from less—and by having a mindset that incorporates the key issues of sustainable development.

Seven Dimensions of Eco-efficiency

Practical experience of implementing these themes suggests that there are seven key dimensions that every business should be taking into account when developing products, introducing process changes, or taking other actions with environmental implications. They are:

1. Reduce the material intensity of goods and services.
2. Reduce the energy intensity of goods and services.
3. Reduce toxic dispersion.

4. Enhance material recyclability.

5. Maximize sustainable use of renewable resources.

6. Extend product durability.

7. Increase the service intensity of goods and services.

The greater the improvement in each of these dimensions—and the more dimensions in which improvement occurs—the more eco-efficient a product or process is (assuming that it also increases economic welfare). Of course, in some cases, innovations may require trade-offs between the dimensions, with improvements in some balanced by poorer performance in others. While the acceptability of this will depend on particular circumstances, such trade-offs should be seen as suboptimal, short-term, expedients rather than long-term solutions. True eco-efficiency requires improvement in most, if not all, the dimensions over the medium to long term with at least maintenance of position in the other dimensions.

The following sections discuss each of the individual dimensions in detail. The appendix to this chapter also provides some questions to stimulate practical discussions about improvement opportunities.

Material Intensity

We live in a material world. The mining, refining, growing, manufacturing, and transport of materials all require energy and create pollution and wastes. The total mass consumed in the life cycle of delivering products or services to consumers can therefore be a useful measure of environmental impact in its own right and also a proxy for others. Much of this mass is usually hidden from the customer's view, such as the overburdens displaced and processed in mining and quarrying or the water consumed during manufacturing.[9]

Mining and processing materials can be expensive, hence they are often costly to buy (although not as expensive as they would be if the full environmental costs were included in their price). Using them more efficiently and sustainably—"doing more with less"—therefore makes sense both for the environment and for business.

Independent of any progress made in response to environmental concerns, advances in technology show promising trends in materials (and energy) efficiency. For example, over the years, the size of computer and telecommunications equipment has shrunk, while its users have come to enjoy a wider and more efficient range of applications. The electronic transfer and storage of documents and data can result in fewer "hard" copies of documents, less air and surface transportation, filing and warehousing. (However, it does sometimes result in additional paper—usually when human systems do not yet mesh with the technology.) Now, with the "data highway," we are beginning to witness a convergence of the equipment and services of the telecommunications, computer, consumer electronics, entertainment, and publishing industries.[10]

But there have also been great reductions in material intensity as a partial or complete result of environmental drivers. Batteries provide an example. After decades as a technological backwater, in the 1990s batteries have seen a flurry of new designs. The aim has been to greatly increase longevity and power-weight ratios to better meet customer needs for portable electronic products while avoiding the toxic heavy metal cadmium, which was used in the most popular nickel-cadmium (nicad) designs. At the start of the decade Hitachi and Toshiba pioneered the introduction of rechargeable lithium-nickel hydride batteries, which gave 50% more energy output than nicads per gram of weight. Sony has since developed even lighter lithium-ion batteries that provide double the power output of nicad from the same mass. Battery technologists look forward to "factor four" improvements in power-weight ratios from the next generation of lithium-polymer devices.

The American crop protection and fertilizer company Cargill is also reducing the material intensity of agriculture through its variable rate technology (VRT). This protects the environment by applying only the required quantity of plant nutrients and agrochemicals in the sections of fields that require them. The innovation is based on a systems approach involving certified crop advisors, trained agronomists, soil testing, and application services that use the latest satellite-linked computer technology. It allows farmers to save money by buying less and benefits the environment through less runoff and contamination of groundwater by surplus products. Cargill loses sales in the short term but in the longer term has a closer relationship with more satisfied customers—and reduces the likelihood of regulatory intervention.

Pervasive changes are occurring too in the packaging area, a subject that has received much attention in recent years.[11] Many innovative companies are now using packaging more efficiently and realizing substantial savings, with no harm to product quality. Meanwhile industrial customers and—in countries with quantity fees for household waste—final consumers enjoy lower disposal costs.

Working with suppliers, Xerox initiated a program of reusable containers and pallets for shipping parts between facilities and suppliers. This avoids the creation of 10,000 tons of waste and saves the company up to $15 million annually, quite apart from saving timber resources.[12]

3M has also tackled the waste generated in its premises by suppliers. It has used a combination of taking supplies in larger quantities or in reusable drums and tote tanks to greatly reduce the amount of waste it has to dispose of.

The Swiss pharmaceutical producer Roche has taken a similar initiative for the companies it supplies. It now uses a reusable transport package for the delivery of its products to hospitals and pharmacies. The new packaging avoids waste disposal and saves the company money by reducing the annual use of corrugated cardboard and paper by 50 tons. This translates into a competitive advantage for Roche, a cost savings for their customers, and an overall reduction of the material intensity of the chain.[13]

At Johnson & Johnson too, packaging is recognized as a key customer concern. The company's target is to reduce its consumption of packaging materials by 25% over the period 1992–2000. Such reductions are one of the fastest ways for the company to impact its bottom line and reduce the disposal burden for its customers. In many of its businesses asepsis assurance and product protection have been central to quality and brand equity. The challenge has been to maintain these standards and provide tangible solutions to overpackaging—both real and perceived.[14]

Three initiatives exemplify simple yet highly successful approaches to source reduction. One has been folding surgical gloves, which reduces package size by 40%. This translates into 625,000 lb estimated waste reduction when fully implemented and annual cost savings of $1.3 million. Shipping packages of 300 rather than 72 vials to pharmaceutical customers also means 73% less packaging by weight, a 143,000 lb reduction in packaging waste, and $217,000 cost savings annually.

Energy

Energy is consumed during all stages of the life cycle of any product or service. Producing and consuming this energy creates enormous amounts of pollution and waste materials and, at present, often depletes nonrenewable fossil fuels. Making life cycles more energy efficient therefore creates great environmental benefit.

Most technologies become more energy-efficient with time, so progress in this area has been very positive in recent decades. However, population and economic growth has meant that overall energy consumption has increased. Even greater effort is needed if we want to move beyond running to stand still.

The energy intensity of a product includes both the energy needed to assemble and use raw materials and the energy used during its consumption and disposal stages. This is net of any energy credits realized through incineration of waste material. The business opportunity is to identify the parts of the system and the life cycle that use the highest energy intensity, and redesign the product or its use to make significant energy reductions. As energy is costly even today, this will also create economic benefits. These benefits will almost certainly rise with time as subsidies are removed or economic instruments are introduced to reflect the full environmental costs of energy production.

Manufacturers can decrease energy intensity by better process monitoring and control, equipment insulation, utilizing waste heat, and other means. The Chieng Sang Industry Co., for example, is a medium-scale textile dyeing plant in Thailand. Its processes—which include hot bleaching and dyeing stages as well as drying—consume a great deal of energy. A cleaner production initiative involving insulation of steam pipes has now cut heat losses from these by 80%. Energy requirements have been cut further by recycling warm condensate from spent steam back to the boiler, thereby reducing both heating requirements and water consumption. Installation of a computerized spectrophotometer—which matches production and design colors more accurately—has also reduced the amount of redyeing by 70%. The net result is savings in energy and water consumption and treatment costs alone of 284,000 baht ($11,000) a year from a capital investment of 1 million baht

Eco-efficient Detergent

Procter & Gamble first introduced compact powdered detergents, known as Ultra formulations, in 1989. These generally require consumer use of half the volume or less of traditional laundry powders as a result of combining a denser product and 30% fewer product raw materials. Consequently, the smaller volume requires 30% less packaging, and less energy is used to ship and distribute enough powder for a given number of washloads. In fact, P&G estimates that trucking needs have decreased by 40% worldwide for compact detergents vs. traditional detergents.

Since their introduction, further improvements in the manufacture and packaging of Ultra detergents have resulted in additional gains in resource efficiency. Switching from a "wet" to a "dry" process reduces by half the amount of energy needed to produce the detergent, as well as reducing water consumption. Plastic refill bags, now available for powdered laundry detergents in the United States and Europe, utilize 80% less material than traditional cartons, and require less energy to make and ship the product or package. They also contain 25% recycled content. In other parts of the world, detergent is sold only in plastic bags.

P&G uses life cycle inventory to understand the amount of energy and waste produced throughout the life cycle of its products—beginning with raw material extraction to final disposal of the product and packaging.[15] P&G's compact detergents offer multiple environmental benefits throughout their life cycle, some of which are not immediately apparent. For example, if fewer raw materials and less packaging are used per washload, fewer raw materials are mined, processed, and transported. This requires less energy and produces less solid waste.

A life cycle study of laundry detergents conducted for P&G under American conditions indicates that Ultras save approximately 664 thousand British thermal units of energy for every 1000 washloads and a total of 500 tons of solid waste per year compared with traditional powders. If all washloads in the United States were done with Ultra detergents, this would save energy equivalent to 140 million gallons (over 700,000 liters) of gasoline per year and cut the solid waste generated in a year by an amount equivalent to that generated by 765,000 people.[16]

($40,000). Considerable additional benefits have also accrued from reduced use of chemicals and increased productivity.[17]

Energy efficiency is especially important in China, which is now one of the world's largest users of energy. The Yantai Second Distillery shows what can be achieved. This is a state-owned, medium-sized enterprise that produces grain liquors and red potato wine. The distillery participated in China's first Cleaner Production Programme, which was sponsored by the National Environmental Protection Agency and supported by UNEP and the World Bank. Yantai's most important environmental problem was the generation of 14 tons of distiller's grain (a wastewater residue from the distillation process) per ton of alcohol. This was broken down in an anaerobic wastewater treatment plant. An assessment revealed a number of low cost options, including additional distillation of the distiller's grain to recover more alcohol, introducing continuous rather than batch fermentation to eliminate washout (and increase production efficiency), and installation of a new coal-fired boiler, which is both more efficient and able to utilize methane produced from the treatment plant. The outcome has been greatly reduced energy and water consumption and costs, and improved product quality, so that the liquor can be now be sold at a higher price.[18]

Cooling, heating, and lighting buildings, and powering the equipment within them, uses around a third of world energy consumption. A number of studies suggest that this can be greatly reduced. Britain's National Westminster Bank shows what can be done. Its 1991–95 plan set a target of reducing its absolute energy consumption by 15% over the period. The target has been achieved—despite an increase in turnover during the period—and has created cumulative net savings of £42 million. The savings have been achieved through a combination of energy-efficient lighting and equipment, more efficient space heating and thermostatic controls, more effective insulation, and improved standards of housekeeping. The advantages of sophisticated energy management systems are also apparent at the Japanese electronics manufacturer NEC. It developed an electronic system for its Tokyo headquarters that has not only reduced energy consumption by 40% but also provided a product that is now sold commercially.

Increasing the energy efficiency of buildings can also benefit productivity. As labor costs are usually the major component of total building occupation costs—around $130 a year per square foot in the United States, compared to $21 for rent, maintenance, energy, and other expenses—this can provide substantial bottom-line advantages.[19] An energy efficiency program at Reno, Nevada's post office involved lowering a high ceiling to improve heating, cooling, and acoustics, and installation of more efficient and less intense lighting. The expected result was a $50,000 saving in annual energy costs. The unexpected result was a 6% improvement in the productivity of letter sorting—to the point where Reno suddenly became the most productive and least error-prone office in the western United States. As nothing else had changed during this period, the better lighting and improved acoustics were almost certainly responsible. A study co-authored by a U.S. Department of Energy official noted similar examples at Boeing, Pennsylvania Power & Light, Wal-Mart, West Bend Mutual Insurance, and other organizations.[20]

Appliances are major users of energy and here too there are great opportunities for improvement. The German appliance manufacturer Bosch-Siemens estimates, for example, that the energy requirements of its products have been reduced by more than 40% over the last two decades. The American competition—financed by over thirty utilities—to develop a superefficient refrigerator program (SERP) suggests that more is possible. SERP offered a prize of $30 million for development and production of a low energy refrigerator. The competition was won by Whirlpool, whose design was 40% more energy-efficient than the national average. As its design utilized only existing technologies, new designs may offer even greater potential for improvement.

Transportation is also a major user of energy—and an equally important source of eco-efficiency opportunities. Lighter components can make a considerable difference. The Airbus A320 aircraft, for example, uses a composite rather than an aluminum finbox in its tail. According to its makers, Novartis, this weighs 20% less—which translates into a saving of 200 tons of jet fuel and 800 tons of carbon dioxide emissions over the 20-year service life of the aircraft.

Toxic Dispersion

Some toxic or otherwise harmful substances that are emitted to the environment can be quickly broken down. But others will remain unchanged (or, occasionally, are converted to even more toxic forms) and spread through the biosphere. They can then cause negative environmental and health impacts in those cases where exposure is at, or accumulates to, a level beyond that generally considered to cause risk. The opportunity is to significantly reduce and control such dispersal.

One means of doing this is to redesign products and delivery systems. The Swiss life sciences company Novartis, for example, has an objective of developing ways of using smaller quantities of active ingredients in better-targeted ways to reduce any toxic effects. Its Egyptian Plant Protection division achieved this for cotton insecticides. A new product, Sirene, combines insecticide with pheromones (scents) that attract the targeted insects. The compound is sprayed onto crops from short distances in much smaller quantities than with previous, aerial, spraying. The method uses less material, avoids contamination by drifting spray, reduces risks to workers, and eliminates large-scale disposal of agrochemical containers.

ICI Autocolor, a subsidiary of the British chemical producer ICI, has also developed a new product to reduce emissions of VOCs, which can be hazardous in their own right and are also precursors to ground-level ozone. Aquabase paint was developed in response to growing demand for metallic car paints. These have traditionally required large amounts of organic solvent and required drying at high temperatures. Aquabase paint is a largely water-based product that can be dried with a simple air blowing system. It therefore reduces emissions and saves energy. It is also particularly suitable to small car repair shops that have previously had difficulty in making environmental improvements. The innovation won ICI a Queen's Award for Environmental Achievement in 1995.

A collaboration in Tunisia between the Environmental Pollution Prevention Program and local sheepskin tanners illustrates the potential for reducing toxic emissions in a developing country. Traditional tanning processes make inefficient use of dyeing and tanning chemicals, create noxious smells, and produce water contaminated by chromium and other hazardous substances. All these problems have been reduced through separation and individual treatment of different waste streams and better control of process temperatures and conditions to improve yields. By doing this, one plant has reduced consumption of chromium sulfate to only a quarter of its original level and saved $50,000 a year on an investment of only $20,000.[21]

Developing a New Product from Waste Water

Coconut palms create a picture of unsullied desert islands. Yet coconut processing can create large amounts of wastewater. This has a high organic content—which robs rivers and lakes of ecologically vital oxygen—and is also highly acidic. The latter prevents it from being used for another possible purpose, irrigating rice paddies. These were problems for the candy company, Peter Paul Philippines Corporation. Its desiccated coconut plant at Barrio Pahinga, Quezon Island, produces 22,000 tons of desiccated coconut a year. And, until recently, it created over 100,000 liters a day of waste coconut liquid. This killed most of the aquatic life in the local river.

Under regulatory pressure to clean up, Peter Paul took part in the government-sponsored Industrial Environmental Management Project (IEMP). With cooperation from the UNEP Industry and Environment program, the project conducted a pollution management appraisal of its plant.[22] Its recommendation was to segregate different wastewater streams. This avoided contamination of rainwater and also created a potential resource, in the form of separated coconut water.

Peter Paul now makes use of the coconut water in a joint venture with a Taiwanese drinks company, Chia Meei. The venture exports concentrated, frozen coconut water as an ingredient in Chia Meei products. Peter Paul pumps 40,000 liters a day of separated coconut water into the joint venture's processing plant—and gets additional revenue from it. The near halving of its wastewater generation also reduces the operating costs of its waste treatment plant. Best of all, Peter Paul's initiative has created higher yields of its main product, desiccated coconut. To capture the water more effectively, coconuts are now cut open and pared by machine rather than hand. The liquid is filtered off and pumped to the Chia Meei plant. The new process means less waste of coconut meat and creates an extra 30 pounds of desiccated coconut for every ton processed.

Peter Paul has had to make only small investments in new equipment to achieve these benefits but is achieving annual savings and output improvements of over $370,000 a year. Most of this is from increased yield of desiccated coconut.

The estimated biological oxygen demand (BOD) of wastewater from the Peter Paul facility has also fallen by 50%, allowing some restoration of river quality. The use of waste coconut water also avoids the material, energy, and other impacts of producing alternative ingredients.

Peter Paul shows the potential of biologically toxic wastes to become valuable raw materials. It also shows how a drive for environmental improvement can result in increased yield and other production benefits. Overall, Peter Paul's general manager, Frank Klar, is delighted that "we've saved money and at the same time been able to produce in a more ecological manner. We're encouraged to look for similar opportunities in other areas."

Recyclability

Material and energy utilization can be improved by reuse in the same or another system. This avoids the energy and waste costs of mining or creating virgin materials. The potential savings from this have always been realized for many expensive materials, which have been recycled for decades or centuries. There is now the opportunity to extend the principle into all business sectors, including the manufacturing, construction, office, retail, and service sectors, as well as to individual households.

It is important to realize, however, that eco-efficient recycling is that which maximizes the financial value of materials and minimizes the environmental effects of their processing. Recycling is environmentally unproductive when the amount of energy, materials, and pollution used in collecting, preparing, and processing the recyclate exceeds the impact of the system that delivers the primary materials. This can be determined by a life cycle analysis (LCA). Financial costs and benefits can be assessed by traditional methods. Of course, there are situations where recycling is environmentally justified but unprofitable. It is difficult for individual companies to take action in these circumstances—experience suggests that the best response is some combination of partnership with other companies, communities, or governments and/or redesign of products to change the economics.

There are also different kinds of recycling. One option is to reuse components or materials. This retains the value created by their original manufacture and avoids the environmental impact associated with making them suitable for other uses and with producing replacements. Another is remanufacture, which also has these benefits—albeit with the higher cost and impact associated with the remanufacturing processing. Four further options are recycling the material to an alternative use, incineration to utilize its energy content, composting, and biogasi-fication. The best option for a particular situation will vary, for example, if reuse, remanufacturing and recycling involve long-distance transport of low-value materials.

Companies such as Hewlett-Packard and Xerox have certainly found that reusing equipment and parts makes both environmental and business sense. Other electronic manufacturers are likely to follow them as economic incentives are joined by takeback legislation making them responsible for the final disposal of their products.

Hewlett-Packard, for example, created its Hardware Recycling Organization to process excess products and parts into useful service parts by disassembling and refurbishing them. This program improves HP's service levels by increasing the availability of parts, while lowering costs. Parts that cannot be used for service are sorted and diverted to lower-level, noncompetitive recovery channels. Examples include:

• Generic memory and microprocessors are removed and sold into markets such as the toy industry.

• Printed circuit boards and cables are refined to recover precious metals.

• Plastics are recovered for reuse in the manufacture of new HP products.

Overall, 98% of the materials received each month are reused or recycled.[23]

Worldwatch Institute's *State of the World 1995* cites several examples that demonstrate the environmental and economic advantages of rehabilitating old buildings for reuse compared with new construction.[24] In Denmark, for example, a nonprofit housing group upgraded some apartment buildings and added another floor on top to increase floor space by 33%. The renovations used significantly less material than new construction and were done at two-thirds the cost. Even with the expanded capacity, the total use of energy and water in the building stayed the same, thanks to conservation improvements.[25]

Industrial pollution prevention initiatives have also resulted in various recycling developments, for example, using the energy content of waste gases, closed-loop systems that continuously recycle process chemicals (dry cleaning equipment is one typical instance of this), and waste exchange programs that match waste generators with businesses looking for a source of raw materials.

The Mexican carbon black producer NHUMO has benefited greatly from capturing the energy content of waste gases. Until 1993 all the waste gas from its production process was released into the atmosphere. Now the gas is captured and used for drying the product—thereby avoiding the consumption of large quantities of natural gas previously used for this purpose.

The Spanish metal finishing company DECORAL provides an example of continuous recycling. Its old aluminum finishing technology used large quantities of caustic soda and sulfuric acid and generated wastewater and sludge, which required costly disposal. Working with the Center for Cleaner Production Initiatives in Barcelona, the company introduced new separation techniques to its process. This allows treatment chemicals to be recovered and water to be recycled. Consumption of caustic soda and sulfuric acid has fallen by 60% and water by 20%. The amount of sludge for disposal is also down by 70%. The net result was a cost saving of $240,000 a year on an investment of $400,000, giving a payback of twenty months.[26]

Du Pont's Altamira, Mexico, facility has also saved over $6 million a year from two initiatives. One is installation of separation equipment to recover wasted raw materials from its titanium dioxide production process. This has greatly reduced waste volumes and saved $5 million a year in raw material costs alone. Secondary reactions in the process also form hydrochloric acid, which was previously vented at low concentrations. This is now recovered and reused in another process, saving raw material purchases of over $1.25 million per annum. This and other Du Pont initiatives have convinced Paul Tebo, the company's senior EH&S manager, that recycling and other actions to reduce waste and increase yield represent an enormous future business opportunity worth at least $3 billion.[27]

Used packaging boxes are also being used for construction purposes in Central America. In 1980 the Swiss Eternit Group decided to phase out asbestos from the fibercement products it was producing in several Central American countries. However, conventional asbestos substitutes were too costly for local markets and, if imported, would exacerbate balance of payments problems. After several years of research, teething problems, and skepticism about the feasibility of finding local substitutes, the group's Costa Rican subsidiary, RICALIT, developed a fiber substitute essentially composed of different grades of cellulose, recycled newspaper, and used banana boxes widely available in the region. Although the manufacturing costs of the recycled fibercement products were more expensive than alternatives, this was more than offset by savings in raw material costs—which have translated into tens of millions of dollars of import savings for the region over the last decade. In addition, the new products have better structural properties than the old and can be used for new markets such as wallboards and roofing. They are now manufactured from local materials in a number of Latin American countries and sold in the United States, providing an example of technology transfer from South to North.

Businesses in the Kanto region of Japan too save money from recycling. They now pay 40% less to dispose of their waste office paper, thanks to the recycling efforts of the Office Neighborhood Association (ONA). ONA was established in 1991 as a cooperative endeavor to collect and recycle waste paper from local businesses. It has grown from thirty-eight participating business establishments in 1991 to over 200 today. During the same period, wastepaper collection has risen from 100 tons to nearly 550 tons a month, and it currently supports forty-three wastepaper collectors. The association has also expanded its activities to the sale of products (toilet paper) made from wastepaper.[28]

Renewable Resources

The fossil fuels and some of the key materials on which our modern world is built are finite. It is difficult to predict how long they will last, for the limits to their extraction depend upon rising prices and the rate at which technical innovation allows more and more difficult sources to be tapped. But sometime in the future we will have to replace them with alternatives.

Using renewable rather than nonrenewable resources—for example, solar power rather than fossil fuels, or sustainably produced timber rather than clear-cut timber—therefore anticipates future trends. It also—although not always—tends to create less environmental impact over the entire life cycle.

The most obvious renewable resource is solar power, whether captured directly through sunlight or indirectly through biomass, waves, and winds. Solar power is probably the key to satisfying the unmet needs of the 2 billion people without access to electricity. Some also believe that it can play a major role in generating electricity even in developed and developing countries with good conventional sources. Although similar predictions have been made in the past—and failed to materialize—years of R&D are beginning to produce results.

What is already feasible—and has been long used in traditional architecture—is "ecological design" of buildings to maximize natural cooling, heating, and lighting. According to Malaysian architect Dr. Ken Yeang,

> If you configure the building right in the first place, then you don't need expensive energy saving devices to correct mistakes. Instead, you use design to lower energy costs with passive devices like orientation, planting and natural ventilation.[30]

Yeang has put the principles into practice in the new Kuala Lumpur headquarters of IBM's Malaysian affiliate. Tall atriums encourage natural ventilation. Movable blinds and curtain wall glazing minimizes solar gain. And natural lighting reaches most areas of the building. The result is an estimated 40% savings in energy costs—and a more relaxing and aesthetically pleasing environment.

Substituting biological materials for synthetic ones can also help the environment. Novo Nordisk is a Danish biotechnology company whose entire business has been built on fermentation-based processes using biological materials. It is now the world's leading supplier of insulin and industrial enzymes and a major producer of pharmaceuticals. One of its products is Terminox Ultra, an enzyme that can degrade hydrogen peroxide into oxygen and water. A small Danish textile dyeing house, Sjkern Tricotage-Farveri, uses hydrogen peroxide to bleach fabric and must remove all traces prior to dyeing. It recently substituted Terminox for a chemical agent, sodium thiosulphate, which it previously used. The change has not only substituted biological for synthetic materials, it has also reduced the amount of water needed for rinsing and saved energy by permitting bleaching at lower temperatures. In total, the company has saved over $100,000 at a minimal additional cost.[31]

Recycling at Saturn

Saturn, a division of the U.S. automaker General Motors, provides many examples of recycling. Through its roughly 300 dealers, Saturn collects used and damaged plastic materials from its automobiles for reprocessing and reuse in new vehicles. New Saturn cars now contain several parts (e.g., wheel liners) made from recycled fasciae, fenders, and doors. To transport these used parts, Saturn relies on a reverse distribution system using trucks that previously returned from dealers empty. Saturn saves $10 in raw material costs for each new car built with parts manufactured with recycled materials, equivalent to $3 million annually, based on sales of 300,000 cars.

In 1995, Saturn made another decision that will alter the life cycle of its vehicles—it decided to tap into the used car market. Since used cars generally appeal to a different market segment from new cars, the company is not really concerned about the effect of its used car program on new car sales. Rather, the company's goal is to develop partnerships with potential new customers—people who might be in the market for a new car in the future—in order to expand market share in the long run.

To qualify for Saturn's "certified used car program," the vehicle's safety and emission systems must, at a minimum, pass inspection. Additional repairs and reconditioning are also undertaken as needed to deliver a used car that meets Saturn's quality standards of durability and dependability.

In the future, the company expects one of its biggest challenges will be getting used parts and automobiles back into the system to provide a reliable source of "raw materials" for the production of new parts, or to sustain its used car program. To overcome this obstacle, it is looking at leasing or service programs that will provide greater access to used cars and parts.[29]

Similarly, Roche's Fukoroi, Japan, site now produces vitamin B_2 directly from fermentation of a natural raw material, glucose. The previous process was based on synthetic materials and processes that used volatile organic solvents.

A small British company, Pronatur, has even made use of waste orange peel to create a substitute for trichloroethane and other synthetic solvents. The product is based on oils distilled from the peel. It is also immiscible with water, which, with other properties, makes it very effective for separating oil based contaminants from wastewater. It is particularly effective when mixed with oil-consuming bacteria. Pronatur holds the oily contaminants in solution while the bacteria go to work. The only products from the process are carbon dioxide and water.[32]

Durability

One way of extending resource productivity is by extending the useful life of products. This results in less frequent replacements, which in turn can mean less waste and the use of fewer material and energy resources. Easily accessible and detachable parts, as well as the availability of replacement parts, allow equipment to be replaced, repaired, and maintained instead of the more wasteful practice of "buying new" each time.

Some companies have employed product-life optimization strategies for some time to gain competitive advantage. For example, a significant part of the market appeal of the Volvo automobile is its life expectancy. Or again, Northern Telecom's Meridian telephone system can be easily upgraded to provide enhanced communication capabilities, a strategy that promotes customer loyalty, while maintaining profits, since it is less expensive to upgrade than to replace the entire system.

Durability can be achieved by actions at all stages of the life cycle—from design, through production, to use and disposal.[33]

Anticipating future uses during the design stage can give many products a useful "afterlife" after their original function has been performed. The Malaysian architect we cited earlier, Dr. Ken Yeang, designs office blocks with open floor spaces, terraces, and suitable windows so that they can easily be converted to residential use if they become unsuitable for business.

The way in which products are made can also have major implications for their durability. For example, robust materials can more easily withstand wear and knocks.

The small Tunisian battery manufacturer, La Societé Tunisienne de l'Accumulateur NOUR, illustrates the point. The life of lead acid batteries is affected by temperature and humidity in manufacture. The more appropriate these are, the greater the service life, cold cranking power, and reserve capacity of the batteries. Following an assessment by the USAID-sponsored Environmental Pollution Prevention Project, NOUR introduced nineteen initiatives. These allow better control of manufacturing so that product durability and quality are greatly improved. They have also cut consumption of energy, materials, and water and reduced creation of toxic emissions, slag, and waste. Most of the initiatives have paybacks of under a year and many are under three months.[34]

Another important way of achieving durability is by more careful utilization and maintenance of equipment. Take Sager Surgicals, a small Indian lead oxide manufacturer. A waste minimization audit in collaboration with the Indian National Productivity Council found that much of the energy input to its melting furnace was being lost as a result of radiation through its sides and top. This was not only expensive but also shortened the furnace life and made it difficult to achieve the necessary temperatures for high lead oxide yield and quality. The solution was modifying the furnace design and installing better insulation. This halved fuel consumption. It also reduced cycle time by a quarter—thereby increasing capacity—and gave a 10% improvement in yield. Best of all, the furnace life has increased from 6 months to an estimated 5 years. The result of these changes is that Sagar is achieving annual savings of $40,000 on a $10,000 capital investment and $5000 per annum additional operating costs.[35]

Canadian based TransAlta Utilities is also taking steps to increase the durability of the over 1 million wooden poles that carry its wires. These are both a major corporate asset and—through their growing, treatment when in use, and disposal—have a significant environmental impact. In 1995 the company initiated a study of their entire life cycle to find opportunities for eco-efficient action.

One outcome of the study is adoption of more environmentally benign pesticides and preservatives. Another is work with pole suppliers to develop quality assurance programs in manufacturing plants. The result is fewer wasted trees and a reduced need for third-party inspections. A pilot project was also undertaken on poles scheduled for removal and landfill disposal to see if they could be reused. In fact, 40% could be. Revised guidelines and practices have since been put in place to spread this learning across the company, generating estimated annual savings of over $1 million. And the poles that cannot be reused are sold or donated for use in shingles, decking, park boardwalks, and other applications.

Of course, durability is not likely to commend itself immediately to all manufacturers, some of whom may believe that the health of their bottom line depends on the regular "repeat" purchase of their products. However, a longer-life products approach need not automatically imply lower profitability, as the boxed example of Xerox shows.[36]

Barriers to Longer-Life Products

There are several barriers that must be overcome in order to increase the acceptability and availability of longer-life products.[37]

• Financial models for product costing are biased toward single use rather than multiple lifetimes. Robust designs that allow a longer product life generally lead to higher unit manufacturing costs, although the life cycle costs are improved through reuse of the parts.

• Regardless of their actual quality, used products suffer from an image problem, in part due to inadequate or ineffective marketing.

• Customers do not always recognize the value and benefits of services, and therefore are often unwilling to pay for them, whereas they more readily accept the price of a tangible product. This has implications for product leasing as well as for servicing longer-life products.

• Remanufactured equipment, as well as closed-loop recycling, requires a reliable supply of recovered product. Xerox, for example, cannot guarantee recovery rates high enough to meet its production needs.

Several other factors work against longer-life products. In the telecommunications industry competitive trends have led to the demise of durability. First, deregulation of the telecommunication markets in the United States, Canada, and Europe has resulted in fewer durable residential telephone sets because the trend in those markets has been moving away from leasing toward greater ownership. Leased telephones are designed to last longer, as the telecommunications provider expects to get the product back, refurbish it, and lease it to another customer. Second, rapid technological innovation and increased capabilities make equipment obsolete at an increased rate, driving faster product replacement.

Remanufacturing and Recycling at Xerox

Xerox has remanufactured products for over twenty years, although not with the efficiency it does today. The rise of environmental issues on the company's agenda led company officials to rethink product return and remanufacturing issues. As a result, Xerox changed its product delivery procedures to recapture more equipment faster; and it is also now developing more effective product return processes.

New approaches to product design also strive to extend the product life through:

remanufacturing;

equipment conversion (i.e., reintroducing equipment into the market in a different configuration, e.g., by converting a copier into a printer or adding new features to old models);

greater use of common parts in products, which provides greater flexibility in reuse and servicing; and

material recycling.

Xerox is realizing savings from activities that extend from the recycling of low-value toner cartridges to the remanufacturing of high-end reprographic machines. In its copy cartridge program, for example, Xerox has demonstrated profitable equipment recovery and remanufacturing while maintaining quality standards. By reusing parts in its low-volume copier cartridges, Xerox estimates savings in raw material cost of over $ 2 million in 1994, based on a return rate of between 25% and 50%. Even with the costs associated with recovering cartridges, the unit manufacturing cost over the lifetime of the cartridge and its components is lower than single-use cartridges. For this reason, the company is providing customers with a cash incentive to return their cartridges.

Xerox has learned through experience that recycling within smaller loops, that is, maintaining the maximum amount of value-added to manufactured equipment, returns maximum value to the company. Thus, refurbishing demonstration equipment for resale is more profitable than remanufacturing it, but remanufacturing in turn yields greater value than equipment conversion or parts-strip and reuse, with material recycling resulting in the lowest return. Generally speaking, the smaller loops strategy also benefits the environment because it saves on the use of virgin raw materials, and means that fewer parts are manufactured, and that less waste is generated.[38]

Extending the life of products has also been thwarted by the high cost of repair and maintenance services when compared with the cost of buying new goods, and by the consequential disappearance of a repair and maintenance infrastructure in some business sectors. A subsidiary of Thorn-EMI, the largest renter of "brown" and "white" consumer durables in the United Kingdom, has launched a "Create" initiative to deal with this. This involves establishing city-based refurbishment workshops that recycle and remanufacture end-of-life goods such as washing machines and refrigerators, and that employ people who have been out of work for long periods. The refurbished products will be reasonably priced and affordable to low-income households.[39]

Finally, there are important issues of technological progress that can make some longer-life products obsolete from an environmental point of view. The automotive sector provides one of the most obvious examples. The environmental benefits of rapid progress in improving the energy efficiency of new cars coming off the production line would be missed if older cars were not replaced.

The implication is that optimizing durability may require a reevaluation of corporate strategy and services. It may, for example, entail moving to lease models in order to maximize product recovery; or it may require manufacturers to offer maintenance and repair services to extend their product's life. Another possibility is to enter secondary markets, as with the Saturn case discussed earlier.

Service Intensity

Increasing service intensity means creating additional value for customers while reducing or holding constant environmental impacts. It can be achieved in a number of ways, such as shared use, multifunctionality, and easy upgrading. Durability can also be regarded as an example of service intensity.

Shared Use

Resources can be more effectively utilized by sharing them with others or selling access to them. For example, telephone companies now offer a call-answering service that is as convenient as owning your own telephone answering machine. This centralized system is essentially a software feature supported by existing telecommunication equipment in the home and the telephone operating company. Many good examples of resource-sharing exist; they include public libraries, communal laundry facilities in apartment buildings, and a variety of businesses that rent products ranging from videotapes, carpets, and floor covering, to office equipment and heavy machinery.[40]

Multifunctionality

Sometimes functions previously provided by a number of pieces of equipment or trips can be consolidated into a smaller number, with consequent reductions in energy and material intensity. The U.S. Electric Power Research Institute, for example, sponsored work on a new, high-efficiency heat pump that can provide space and water heating and air conditioning. The result is Powermiser, which the manufacturer Nordyne estimates can reduce energy bills by 20% to 40% compared with doing the tasks separately. And according to calculations by the utility, Public Service Electric & Gas, they have a payback period of only three to four years.[41]

The Swedish logistics company ASG has achieved the same objective in transportation. They transport boxes from a Swedish packaging company to one of its customers. Through effective joint planning, the number of deliveries have been reduced to twice a day, creating better utilization of the trucks. The result is lower costs, higher delivery reliability, and less environmental impact. Moreover, the cost savings have created the financial space for investment in state-of-the-art Volvo trucks for the service, which reduces environmental impacts even further.

Upgrading

If equipment is designed for upgrading—for example, by modular construction—the durability of many components can be increased. Although there are some products where technical attributes and prices change so quickly that upgrading has not seemed appropriate—most people who can afford it generally prefer to take advantage of the lower cost and improved performance of new personal computers rather than upgrade existing machines—there are others where careful design can make it a feasible option.[42]

Upgrades can be undertaken by customers, but a growing way of adding value is if products are leased rather than sold to them and then upgraded on return to the manufacturer. Of course, this is not environmentally beneficial if they are disposed of when the products are returned. But if they can be reused, remanufactured, or recycled, the benefits can be considerable.[43]

Interface, Inc., an Atlanta, Georgia, commercial floor covering company, has launched an innovative program aimed at selling functionality of comfort. Working in collaboration with fiber producers, a new product line has been created by remanufacturing products, thereby converting the old product into new carpeting or floor tile. The customer leases the product, or the comfort provided by the carpet. Once the customer's carpet reaches the end of its useful life, a new floor covering is supplied to replace the old, and the spent product is then reintroduced to the marketplace after refurbishment, remanufacture, or a fashion face-lift.[44]

Measuring Eco-efficiency

It is often said that "you can't manage what you can't measure." While this is not always true there are a number of advantages to measuring eco-efficiency. They include:

- Monitoring improvement over time and in comparison with others,
- Providing a good knowledge base for setting the stretch targets that eco-efficiency requires,
- Helping set priorities for action,
- Deciding between alternative courses of action,
- Providing information to external stakeholders.

However, measuring eco-efficiency is not easy.[45] One difficulty is that eco-efficiency is about getting more from less. Measures that only have an environmental parameter such as quantities of substances emitted and resources used are, while valuable for environmental management (as we discuss in chapter 4), not eco-efficiency measures because they cover only one side of the equation. True eco-efficiency measures have to show how more output is being obtained from a given resource input or environmental effect. While this is relatively straightforward for outputs expressed in physical units—as with miles per gallon or fuel consumption per ton of product as a measure of fuel efficiency—it is more problematic for economic outputs. Some companies and analysts relate resource utilization or emissions to turnover, for example. However, while this can be useful, there is a danger that the measures improve not because of real environmental action but because of other changes such as inflation of revenues through price increases, corporate reorganizations, or acquisitions. Similar problems can occur with other output indicators, such as production, profitability, or value added. Whichever one is chosen needs to have a significant relationship with the environmental parameter(s). Decisions also have to be made about the boundaries of the measurement—is it the whole corporation, a division, a site, or a process within the site?

There is also a danger that measuring eco-efficiency improvements in one environmental parameter can obscure a deterioration in another. While this can be reduced by developing a wide range of individual measures covering all the main parameters, many nonspecialists lack the time to absorb such detailed information and therefore seek a single eco-efficiency measure that relates an aggregate indicator of environmental impacts to output. However, this means comparing apples (e.g., the impact of a gaseous emission of sulfur dioxide) with pears (e.g., the environmental impact of producing a ton of copper)—a procedure for which there is no broadly accepted scientific methodology.

A final difficulty is that, even if an individual organization can demonstrate that its activities and products are becoming more eco-efficient, this says nothing about its sustainability. When markets are expanding rapidly, for example, any improvements in the eco-efficiency of making products may be outweighed by the effects of increased numbers in use and/or their greater utilization. The effects of some products and processes will also be unsustainable even with radical improvements in their eco-efficiency.

Eco-efficiency is a new concept and such difficulties are inevitable—after all, it took many decades for accountants to work out the standardized measures of financial performance that we now take for granted. But some companies are at least making initial steps that, for all their imperfections, are providing useful information and a solid foundation for further progress. The following paragraphs examine four such initiatives—one by Novo Nordisk with regard to the eco-efficiency of operations and three others, by Sony Europe, Volvo and Dow Europe on the eco-efficiency of products. In addition, the case study in chapter 6 describes the development of operational eco-efficiency measures at Roche.

Novo Nordisk track their resource productivity through eco-productivity indices (EPI). These relate corporate turnover (adjusted for exchange rate and price fluctuations) to corporate consumption of the key inputs of raw materials, water, energy, and packaging. Its formula is:

$$EPI = \frac{\text{indexed turnover in constant prices}}{\text{indexed resource consumption}} \times 100$$

The higher the figure is, the more eco-efficient Novo Nordisk has been in utilizing the resource. When making the calculations, the annual turnover figure is adjusted for exchange rate and price fluctuations and indexed to the level of 1990, which is set at 100. The resource consumption figure is expressed in physical units and also indexed to the 1990 level.

Novo Nordisk's corporate-level approach is useful for showing broad trends and demonstrating that overall performance is improving. However, it is not an operational management tool, which requires a more disaggregated approach giving site- and raw material-specific data. It can be contrasted with Roche, which has adopted both aggregate and site eco-efficiency measures (see case study in chapter 6).

Another innovative measure is Sony Europe's Resource Productivity Index (see figure 3.2). This relates an economic variable (value added over a product's lifetime) to an environmental one (a composite of energy and material intensity and recycling). Different options can then be compared. For example, Sony used it to compare the resource productivity of three different batteries—nonrechargeable manganese-zinc and rechargeable nickel-cadmium and lithium-ion. Lithium-ion proved to be far the most eco-efficient, with a resource productivity almost 2000

Resource productivity

$$\text{Resource productivity} = \frac{\text{(economic value added)} \times \text{(product lifetime)}}{\text{(material consumed - recycled)} + \text{(energy consumed + (lifetime energy used)}}$$
for production and recycling)

Resource productivity of Batteries (Preliminary Estimation)

Batteries	Resource Productivity	Ratio
Primary (Mn/Zn)	10.77	1
Rechargeable (Ni/Cd)	3750.45	348.2
Rechargeable (Li-ion)	21487.09	1995.1

Assumptions

(1) Sales price as the added-value of a product
(2) Cyclability as the lifetime
(3) Self-discharge and complete discharge before charging (Ni/Cd only) as the energy consumption over lifetime

All of the used cobalt and cadmium are recycled.

Figure 3.2
Sony Europe's measures of resource efficiency.
Source: Sony Yokohama Research Center, Japan.

times that of nonrechargeable and 348 times that of rechargeable nickel-cadmium.

The specific measure has several limitations. It only addresses two of the eco-efficiency guidelines, energy and materials. The use of turnover also means that higher prices would improve the score (although it could be argued that the customer's willingness to pay a higher price reflects the product's increased utility and that the improvement is therefore a real one). There may also be an element of double counting, as increased product lifetime is reflected in the higher price of rechargeables. However, none of these points alters the ranking of the alternatives with regard to energy and material intensity and the measure has proved useful to Sony Europe in demonstrating to internal staff and others just how much more eco-efficient rechargeables in general, and lithium-ion versions in particular, are on these dimensions.

A number of companies, including Philips and Volvo, have also worked in collaboration with government research centers to develop eco-indicator schemes.[46] These assign eco-points—reflecting the seriousness of environmental impact—to standard quantities of materials, emissions, and wastes. A software package can then be used to calculate the total eco-points for different approaches to delivering the same output—that is, a product delivering a given performance. As well as making final choices between different variants, the packages can also be used to examine the effects of varying material compositions and product configurations in order to achieve an environmentally optimal design. The main strength of such schemes is their conversion of environmental "apples and pears" into a common unit. However, this is also their weakness, as there is often a lack of consensus about the weightings that should be given to different impacts. For example, how should a unit of nuclear-generated electricity be weighted relative to one from hydro? And how should substances about which there is considerable scientific and public controversy, such as hormone-mimicking chemicals, be assessed? Environmentalists will usually have very different views from industrialists on such topics and there will often be disagreement even among scientists. Nonetheless, the companies that use eco-indicators do find them to be useful ways of making broad comparisons between products.

Volvo has used an eco-points scheme—which it terms the Environmental Priority Strategies (EPS) system—to assist design engineers in the selection of environmentally preferable materials for product construction. In one such case, two technically equivalent constructions for the front end of a car, one using a plastic composite and the other galvanized steel, were compared. Eco-points were calculated for production, product use, and product disposal at end of life for each material. The plastic construction proved to have a lower overall environmental impact. The galvanized steel received a less favorable score because its heavier weight increased fuel consumption during product use.[47]

Dow Europe has developed an "eco-compass" to compare different products (see figure 3.3).[48] This scores six dimensions, which broadly cor-

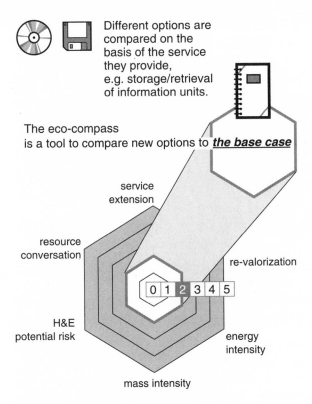

Different options are compared on the basis of the service they provide, e.g. storage/retrieval of information units.

The eco-compass is a tool to compare new options to **_the base case_**

service extension

resource conversation

re-valorization

0 1 2 3 4 5

H&E potential risk

energy intensity

mass intensity

Figure 3.3
Dow's eco-compass.
Source: Claude Fussler with Peter James, *Driving Eco-Innovation* (London: Pitman, 1996), p. 153.

respond to the seven listed on pp. 56–57. (For convenience, Dow treats durability as part of service intensity—which it terms service extension. It also uses the term "revalorization" to cover the potential for recycling, reuse, or remanufacture. The other difference is its substitution of resource conservation for renewable resources.) The new or revised product is scored for each dimension on a scale of 1 to 5. The scoring is relative to a base case (usually an existing product), which is always scored as 2. To ensure that comparisons are fair, each score is based on the environmental impact of delivering a standard unit of service (e.g., 1MB of data storage or passenger-kilometer of transportation). The precise scale is:

0   performance per functional unit decreases by 50% or more

1   performance per functional unit decreases by up to 50%,

2   there is no significant variation from the base case,

3   up to 100% improvement per functional unit,

4   up to 300% increase in performance per functional unit,

5   a more than 300% increase in performance per functional unit.

This scoring is more logarithmic than linear to stress the point that sustainable development requires radical product innovations. New products only receive a 5 if they provide "factor four" levels of improvement over existing ones—the level that a number of environmental thinkers believe is the minimum required for true sustainability.[49]

The scores of the base case and the alternative(s) can then be mapped onto the compass to provide a visual comparison of their eco-efficiency. Dow then uses these as inputs to "eco-innovation workshops" that consider ways in which the eco-efficiency of new or existing products can be further improved.

The workshops bring together people from a wide range of backgrounds—R&D, production, marketing, environmental—from both within and outside the company. Their premise is that eco-efficiency is not just an idea and set of techniques but a process that involves generating and maintaining enthusiasm and commitment so that the ideas and outputs of the techniques are actually implemented. In the words of Claude Fussler, a vice president at Dow Europe,

Eco-efficient innovations only add value when they respond to future market needs and openings, create genuinely new ideas for meeting those needs and achieve outstanding implementation.[50]

The message of this chapter is that such outstanding implementation rests upon clear and measurable eco-efficiency objectives. These guide progress and provide the benchmarks that allow progress to be charted and different alternatives to be compared. They also set the boundaries for concern and actions—often beyond organizational boundaries to consider interactions with suppliers and customers throughout the product life cycle.

The next chapter examines these other aspects of implementation in greater detail.

Appendix: Checklist Questions for Eco-efficiency[51]

Material Intensity

Can the product or service be redesigned to make less use of material inputs?

Are there less material-intensive raw materials?

Can existing raw materials be produced or processed in less materially intense ways?

Would higher-quality materials create less waste in later stages?

Can water consumption be reduced?

Can water, wastewater treatment, or waste disposal costs be allocated to budgets to encourage greater control?

Can yields be increased by better maintenance, control, or other means?

Can wastes be utilized?

Can products be made of smaller size, or a different shape, to minimize material and packaging requirements?

Can the product or service be combined with others to reduce overall material intensity?

Can packaging be eliminated or reduced?

Can the product be reused, remanufactured, or recycled?

Energy

Can raw materials be produced or dried with less or renewable energy?

Would substitute materials or components reduce overall energy intensity?

Can energy costs be directly allocated to budgets to encourage better control?

Can energy be exchanged between processes?

Can waste heat be utilized?

Can processes be integrated to create energy savings?

Can processes or building energy consumption be better monitored and controlled?

Could better maintenance of boilers and other equipment improve energy efficiency?

Can processes or buildings be insulated more effectively?

Can more energy-efficient lighting be installed?

Is there scope for better energy housekeeping?

Can the energy efficiency of products in use be improved?

Can the product or services be combined with others to reduce overall energy intensity?

Can wastes and end-of-life products be reused, remanufactured, recycled, or incinerated?

Can products be made biodegradable or harmless so that less energy is required for disposal?

Can transport be reduced or greater use made of energy-efficient transport such as rail?

Are there incentives for employees to cycle, walk, use public transportation or car-pool?

Toxic Dispersion

Can toxic dispersion be reduced or eliminated by using alternative raw materials or producing them differently?

Are products designed to ensure safe distribution, use, and disposal?

Can harmful substances be eliminated from production processes?

Can harmful substances generated in use be reduced or eliminated?

Can any remaining harmful substances be recycled or incinerated?

Are remaining harmful substances properly handled during production and disposal?

Are equipment and vehicles properly maintained so that emissions are kept to a minimum?

Recyclability

Can wastes from raw material production be reused or recycled?

Can process wastes be remanufactured, reused, or recycled?

Would separation of solid and liquid waste streams make recycling easier or reduce treatment costs?

Can product specifications be amended to enable greater use of recycled materials and components?

Can products be made of fewer or marked and easily recyclable materials?

Can products be designed to facilitate customer use or revalorization?

Can products be designed for easy disassembly?

Can product packaging be made more recyclable?

Can old products and components be remanufactured or reused?

Are there any opportunities to participate in waste exchange schemes?

Can energy be recovered from end-of-life products?

Resources

Can renewable or abundant materials be substituted for scarce, nonrenewable, ones?

Can more use be made of resources that are certified as being sustainably produced?

Can more use be made of renewable energy in production or processing?

Are new buildings and refurbishments maximizing use of passive heating and cooling?

Can products be designed to utilize renewable or abundant materials in use?

Durability

Can materials or processes be altered in order to improve longevity?

Can products or components be made more modular to allow easy upgrading?

Can whatever aspects of the product that limit durability be redesigned?

Can maintenance of the product be improved?

Can customers be informed or educated about ways of extending product durability?

Service Intensity

What service are customers really getting from your product? Can this be provided more effectively or in completely different ways?

What services will customers need in the future? Can you design new or develop existing products to meet them?

Is your product providing other services as well as the most obvious one? Can these be accentuated or enhanced?

Can the product or service be integrated or synchronized with others to provide multifunctionality?

Can customer's disposal problems be eliminated by providing a take-back service?

Can the properties of the product be accentuated or developed for greater customer value?

Can products be designed to facilitate customer reuse or revalorization?

Can products be redesigned to make distribution and logistics easier?

Can the product be made easier for customers to dispose of?

Can production be localized to both enhance service and reduce transport needs?

Can products be transported or distributed by alternative means to enhance customer value and reduce environmental impacts?

Summary

The full definition of eco-efficiency:

Eco-efficiency is reached by the delivery of competitively priced goods and services that satisfy human needs and bring quality of life, while progressively reducing environmental impacts and resource intensity throughout the life cycle, to a level at least in line with the earth's estimated carrying capacity

has five core themes:

An emphasis on service—by focusing on what services to provide, not just what products to supply, companies open up opportunities to deliver less eco-intensive, higher value applications.

A focus on needs and quality of life—the key to improved service is understanding customer's real and often unarticulated needs.

Consideration of the entire product life cycle—companies have a responsibility to consider the upstream and downstream implications of their activities and take action to mitigate them.

A recognition of limits to eco-capacity—our planet's capacity to assimilate pollution and wastes and maintain resource yields is near or at its limits.

A process view—eco-efficiency is as much a journey as a destination.

There are seven key dimensions that every business should take into account when developing products, introducing process changes, or taking other actions with environmental implications. They are:

Reduce the material intensity of goods and services—many experts believe that we must reduce material intensity by a factor of four or greater in the medium term.

Reduce the energy intensity of goods and services.

Reduce toxic dispersion—achieved by such means as removing hazardous substances from products and delivery systems and/or their more effective utilization.

Enhance material recyclability.

Maximize sustainable use of renewable resources.

Extend product durability.

Increase the service intensity of products—that is, creating additional value for customers while reducing or holding constant environmental impacts through means such as shared use, multifunctionality, and easy upgrading.

Eco-efficiency is more than business as usual. It requires major changes in philosophy, products, and processes. As chapter 1 discussed, there is growing evidence from the companies that have begun to implement it that this change is possible—and that environmental impacts are reduced and sustainability is increased as a result.

However, their experience demonstrates that there are both external and internal barriers to eco-efficiency. As chapter 7 notes, some of these barriers are created by the framework conditions within which business operates. Such barriers are out of the control of individual companies and can only be overcome by concerted actions by government, financial institutions, business, and other parties.

There are also internal barriers to eco-efficiency that companies can influence, for example:

- Lack of awareness about environmental and other sustainability issues and of the scale of change needed to achieve sustainable development,
- Despair about the enormity of environmental problems and the apparent inability of individuals to deal with them,
- Short-term decision-making perspectives that mean that all long-term trends are ignored or underestimated and the future benefits of environmental actions are heavily discounted,
- Organizational structures that inhibit the cross-functional interaction necessary to fully integrate environment into key areas such as product development,
- An absence of senior management commitment,
- Lack of motivation and awareness among middle- and lower-level staff,

- A lack of systems and tools to bring environment into business decision-making processes,

- A focus on the company's own impacts and lack of knowledge about those of its suppliers and customers.

The box provides examples from one project of how these barriers can be overcome and the benefits of doing so. The following pages provide further examples and demonstrate that action is possible in every kind of company, from large multinationals to small companies with a handful of employees. They also show that the process of overcoming internal barriers is both radical and incremental. It is radical because it involves a complete change from business-as-usual thinking. It is incremental in that the operational transition to eco-efficiency is a step-by-step process. In either case there are nine key elements that allow progress to be made:

1. Leadership,
2. Foresight,
3. Culture,
4. Management tools,
5. Life cycle management,
6. Research and development,
7. Production and operations,
8. Marketing and procurement,
9. Aftersales service and disposal.[2]

Leadership

Effective leadership is perhaps the single most important requirement for eco-efficiency. If top management does not support it through words and action, change simply will not happen. Supporting it effectively involves five essential tasks:

1. Alerting staff to the long-term challenge of sustainable development,

2. Creating and communicating a shared sense of how these challenges can be met,

Barriers to Environmental Improvement

The U.S. President's Commission on Environmental Quality established total quality management (TQM)-based environmental improvement demonstration projects at twelve sites.[1] All created one or more of four main categories of benefit:

Potential cost savings. Procter & Gamble estimated that its waste minimization efforts had generated benefits of $25 million at one of its plants alone.

Technological innovation. AT&T invented a new dispenser in order to move from soldering fluxes that required subsequent cleaning to remove residues to a "no-clean" product and is now selling it other companies.

Increased public acceptance. Several of the U.S. sites rated this as their greatest benefit. DuPont was facing considerable public hostility because of a high level of toxic emissions from one of its plants. This was greatly reduced as a result of the reductions achieved by its quality program.

Better relations with regulators. Environmental quality programs signal that companies are taking their environmental responsibilities seriously and can mean that companies are given the benefit of the doubt if any accidents occur and are inspected less frequently.

However, the projects also revealed a number of barriers to environmental action—and demonstrated means of overcoming them.

Limited resources. Dow's solution to this barrier was to prioritize low-cost or no-cost projects, even though many of these were small. By demonstrating the gains that could be made, these "quick wins" built overall support for environmental quality programs and helped generate additional resources for larger projects.

Inertia. Several of the companies overcame this by introducing environmental factors into individual performance criteria and giving awards for innovative projects.

Uninformed management or employees. Training is the obvious means of overcoming this barrier. Experience suggests that the best training does not focus on general environmental awareness but demonstrates the connections between work activities and environmental activities—for example, the role of maintenance in avoiding leakage or spills—and the concrete benefits of actions for the company and employees' families and communities.

Accounting systems that do not measure environmental costs or values. The costs of poor environmental performance are often not calculated or are hidden by being buried in overheads. Identifying and aggregating these can often make a difference to project economics and overall perceptions of environmental programs.

Fear of compromising product quality or production efficiency. A quick-win approach that demonstrated through small projects that these fears were unfounded proved to be useful. So did up-front testing and pilot operation to demonstrate that it was unfounded.

Technology limitations. Several companies overcame these by working with suppliers to modify existing or design new equipment. Chevron, for example, collaborated with a vendor to develop new, low-cost, in-process sampling to provide better data on emissions.

3. Motivating and empowering people to take action,

4. Demonstrating that eco-efficiency is about day-to-day behavior,

5. Establishing and supporting eco-efficiency champions.

A leader's words and behavior can lift people from their immediate tasks and concerns to the wider picture of the organization's future—and help them see how important sustainable business practices are to it. Ken McCready, former CEO of the Canadian power company TransAlta Utilities, has given much thought to this and comments:

A bit of imagery I find useful is that of a fish swimming in water. To the fish the water is invisible. The role of the CEO is to make the invisible visible; to bring into focus the changing context in which the corporation is "swimming," making the possibilities and changes needed visible to employees.[3]

Leaders must also create a shared sense of how their organization should respond to the challenges of sustainable development—and provide a road map of how to get there in order to motivate people to take action. Ed Woolard, until 1996 president and CEO of DuPont and now chairman, has shown how this can be done. In the words of a professional journal:

It was Woolard who coined the phrase "corporate environmentalism," proclaimed that CEO stood for Chief Environmental Officer, and who (as chairman) still stands among corporate America's greenest executives.[4]

The quotes at the beginning of the book show how other CEOs are demonstrating similar leadership. The "zero emissions" targets established by Monsanto and other companies also send powerful messages about what has to be achieved ultimately, while targets such as its commitment to cut emissions by 70% between 1990 and 1995 (which it achieved) provide nearer-term road maps.

These expectations, communicated throughout the organization, encourage everyone to work together along the same lines. This is partly a question of briefing and educating through personal communication. It also can be done more formally through environmental mission statements, policies, goals, and programs. These should be based on proactive targets. 3M's policy stresses the need to prevent pollution and minimize the environmental effects of products. It is also important that policies fit with organizational cultural and environmental objectives. Texas Instruments, for example, links its overall environmental goals to its quality philosophy and emphasis on individual commitment:

Excellence and leadership in environment, health and safety are core values of Texas Instruments and TIers. These values are integrated into our processes, products and services and are key ingredients for sustained competitive advantage.

The implementation of these values in its European plants contributed to TI winning the prestigious European Quality Award in 1995.

AT&T underlines its commitment to a life cycle perspective in its statement that

AT&T's vision is to be recognized by customers, employees, shareholders and communities worldwide as a responsible company which fully integrates life cycle environmental consequences into each of our business directions and activities.

However, leadership for eco-efficiency has to strike a balance between central direction and challenge and local autonomy. Getting this right is the key to a vibrant and vigorous eco-efficiency culture. If you just have top-down initiatives, people wait for things to be done. If there is an exclusive reliance on bottom-up initiatives, the wheel gets reinvented at every location and things become fragmented.

At the end of the day leaders are judged less by words than whether they "practice what they preach" with regard to eco-efficiency. Every action sends a message about what is and is not of importance to the organization. Frank Riddick, a DuPont EH&S trainer with many years of line EH&S experience, notes that

What managers do and say with respect to the environment is reflected in the way their people do their jobs. If the first question the boss asks every day is how much did we make last night, everybody understands that production is important. If he asks did we have a safe night, did we have any environmental incidents, he makes safety and environment a routine part of the day-to-day job, just like production, quality and cost.[5]

Practicing rather than preaching eco-efficiency also requires operational champions, with clear lines to top management and a broader vision than that of traditional, compliance-driven or technically focused environmental staff. Indeed, W. Ross Stevens, DuPont's manager of Environmental, Safety and Advocacy, believes that eco-efficiency and sustainable development are increasingly the province of the line and business development expert rather than just the environmental manager. However, the latter remains important because "Somebody has to inspire the line management to understand these issues, and nobody is better positioned than the outward thinking EHS manager."[6]

One study has also found that, in addition to being knowledgeable about environmental issues across the life cycle, "next-generation" environmental or eco-efficiency managers must be:

Outward looking, to effectively manage product chains and deal with the changing needs of external stakeholders.

Organizationally adept, to develop and maintain support across the company, particularly among senior management.

Capable of managing tension, for example, between the need to be an internal critic but an external defender of environmental performance.

Business oriented, so that the costs of environmental management can be minimized and the potential benefits maximized.

Visionary, in directing organizational attention toward the long-term challenge of sustainability.[7]

In 1990 Dow achieved these objectives by creating a board-level vice president of EH&S, reporting directly to the CEO—and filling it with a highly regarded general manager, David T. Buzzelli, who was previously president of Dow Canada.

3M has moved in the same direction by appointing an eco-efficiency manager (the world's first), Allen H. Aspengren. He sees his role as

> encouraging people to get out of the usual boxes and think about ways of creating value and environmental improvement. Sometimes this means asking basic questions—isn't there anything we could do with this waste? Can we envisage a better process that has lower costs and emissions? At other times, it's providing people with the right information so they can ask and answer the questions themselves.[8]

Foresight

Looking into the future—and translating this into a vision of where the company is going and the competencies and technologies it will require to get there—is essential for eco-efficiency. The eco-efficiency paradigm recognizes that the earth is finite, its capacity for recovery from damage because of resource ill-use is limited, and that public and other pressures to modify business behavior will inevitably increase. Proactive companies will assess the specific impact of these pressures on their industry and markets in order to take timely action to reduce risks and take advantage of business opportunities.

Volvo is one company that is doing this. The Swedish car producer sees that growing congestion and more stringent emissions and fuel efficiency regulation will change the nature of urban transportation. According to executive vice president Per-Erik Mohin,

> Because we provide trucks, buses and cars, we're a natural partner when it comes to providing complete transportation solutions for cities. . . . We will see Volvo participating much more in local traffic/distribution planning: we strongly believe we have to develop these skills. We want our role in traffic planning to be more integrated than merely selling pieces of equipment. We plan to be more active in this type of business development.[9]

A key part of creating a future vision is paying attention to leading-edge thinkers—however remote their ideas seem from current realities. Like all of us, they are not infallible. But experience suggests that many of their predictions will be right—and that the companies that have built their insights into their long-term plans will benefit accordingly.

The American energy analyst Amory Lovins is an example of one such thinker. His predictions in the 1970s that there were massive opportunities to increase energy efficiency and that, in many circumstances, this could be more economically beneficial than expanding supply were scorned. Now they are part of mainstream thinking and thousands of utility staff work on demand-side management and least-cost planning. His record led the *Wall Street Journal* to name him in 1991 as one of 28 people around the world most likely to change the course of business. Today Lovins—and the Rocky Mountain Institute, which he now directs—is predicting a future of much more decentralized energy services and continuing opportunities to save energy in eco-efficient ways through ultralight and fuel-efficient "hypercars," more effective electric motors, and other technical innovations.

Lovins has also linked with Ernst von Weizsäcker, president of Wuppertal Institut, a European center of leading-edge thinking, to identify opportunities for radical improvements in the material as well as energy intensity of goods and services.[10] The Wuppertal Institut's work on dematerialization is the inspiration for the Factor 10 Club. Their ideas are already proving influential in international discussions and setting national government policies, for example, in Austria. They are also being taken seriously by forward-looking businesses—the scoring system of the Dow eco-compass (see figure 3.3), for example, gives full marks only to new products that achieve a minimum of factor four improvement.

How can these future visions be translated into practical action? Scenarios are one way. The international oil company Shell is probably their best-known exponent. During the early 1970s, Shell developed scenarios about oil futures, one of which was based on much higher prices. This prior identification of the problem—and the advance discussion of ways of responding that it precipitated—meant that the company was the best prepared of the oil majors for the quadrupling of oil prices that followed the 1973 Yom Kippur War. And in the 1980s a similar exercise alerted it to the possibility of a collapse in oil prices, which happened in 1986. In the mid-1990s Shell developed new scenarios to take account not only of changed trends in the oil market but also the long-term impact of climate change. The overall conclusion, according to Roger Rainbow, U.S. Shell's vice president for Global Business Environment, is

if you look ahead to 2040 and 2050, we expect to see an energy world that is even more complex than the one we have today, with many more competing fuels, many more niche markets and much more blurring of boundaries. It won't even be clear what the energy industry is anymore.[11]

Much of this complexity will be generated by environmental factors— and one of the definite conclusions is that energy solutions that are eco-efficient will be favored over those that are not.

Thomas Crumm, manager of Envisioning and Alternative Futures Development at General Motors, also spends much of his time developing scenarios of the impact of environmental factors on the automobile industry. Although he expects the fundamental demand for mobility to remain, he sees the possibility of major changes in the ways it is expressed. For example, greater teleworking could mean less commuting while teleshopping may result in more home delivery and less use of cars for errand running. Their source of power is also uncertain:

Some analysts say that fossil fuel reserves are sufficient in light of the fact that we'll get more efficient and effective in how we use petroleum. The other scenario is that we walk away from fossil fuels whether or not reserves are exhausted. I can't predict which way the race will go, but I can say that we are very carefully preparing for both alternatives.[12]

General Motors' preparations include development of alternative vehicles such as electric and hybrid-powered cars as well as continued improvement of internal combustion engines.

Another means of implementing a vision of the future is to translate it into future performance targets. This is a technique used by Philips Sound & Vision, the consumer electronics division of the Dutch multinational Philips.[13] One example concerns the adaptation of television design to takeback legislation and rising waste disposal costs. The company forecast the likely situation in 2005–2010 and translated this into the following targets:

• Average disassembly time halved from a current 15 minutes to 5 to 7 minutes

• Materials recycled at an equal level of application up from 15% today to 85% in 2010

• Costs of $8 to $16 compared to $26 to meet a similar recycling target with current technology

Meeting the cost target requires economies of scale in disassembly and Philips is now planning large disassembly facilities capable of dismantling 250,000 to 400,000 sets a year. The design and technology implications of the targets include improved separation technology for components, new methods of cleaning of glass cullet to remove contaminants, and development of new disassembly tools.

The analysis also revealed that government actions will influence television takeback. The large size of reprocessing plants means that transborder shipments of sets and derived products—which are currently banned in some countries—will be necessary. And governments will need to create a financial framework that recognizes that old sets not designed for disassembly will be very expensive to recycle.

A final benefit of envisioning the future is anticipating "trigger points." According to Noble Robinson, Ralph Earle, and Ronald McLean of consultants Arthur D. Little:

Environmental policy analysis often ignores the likelihood and impact of trigger events—front-page news like Bhopal—that turn existing environmental practices on their head. Trigger events radically change the dynamics of an issue not by turning public attention to an overlooked problem but by bringing widespread anxieties into focus.

A careful analysis of environmental issues can help identify which ones are ripe for dynamic change. Concerns about water-use issues—long important only to water-poor regions like California—are currently very widespread among experts. . . . To date, no specific event has focused a critical mass of public and political attention on the issue. But companies that wait for this focus before addressing an issue like water-use policy are not taking advantage of readily-available intelligence.[14]

Anticipating possible trigger points in advance means that eco-efficient solutions can be put in place proactively—and that the potential for gaining competitive advantage from the changes that result can be maximized.

Culture

Important as leadership and foresight are in setting a direction and establishing expectations and structures, they are no substitute for commitment and action by everyone in the organization. Individual employees make the difference between eco-efficiency happening or not. Carola Teir-Lehtinen, vice president of EH&S at Finnish oil company Neste Oy, puts it this way:

Our environmental management implementation needs to work from the bottom up with involvement from our people. Environmental awareness is high in our company, as it is in all of the Scandinavian countries, but it can be even higher. We want to encourage employees to report both problems and ideas for improvement. This is one of the best ways to ensure that our new products are environmentally superior to their predecessors throughout their life cycle.[15]

Cornell University researchers have statistical evidence of the value of staff involvement. The U.S. Environmental Protection Agency's form for compiling data on companies' emissions of toxic substances—which forms the basis of the Toxic Release Inventory (TRI)—also requests information about employee participation. It asks whether companies are operating pollution prevention programs, formal suggestion schemes, and participative team management. The researchers found a correlation between substantial reductions in emissions and use of one or more means of employee participation. Companies using all three reduced toxic emissions by an average of 16% more than those using none. According to one of the researchers, Ed Cohen-Rosenthal,

If all companies performed at the level of those with strong employee engagement, then hundreds of millions of dollars would be saved and millions of tons of toxic wastes would not enter the environment.[16]

Achieving such a culture of continuous improvement of environmental performance—and ensuring that the improvements are sometimes radical as well as incremental—requires informed staff who feel a personal involvement in eco-efficiency and are empowered to take action to achieve it. As DuPont's Frank Riddick puts it:

Safety and the environment are both people-motivation issues. You want your people to do the right thing because it's the right thing, not because somebody is watching them. At 2:30 in the morning your environmental manager is the operator with a hose who could wash a chemical spill down the drain. He needs to be motivated and understand that's not the right thing to do. That's why our management seminar for line supervisors devotes time to helping them improve their employees' sense of ownership and pride for good environmental performance.[17]

Building this motivation, and a culture that is supportive of eco-efficiency ideas and techniques, takes time. It requires constant reinforcement by committed leaders, regular feedback on performance, and frequent celebration of successes.

Training is also vitally important. At the Danish biotechnology company Novo Nordisk, environmental topics are an integrated part of all the company's general training courses, from directors to new trainees. Volkswagen too believes that

successful environmental protection depends to a large extent on continuously developing a commitment to the environment at all levels of the workforce by providing information and training, and by getting people involved.[18]

Environment forms part of the curriculum for all its apprentices (who are more numerous in Germany than other countries). Activities include a "green factory rally," several days' attendance at a seminar in a nature reserve, and specialist projects. One team of apprentices, for example, designed and built a solar recharging system for electric vehicles. There are also regular courses for workers, managers, and factory committee members and all in-company trainers receive environmental training themselves.

The Canadian mining and resources company Noranda has placed even greater emphasis on training since a 1992 survey of 2,000 of its employees suggested that, although 89% had a favorable opinion of its environmental performance, more could be done to demonstrate its commitment and involve staff in environmental improvement. As a result Noranda has developed an environmental awareness program that focuses on three strategies:

1. Ensuring that frontline employees operating environmentally sensitive systems or equipment fully understand all relevant compliance and regulatory requirements

2. Improving general employee awareness through better communications

3. Training frontline supervisors to provide employees with environmental information

The last has been achieved through the Noranda Environmental Awareness Training program (NEAT). This includes:

• Two-day workshops to help participants reexamine their routines—how they consume energy, produce wastes, and affect environmental performance of other operations

• Learning how to set a personal example and influence others to take action to protect the environment

• Tours of their own operating sites using an input-output model to characterize the operation's relationship with the environment

• A workshop to help employees define how their site's environmental performance measures against regulations and policies

NEAT is designed to enable employees to look at their jobs in a new light, with greater awareness of the environmental consequences of both their actions and inaction. In the final training module, employees also develop a practical improvement project for their place of work, for example, by identifying risks of chemical spills and taking action to reduce them or by minimizing consumption of resources.

Programs like NEAT are a rarity in resource companies and it is still new to Noranda. Even so, more than 2,000 employees have participated in the training sessions since its inception in 1994.

Introducing eco-efficiency and related ideas into further education is also important. This can spread the message to tomorrow's personnel, influence current staff and stakeholders who attend courses and generally influence public and expert debates. Fortunately, more and more business and engineering schools are including eco-efficiency in their courses. In the United States the Management Institute for Environment and Business (MEB—now part of the World Resources Institute) has been a focal point for developing curricula and teaching materials. The Massachusetts Institute of Technology (MIT) has programs both for business graduates at the Sloan School of Management and courses at the School of Engineering about the theory and practice of eco-efficiency. ETH in Switzerland and Tokyo University are cooperating with MIT in both research and education around eco-efficiency, and have formed a long-term research cooperation called the Alliance for Sustainable Development. Management courses at business schools like IMD in Lausanne, INSEAD in France, and INCAI in Costa Rica include special sessions on eco-efficiency. The Norwegian School of Management and the UK's Sustainable Business Centre and Centre for

Sustainable Design are also running courses and activities on the related topic of eco-innovation.

Finally, a company culture will best support eco-efficiency if it is open and transparent. Good ideas can come from any source and it is important to take account of any, from wherever they come, that will add value, and reduce resource input and environmental impact. Too many companies have gone on the defensive when faced with environmental challenges. This is not just unconstructive—it is also counterproductive because defensiveness tends to breed even greater suspicion and opposition.

Quality

Many companies have found that the objectives and tools of TQM are similar to those of eco-efficiency (see chapter 1). This is certainly the view of Michael Cordry, vice president for quality at Weyerhaeuser Pulp, Paper and Packaging. He notes that Weyerhaeuser is

trying to use the total quality framework and quality tools and techniques more in our environmental processes. In the next few years we will be improving in that effort. Because the environmental area is so important to us, we need to

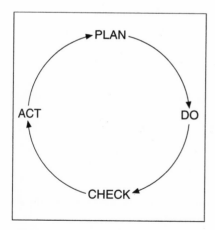

Figure 4.1
The quality cycle.
Source: Peter James, *Continual Improvement,* Croner's Environmental Policy and Procedures special report, February 1996, p. 5.

make sure we continue to incorporate quality thinking into our environmental activities.[19]

Leading U.S. corporations have established the Global Environmental Management Initiative (GEMI) as a forum for sharing and developing knowledge about quality approaches to environmental management. GEMI limits its membership to a small number of leading-edge businesses, but disseminates their experiences of increasing resource productivity and other topics through its annual conferences and other events and publications.

TQM rests on a simple cycle of "plan→do→check→act" (see figure 4.1).

Plan involves the identification of key customers and stakeholders, identifying opportunities for improvement and the development of programs to achieve them.

Do is the implementation of the programs.

Check is the monitoring and reviewing of progress, wherever possible against quantitative targets.

Act involves changing, if necessary, existing programs and using the learning from them to begin the cycle again with new plans.

One dimension of planning is developing an environmental quality infrastructure within the company. This should diffuse responsibility to, and synthesize the insights of, everyone in the organization. One means of doing this is through the creation of quality teams that bring together representatives from all the functions—and any outside parties—involved in a particular environmental problem. Training to develop both environmental awareness and problem-solving skills is also vital.

A cross-functional packaging quality improvement team established by Rank Xerox, the European affiliate of Xerox, indicates what can be achieved. Its aims were to ensure that all packaging was environmentally acceptable, that the company was well ahead of all regulations, and to identify eco-efficiency opportunities. In its first two years its ideas helped cut £2 million per annum from the company's packaging bill. More recently, it has developed a new system of returnable containers for all movements of materials and components between its factories, which should also generate considerable savings.

Identifying improvement opportunities is also a vital part of planning. Insights can come from cross-functional discussions, mapping energy and material flows, and interaction with customers and stakeholders. Monsanto, for example, has a checklist for its marketing and sales staff to identify ways in which it can work with customers to achieve eco-efficiency. The current costs of poor environmental performance (such as high energy, materials, and waste costs) and potential future costs, such as liability for contaminated land, can also be analyzed to reveal "win-win" opportunities.

Defining objectives and setting detailed targets is a third aspect of TQM planning. Eco-efficient companies will have a bias toward ambitious "stretch" targets to stimulate set change improvements.

For the do stage, quality practice is to implement on a pilot or experimental basis to maximize learning. Many organizations that have introduced environmental management systems did so by implementing them at just one site before extending them to the remainder of the organization. Full implementation then requires assignment of responsibility for action and establishment of performance measures.

Checking can occur in a variety of ways of varying formality, ranging from formal audits to informal team discussion. What is important is that performance is monitored and analyzed and that there are feedback mechanisms in place so that necessary changes can be made. It is also important that successes are recognized by awards, publicity, or other means.

The fourth, act, stage can integrate the whole cycle and prepare the ground for further improvement. In the late 1980s, for example, the U.S. health care services provider Baxter set itself a target of becoming a state-of-the-art company in environmental management. To achieve this it commissioned the consultants Arthur D. Little to define state-of-the-art standards for facility and divisional management and encouraged their implementation, with a target of 100% conformance in the United States, Canada, and Puerto Rico by 1995. In the first round only 35% of sites met the target. The importance of meeting the standards was recommunicated and peer group pressure from good performers was encouraged. The standards were also recalibrated to reflect continuing improvements in state-of-the-art performance around the world. Training and other support were also provided. After several further cycles, Baxter achieved

---

Five Signs of Good Environmental Performance

Companies like Dow who have made formal, public commitments to continuous improvement in environmental performance are increasingly looking to do business with companies who share similar values. To assess whether there's a good fit, five essential signs are considered.

The first sign is employee health and safety. Does the company have written health and safety programs? Does it monitor and assess the exposure of its employees? Does it provide employees with the appropriate safety equipment?

The second sign is the quality of facility management and basic housekeeping. Does the company have a formal pollution prevention system that signals its importance to all employees? How do they handle waste from their facility?

If these first two aspects are strong, the companies at least have a firm grip on environmental programs.

The next sign relates to a company's commitment to the safe handling of products throughout their life cycles. Does the company maintain information on EH&S hazards and evaluate exposures throughout the life cycle of its products? Is all relevant product environment and safety information provided to customers and other downstream users?

The fourth sign relates to a company's emergency preparedness. Does it have written emergency communication plans? Does it hold regular emergency response drills? Does it have plans for distribution incidents?

The final sign is whether the company is looking beyond compliance. Does it have an EH&S policy that sets a long-term direction? Does it proactively communicate its environmental performance? Does it have a system to follow up on concerns and complaints about its operations? Is it building new skills and strengthening its hand?

---

its target of 100% compliance by 1995 and is now putting its efforts into achieving state-of-the-art performance at all its operations worldwide.

Creating a Global Common Culture

It is also important that culture is shared in all places where an organization operates. Dow, for example, has a global EH&S council that brings senior staff together from around the world on a quarterly timetable. According to EH&S vice president Dave Buzzelli, we have to get input from around the world; we have to reach a consensus, because we cannot afford to be inconsistent. That is the one thing that would kill us: inconsistency in performance or strategy. Critics of the industry would say, "Yes, that's great for Midland, Michigan, but what are you doing in Thailand?"[20]

The Canadian mining and natural resources company Noranda has a similar policy. David Kerr, its chairman and CEO, believes that

environmental protection should have no political borders. As a global corporation committed to sustainable development, we cannot justify environmental double standards. When we are invited to participate in international projects where the standards are suspect or obviously objectionable, we decline. It's that simple.[21]

Management Tools

There are a number of management tools that help to identify and select eco-efficiency opportunities. They include environmental management systems, environmental assessment, environmental performance measurement, and environmental accounting.

Environmental Management Systems

These can vary from simple broad-brush exercises to sophisticated systems, with thorough reviews of impacts, detailed documentation of procedures and environmental problems, and regular auditing of the system's operation. As the box on environmental management systems discusses, formalization is required to achieve accreditation to the two main standards that now exist—International Standard 14001 (ISO14001, which has already or will in the future subsume most national standards such as British Standard BS7750) and the European Union Eco-Audit and Management Scheme (EMAS).

In practice, all environmental management systems share five main elements:

1. Identifying company impacts on the environment
2. Understanding current and future legal obligations
3. Developing plans for improvement
4. Assigning responsibility for implementation of plans
5. Periodic monitoring of performance

Environmental Management System Standards

There are now two international standards for environmental management systems (EMS)—those of the International Standards Organization (ISO) and that of the European Union, which is the Eco-Management and Audit Scheme (EMAS). These build on the earlier experience of national EMS standards, notably British Standard 7750 (BS7750), which are now being withdrawn and replaced by ISO14001. They are also inspired by the ideas of total quality management and the international standards on quality management systems (the ISO9000 series).

A number of ISO standards and guidelines (collectively known as the ISO14000 series) deal with EMS and related topics such as auditing and performance evaluation. The most important is ISO14001, which sets out the criteria for accrediting the EMS itself. It focuses on the existence and adequacy of the key processes (see flow chart) and whether these are thoroughly documented.

ISO certification can be gained in any country and, in principle, can be obtained for any organizational level—site, division, or the entire organization. This is a key difference with EMAS, which is only applicable to sites within the European Union (and at present only those engaged in industrial activities, although it may be extended). Another difference is that, although the existence and adequacy of the EMS is a major criterion for EMAS accreditation (and in practice ISO14001 accreditation is accepted as meeting the EMS requirements of EMAS), EMAS introduces an additional requirement of a public environmental statement. This must contain details of emissions, wastes, and other impacts; targets and actions to meet them; and, over time, information about performance.

A number of companies around the world have now been certified under such schemes and their precursors. In Argentina, for example, two companies—ARCIOR and Petroquimica Cuyo—were accredited to BS7750 in 1996, as were Mitsubishi Electric and Samsung in East Asia.

Some critics feel that the requirements of EMS standards create a bureaucratic, rule-based, approach to environmental management and that it is possible to meet them without major improvements in environmental performance. These dangers are real, not least for companies with long-established environmental, health, and safety systems. It is important to see an EMS as just one strand of an overall approach to eco-efficiency, which needs to be complemented by the other features discussed in this chapter. This is the approach at Philips, which has a target of achieving ISO14001 accreditation at all of its 250 plants around the world by 2000. Although this will be expensive Henk de Bruin, Philips corporate environmental director, believes that waste reductions and other benefits will give a payback period of only two years.[22]

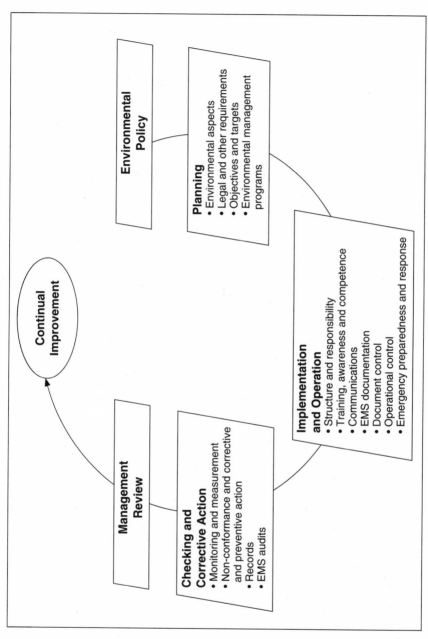

Introducing these elements can be costly. Some companies with long experience of environmental management have found that incorporating environment into existing high-performance work systems can avoid these costs and still achieve equivalent performance. However, an increasing number of organizations are finding environmental management systems to be useful and a valuable means of fostering eco-efficiency. The benefits include:

- Identification and control of business risks
- Identification of environmental and business improvement opportunities
- Early warnings of future environmental problems and costs
- More effective implementation of environmental policies
- Greater environmental awareness among staff

Accreditation of an environmental management system can bring the additional benefits of enhanced reputation with customers, regulators, and other stakeholders. A number of countries are also considering introducing less onerous regulatory regimes for companies with accredited environmental management systems.

The British pest control company Renlon—which has 60 staff—provides an example of these benefits.[23] Renlon's business was built on spraying toxic substances dissolved in organic solvents. Realizing that environmental pressures posed a threat to its continuation, the company decided to introduce an environmental management system and seek accreditation to BS7750, It reduced costs by integrating environment into its existing quality and health and safety system, but setting up and training still involved an expenditure of about $45,000 and several hundred hours of staff time. The process triggered a strategic reappraisal of Renlon's business. The company offers long-term guarantees against the return of problems and suffers high costs if rework is necessary. Building users are also inconvenienced. The best way to avoid rework is to change the underlying cause—such as damp or poor ventilation—of the initial problem. Renlon is now repositioning itself as a provider of a pest control service, offering advice about long-term preventive measures rather than simply providing treatment after the problem has occurred.

Introducing BS7750 also created immediate savings—including $26,000 a year from an energy efficiency program and $6000 a year from more effective control of stationery and printing. There are also continuing, unquantified, benefits such as the favorable publicity its initiative has received and the goodwill it has created with customers.

Hipp, a small German food producer that uses only organic materials, has also benefited from EMAS accreditation.[24] The company found that the introduction of the system developed employees' environmental awareness and motivation. Accreditation has also proved to be a good tool for communicating with customers and suppliers. The fact that Hipp received over 1500 requests for its EMAS environmental statement (which sets out its impacts and improvement targets) within 3 months of accreditation also demonstrates the high level of business and public interest in environmental management systems in some countries.

The 3M case in chapter 6 also provides details of its environmental management systems.

Environmental Assessment

At the heart of sound environmental management is the assessment of effects, real or potential, on the environment as a consequence of business activities and the planning and implementation of measures to reduce that damage. There are a number of systematic tools and procedures for performing such assessments, ranging from company-wide to site-, process-, or product-specific. They include:

Life cycle assessment (LCA)

Environmental audits

The formal assessments of environmental effects required for environmental management systems (e.g., ISO 14001/3)

Product stewardship assessments

Design for environment (DFE) assessments (see below)

Environmental risk assessment of products

Environmental impact assessment

All of these involve five essential steps (see following box). They are likely to be of most value when the results are integrated into environ-

How to Do Environmental Assessment

A WBCSD report on the topic identifies five main stages and makes these recommendations:

1. *Goal definition and scoping.* As a minimum comply with legislation and internal guidelines. Be clear, transparent, and cost-effective. Define the important stakeholders, key environmental impacts, and main alternatives. Do not define the study area too broadly—focus on the key primary and secondary impacts.

2. *Data collection.* Recognize all environmental impacts, including socioeconomic. Focus on the main features of the system or product that have environmental implications. Be reproducible and auditable. Adjust the precision reporting to the weakest data to avoid a false sense of accuracy. Use existing data wherever possible, but fill in the information gaps.

3. *Impact assessment.* Predict the scale and significance of the effects. Be clear about the criteria used to assess them. Quantify the impacts, positive and negative, direct and indirect. Provide stakeholders with the necessary quality of information, but be simple and understandable.

4. *Control of effects.* Address options for improvement—preferably process or design modifications but end-of-pipe solutions if necessary. Consider the environmental and ecological significance of the various alternatives. Action measures should be presented as commitments, not recommendations, wherever possible—and should be part of an implementation plan.

5. *Communication.* Build an early and continuing dialogue with stakeholders. Understand that different stakeholders have different information needs at different times. Their perception can be as important as the reality. Validate information. Never underestimate the audience—and recognize that their contribution can be invaluable.[26]

mental management systems or other regular management procedures rather than being one-off exercises.

Peter Langcake of Shell International led a WBCSD task force on the use of environmental assessment.[25] He believes that assessment can create better decision-making and reduce both environmental impacts and time and money by:

Helping to identify problems and issues associated with gaining internal or external approval of projects

Avoiding conflict and developing consensus with stakeholders at the start of projects

Allowing environmental requirements to be developed at an early stage

Identifying waste streams and evaluating ways to eliminate or minimize them beforehand

Reducing corporate risk—which results in better, cheaper insurance coverage, enhanced shareholder value, better loan conditions, and improved investment worthiness

Helping to identify new opportunities

Enhancing reputation and trust

Avoiding costly options and reducing retrofitting costs

Providing a better fit between products and services and their markets

Anticipating future stakeholder concerns and requirements

However, it is important that the time involved in conducting assessments and gathering data for assessments is commensurate with the benefits. Many companies have found, for example, that full life cycle assessments cost thousands of dollars and months to prepare. Although they can be useful for guiding major decisions, or in convincing skeptics about a product's environmental benefits, many companies find that simpler versions can provide sufficient information about major impacts and improvement opportunities.

Measurement

It is a truism that what gets measured gets managed. Measuring environmental performance ensures that long-term visions and policies are implemented on a day to day basis. Specific internal reasons for measuring include:

• To monitor the organization's success both in improving over time, and in comparison with others

• Expectations from other managers who are accustomed to meeting demands for rigorous measurement of performance in their own areas and expect no less from environmental management

• To make the business case for proenvironment policies and actions

- To demonstrate that the financial resources available are being applied to the best possible effect
- To help to set priorities for action

Measurement is also necessary to achieve accreditation of environmental management systems and to meet the demands of regulators and stakeholders for more information about environmental performance.

Rodney Chase, managing director of British Petroleum, believes that in his company,

The result of better measurement of our emissions and wastes has led to success in reducing them, and being creative in targeting further reductions. The answer is not only to deal with the extremities, but also to go back to square one and see if you can design a process or a product that prevents the problem from arising in the first place.[27]

A subsidiary, BP Chemicals, provides a practical illustration of the advantages not only of measurement but also of ambitious target-setting. It set a stretch target of halving its hydrocarbon emissions over seven years—and then looked for ways to make this happen. BP Chemicals measured the sources of emissions within its own business and traced 8% of the company total to the decay over time of packing material in a particular valve. The "unbelievably simple" solution (an extra layer of graphite packing in the valve) not only eliminated the emissions but continues to save over a million dollars per annum in reduced materials and maintenance costs—and has prompted searches for further potential gains.

The French chemicals producer Rhone Poulenc also reduces costs by tracking waste emissions at all its plants around the world and compiling the results into an environmental index. This allows good and bad performers to be identified and highlights opportunities for eco-efficient actions.

A wide variety of measures can be used, although most focus on three core areas—inputs (such as materials), processes (such as existence of management systems) and outputs (such as emissions and wastes).[28] Many advanced companies also supplement absolute measures with normalized measures that relate environmental impacts to some aspect of business activity such as production or turnover—for example, energy consumption per ton of output. This allows extraneous factors such as increases or falling production to be screened out.

Normalized comparisons also make it easier to undertake either internal—for example, between plants—or external benchmarking, which can be a powerful driver of improvement. A study by the Dutch National Institute of Public Health and Environmental Protection found up to a tenfold difference in emissions from similar processes in several industries. Both the worst and the best performers were frequently unaware of how they compared relative to others in their industry. Further investigation often showed that the reasons were trivial: for example, minor differences in process controls that could be easily changed to produce substantial improvements.

Environmental Cost Accounting

Various methods of accounting for environmental costs are employed today.[29] It is not unusual for ongoing operating costs to be aggregated in a cost category called "Environmental Costs," collected at a central or corporate level within an organization and then spread back out to individual products or businesses in a way that may or may not reflect the actual cost that product or business should bear. In like manner, environmental capital budgets can be managed in a central fashion such that it is not easily apparent to corporate decision makers exactly what businesses or products within their organization require more extensive capital investment to maintain compliance. These types of accounting systems smooth out the impact of individual businesses and products on the overall bottom line so that high environmental costs are effectively unnoticed.

As businesses begin to redirect environmental cost allocation from more centralized collection approaches back to the actual business or product that uses that particular service, the "full" environmental costs start to become measurable. Organizations looking to expand their efforts to implement full cost accounting must first identify all the environmental and environment-related activities associated with running a particular business or making a particular product. These activities must then be assigned a specific value such as dollars per pound of waste managed or dollars per hour of environmental expert support time needed for that permit or legal work. Once an activity-based cost framework is put in place and the tangible costs are being tracked back to the users, the less tangible costs can be factored in. These can include anticipating the future costs of clean-up of a historic site, cost of a new landfill or waste treatment device to meet future regulations, and so on.

Full-cost accounting is simply about allocating the full cost—including environmental costs that arise during use and disposal—to a given product or process. It ensures that the best process is put in place—and that organizations avoid subsidizing the things that look good on paper, but have a long-term negative impact.

In the long term, full-cost accounting will need to take into account the total environmental costs of making a product, if only because the "polluter pays principle" means that these costs will eventually be internalized by taxation or other means. Ontario Hydro has started to do this by considering the social costs of its electricity generation. In the short term, however, there is much to be done in considering costs that are currently being borne by individual companies or their customers and suppliers but are hidden in overheads or otherwise unaccounted for. These can often be substantial, as chapter 2 demonstrates.

A study by Tellus Institute for the U.S. Environmental Protection Agency demonstrated the difference that identifying such costs can make to capital investment decisions.[30] They examined two pollution prevention investments in the paper industry that had failed the normal rate of return criteria. However, both investment cases had underestimated or ignored the normal operating costs of energy and water consumption and waste management and disposal. Doing this—and then calculating the savings that could be achieved by the pollution prevention schemes—changed the picture to the point where both projects were found to have very positive returns.

Once environmental costs are identified they can be allocated to individual budgets. Revealing the costs of poor environmental performance this way can often have immediate effects. Dow, for example, was worried that its in-house landfill site was filling too quickly. It therefore raised the internal charge for using that facility. The result was a rapid fall in internal waste generation, and the freeing of several decades of additional landfill capacity. A product analysis at one 3M division also found that pollution control costs were lost in overhead and therefore allocated to products on a turnover basis. However, close analysis revealed that 90% of the costs were driven by only one product—and provided a powerful incentive for the product "owner" to take action to reduce them.

Life Cycle Management

The aim of eco-efficiency is to optimize the total life cycle rather than any individual part of it. Life cycle management is concerned with understanding and managing the entire life cycle of products—from cradle (creation and processing of raw materials) to grave (final disposal)—to achieve this objective.

One key aspect of life cycle management is product use, which often accounts for the majority of life cycle impacts. Procter & Gamble, for example, has found that 95% of the materials that enter its production processes go to the final consumer, where they are used or discarded. And Asea Brown Boveri (ABB) calculates that the use of one of its electric motors has 300 to 400 times the impact of its manufacture. Talking to and involving customers in life cycle management is therefore a prerequisite for success.

A specific tool that can help with life cycle management is life cycle assessment (LCA). In the past, many companies have found this to be too costly and difficult to interpret for day-to-day decision-making, but desktop software and the development of standardized databases by research bodies and consultants is making its use cheaper and easier. The important point is gaining reliable information that is good enough for management purposes.

A number of companies are now developing linking LCA data to cost data to generate information about life cycle costs. As with environmental accounting, the costs that are identified can either be confined to those borne by an individual company or its supply chain partners or also take broader social costs into account.

The U.S. car manufacturer Chrysler is one of the leaders in life cycle management.[31] It has developed a computerized model that contains data on four key parameters for selected products and components. One parameter is recycling, and includes data on disassembly, material composition, and substances of concern. A second is environmental control, disposal, and administration. The third is health and the fourth, safety.

A wide range of staff at Chrysler have access to the database, which provides a more systematic way of ensuring that EH&S issues are considered during R&D and product development than during previous, informal, means. The value of the tool is demonstrated by a decision concerning an underhood lamp assembly. Traditional lamps contain a mercury switch, which is cheaper to purchase than alternatives that do not contain mercury. However, some countries and states are either banning their use or requiring labeling or their removal before recycling. When the costs of the additional disassembly time and of meeting labeling, permit, and reporting requirements created by the switches are taken into account, nonmercury alternatives are considerably cheaper.

The medium-sized Dutch office furniture manufacturer Ahrend Zwanenburg provides another example. A life cycle costing of office chairs revealed that the company's costs were likely to rise substantially as a result of takeback legislation and rising waste disposal charges. As a result, the chairs were made easier to disassemble and substitutes found for hazardous and difficult to recycle materials. The redesigned chair is estimated to have only half the cost of the previous model by the year 2000 and the company found that the whole project had a payback of only two years.[32]

Design for Eco-efficiency

Design determines the manufacturing and performance parameters of most products. It is therefore a major determinant of environmental impacts over the product life cycle and an important part of life cycle management. This in itself is a major reason to consider environment during the design stage. An equally compelling reason is that it is much cheaper to design environmental problems out of products and processes than to deal with them retrospectively, for example, by retrofitting pollution control equipment.

Design for eco-efficiency includes, but is broader than, the increasingly utilized techniques of design for environment (DFE). This has been defined as "systematic consideration of design performance with respect to environmental, health, and safety objectives over the full product and process life cycle."[33] Design for eco-efficiency emphasizes providing value for the customer as well as reducing environmental impacts.

One of the most substantive eco-design initiatives is the PROMISE project created by several Dutch public agencies and UNEP.[34] The project involved case studies of eco-design initiatives and development of a manual for general use by designers. The manual identifies eight main ways of achieving eco-design, which broadly correspond to key stages in the product life cycle:

1. Development of new product concepts
2. Selection of low environmental impact materials
3. Reduction in material use
4. Optimization of production techniques
5. Efficient distribution
6. Reduced environmental impact in use
7. Optimization of initial lifetime
8. Optimization of end-of-life system.

The box also contains the "five fast questions" that Philips designers and engineers use to identify key environmental issues before turning to more complicated quantitative analyses (see Philips case in chapter 6.)

Many other companies have also used these and similar techniques to achieve more eco-efficient products. SC Johnson Wax, for example, runs design for eco-efficiency workshops. IBM has achieved better energy efficiency and materials management, and more environmentally responsible packaging for its AS/400 computers. Greater use of "snap-on" components, use of a restricted number of clearly marked plastics, and elimination of embedded materials in plastics also make disassembling and recycling them much easier.

Fiat Auto's Design For Recycling (DFR) plan uses similar techniques to maximize the recycling of components and materials used in its cars. Its cars now use soft dashboards and door panels made from a single recyclable polymer, polypropylene, rather than the hybrid materials that were previously used. Each virgin material also has its "reutilization cascade"—that is, the use to which it can be put when recycled—considered in advance. This allows maximum advantage to be taken of

**Philips Five Fast Questions Highlight Design
for Eco-Efficiency Issues**

The Philips manual explains them in this way:

A reference product should be identified. This should be the closest
existing product to the one that is being designed. It can be a previous
Philips product, or a competitor product that is dominant in the market. A new product is proposed and the major differences between it
and the reference product are noted. More than one concept or feature
can be considered.

1. Energy: Does the proposed design require less energy than the reference product? Consider manufacturing, transportation, using the product (both normal and stand-by operation), and disposal. In most cases,
the use of the products consumes the most energy.

2. Recyclability: Is the proposed design more recyclable than that of the
reference product? Consider whether the larger components can be easily separated into monomaterial subassemblies. Are noncompatible metals easily separable? Are noncompatible plastics easily separable? Are
recyclable plastics used?

3. Hazardous waste: Does the proposed product design produce less
chemical waste than an alternative design? Consider whether any restricted materials are used in the products (such as halogenated flame
retardants in plastics, cadmium pigments, or ozone-depleting chemicals). Consider whether batteries are used, and if so, whether they are
rechargeable.

4. Durability, repairability, and preciousness: Does the proposed design
have a better durability, repairability, or affection level than the reference
product? Consider whether the new design will last longer or be easier to
upgrade than the reference. Also consider whether the precious qualities
of the new design (such as the customer's affection of the design) will
make the consumer keep the new product longer than the reference.

5. Alternative ways to provide service: Are there ways of providing the
product service that have much lower ecological loads? Consider
whether there are techniques that require much less energy or material,
but that provide the service at the same level of quality.

The manual suggests that 1–2 hours time spend on the exercise will
highlight most important eco-efficiency issues, which can then be analyzed in depth by other methods.

the residual properties of materials that can feasibly be reused for their original purpose. In the case of car windows, for example, the cascade is designed so that the recycled material can be used in containers and bottles. Reuse in new windows would be uneconomical because of the need to remove the various colorations and impurities in the glass.

Plants and processes can also be designed for greater resource productivity. Dow recently dedicated a new ethylene plant at its site in Fort Saskatchewan in Canada. As a result of state-of-the-art technology and careful planning it is 20% more energy-efficient than its predecessor. It didn't cost more or take longer to design efficiency into the plant. But the payoff will be a competitive advantage in the long run.

Arthur D. Little consultants Robert Shelton and Jonathan Shopley have examined a number of DFE initiatives and developed six criteria for their successful implementation—and, by extension, implementation of design for eco-efficiency. They are:

1. Design the DFE initiative to fit the product development process, not the other way around.

2. Keep in mind that the DFE goal is to create more competitive products, not green products.

3. Build collaboration among the product development and EH&S staff.

4. Ensure that DFE belongs to the design team, supported by EH&S.

5. Simple, flexible, easy-to-use DFE tools and management systems are mandatory—especially at the beginning.

6. Remember that DFE is not life cycle analysis. Develop simple, flexible DFE tools that capture the life cycle approach.[35]

R&D

R&D provides key inputs to design and life cycle management. Its effects—in the form of products and processes—can last for decades or even centuries so it is vital that work in the field be influenced by the long-term vision we discussed earlier. This enables tomorrow's environmental challenges to be dealt with as well as today's. Dow Europe's vice president Claude Fussler believes that researchers and managers must think in time scales of 20 or 30 years. Only then are they likely to understand the scale of the performance improvements required for the

---

Design for Environment at AT&T

The U.S. telecommunications company AT&T has made DFE the capstone of its entire environmental policy, which was amended in 1993 to read:

AT&T's environmental vision is to be recognized by customers, employees, shareowners, and communities worldwide as a responsible company which fully integrates life cycle environmental consequences into each of our business decisions and activities. Designing for the environment is a key element in distinguishing our processes, products and services.[36]

To implement the policy, it established a DFE coordinating team and subteams to examine what it saw as seven key issues in a successful DFE strategy:

1. *Green accounting*—getting financial systems to allocate environmental costs on a product-by-product and process-specific basis

2. *Energy*—identifying the issues affecting operations and products, and supporting the development of energy-efficient products and operations

3. *International environmental standards*—helping contribute to the coming generation of environmental performance standards

4. *Supply-line management*—ensuring that the company is partnering with suppliers to obtain environmentally appropriate materials, components, and subassemblies for its products

5. *Takeback*—preparing AT&T for the changes that will be required by voluntary and mandatory return of products to their manufacturer at the end of their useful life

6. *Life cycle assessment*—developing technical methods to aid in understanding the environmental impact of processes, operations, products and services

7. *External relations*—being active collaborators and leaders of industry, governmental, academic, and nonprofit environmental organizations

One product is a software package to score the environmental impacts of products. For example, a business telephone initially scored 86.3 out of 100 for physical design and 55.6 for electrical design. The scoring demonstrated improvement opportunities in marking of plastics, printing the user's manual on recycled paper and replacing tin-lead solder with other means of connecting components. Once these changes were made the physical score increased to 93.6 and the electrical one to 72.2.

---

product or process they are concerned with—and to draw the conclusion that radically new approaches will be required rather than incremental improvements.

This is the philosophy at the German auto producer Mercedes Benz. Gerritt Huy, senior manager and commissioner for the environment, believes that

There are many aspects to the subject. Decreasing fuel consumption is one, of course, and we're working intensively on that. But you can save energy, for example, by constructing a lighter car. We're carrying out bionic research, that is, we're looking at nature, at how nature has optimized material use. We're looking at all types of light-weight materials: optimized steel, aluminum and especially at carbon fiber compounds . . . [as] cars will be small and light, they will no longer have a buffer zone of material, so you have to ensure safety in other ways. Imagine an electronically controlled distance-keeper, cars driving very close to each other in a convoy. They hook up on the conveyor electronically, they're steered electronically at a close distance from each other, and that way you can increase the number on the highways considerably.[37]

The chemical industry too has much scope for fundamental improvements in the eco-efficiency of its products and processes. Catalyst research is one area where these improvements are starting to be realized. Hartmut Verren of Hoechst summarizes their advantages:

With less initial raw material, the same amount of product can be manufactured, with only a fraction of the former residual waste. It's a little bit like magic.[38]

At Hoechst's Griesheim plant, which produces aromatic amines, a building block for dyes, pigments, and other products, the old process created 17,000 tons a year of solid waste and large amounts of wastewater. A new catalyst has now eliminated the solid waste, reduced wastewater by 90%, and increased product yields.

Although the long-term need is for new products and processes that radically improve environmental performance, there is much to be done in the short to medium term to improve existing products and processes. Philips and Sony, for example, are improving the environmental acceptability of current TV sets by using recyclable materials, reducing the type and variety of plastics, making the sets lighter, and eliminating hazardous substances from the product and during production.

Improvement is particularly important for capital equipment in developing countries that will be in operation for years or decades. The

Swedish-Swiss electrical engineering company ABB is making a contribution here by reducing carbon dioxide emissions and power generation costs through forcing the performance of coal-fired power stations. Its supercritical technology uses high pressures and temperatures to increase their energy efficiency. A new plant at Shidongku near Shanghai was recently rated as one of the top three plants in the world. It also involved considerable transfer of technical know-how so that the station is staffed entirely by Chinese workers.[39]

Production and Operations

The cleaner production program of the UNEP Industry and Environment Office is a good starting point for any consideration of eco-efficiency in production. It defines *cleaner production* as "the continuous use of industrial processes and products to prevent the pollution of air, water and land, reduce wastes at source, and minimize risks to the human population and environment."[40] Cleaner production therefore encompasses the entire product life cycle, from raw material extraction, through manufacturing and use, to the "ultimate" disposal of the product. As the box shows it also encompasses the service sector. However, a large part of UNEP's practical work has been with manufacturers, with a particular emphasis on small- to medium-sized companies in developing countries and transitional economies.

This experience has shown that cleaner production can be achieved in three main ways: (1) changing attitudes, (2) applying know-how, and (3) improving technology.

As previously discussed, developing motivation and a sense of personal responsibility for environmental improvement is a prerequisite for eco-efficiency. UNEP has found that this change alone can produce significant reductions in pollution and waste in many companies.

Applying know-how means improving efficiency, adopting better management techniques, changing housekeeping practices, and revising policies, procedures, and institutions. Timely and preventive maintenance, for example, can often reduce leakages and improve yields and energy utilization. Good inventory management can also reduce waste, while better scheduling can often reduce the need to clean equipment between batches.

Experience also shows that there are four principal means of improving technology.

1. Changing process or manufacturing techniques. Fundamental changes to production processes normally require R&D but even simple modifications can often produce positive results.

2. Changing input materials. For example, water-based processes can be substituted for ones using organic solvents.

3. Changes to the product, such as eliminating heavy metals or other hazardous materials from their design.

4. Reusing materials on site, as with separation or treatment techniques to recover useful materials from wastes.

Although cleaner production and eco-efficiency go well beyond waste minimization, initiatives in this area can be a useful starting point. Every organization creates waste and the basic principles of reducing it appeals to widely shared values such as thrift. The approach can be applied in service as well as manufacturing companies and is relevant to inputs, processes, and outputs. The careful analysis of "how we do things"—and the subsequent question, "can we do them better?"—which is a prerequisite of waste minimization can also create spin-off benefits such as yield improvements. Finally, waste minimization initiatives can also produce the "quick wins" that build support and enthusiasm.

Waste minimization is not only confined to manufacturing and offices. Fletcher Construction, an Australian subsidiary of the New Zealand holding company Fletcher Challenge, has shown that it can be applied to the building and demolition sector too. Its RECON system aims to avoid waste creation wherever possible and increase recycling of steel, concrete, timber, cardboard, and plasterboard. The initiative has reduced the amount of rubble sent from a trial site to the tip for landfill by 43%, and saved 55% in waste removal costs. According to Fletcher Construction's managing director Graham Duff:

The scheme demonstrates what can be achieved with a commitment to environmental care. Importantly, the benefits have also been financial, proving the economic viability of recycling.[41]

Australia-based Western Mining has also shown that "best-practice" mining can minimize destruction of land and biodiversity and prevent leaching of hazardous materials. The company's Hog Ranch gold mine in Nevada was home to a rare plant called Crosby's buckwheat. To preserve its numbers, specimens were transplanted to a nearby area where they are now thriving. The company also developed new techniques for reclaiming the site that both recovered gold from the wastes and created greater environmental benefits. As a result, it received an Excellence in Reclamation Award from a joint grouping of the U.S. Bureau of Land Management, the U.S. Forest Service, and the Nevada Divisions of Environmental Protection, Minerals and Wildlife.[42]

Marketing and Procurement for Eco-efficiency

For many companies the environmental impact of their own activities are dwarfed by those of their suppliers or the users of their products. Eco-efficiency therefore requires that upstream and downstream impacts be addressed.

Marketing
Sustainable production and consumption require changes in the usage and consumption patterns of millions of individuals and businesses. It means that business will increasingly be challenged on the actual value it provides. People will ask whether the function is really needed; and if it is, whether particular products and services are the right answer to that function, or whether there are alternatives.[44]

They will also demand that advertising and marketing not make exaggerated claims about the environmental impact of products. Most companies know this and many have internal procedures to deal with it (see box for 3M's policy, which was introduced in 1990). Companies in a number of countries are also bound by truth-in-advertising regulatory systems. The best contribution of advertising and marketing to eco-efficiency is to provide consumers with the clear, accurate, and reliable data need to make informed purchasing decisions, and to help develop a pull from the marketplace. However, its importance should not be exaggerated. Generally speaking, advertising can get a product bought

3M's Policy on Environmental Marketing Claims

All new and existing product environmental claims, symbols, and slogans must be submitted to the Environmental Marketing Claims (EMC) Review Committee for approval. Approval will be based on:

technical accuracy and substantiation

clarity; that is the likelihood not to mislead 3M customers or the general public

Guidelines

When submitting environmental claims to the EMC Review Committee for approval, avoid using:

slogans or symbols that make broad environmental claims, such as "safe for the environment" or "environmentally friendly." Such broad claims are ambiguous and impossible to document.

claims whose meanings have not been clearly defined.

The procedures for gaining approval are:

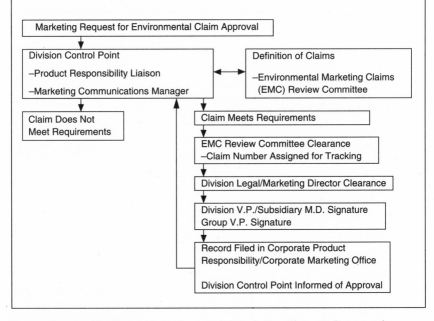

Source: Courtesy 3M Corporate Environmental Marketing Claims Policy, issued September 4, 1990.

once, to try it. If the product does not fulfill expectations, it will not be purchased again. This is especially the case for fast moving consumer goods.

A WBCSD report on the topic concluded that companies should

• Improve the quality and value of the information they provide about products and services, to make it easier for consumers to use the information.

• Provide clear, consistent, and accurate environmental messages.

• Enlist the assistance of marketing staff to gauge the market's environmental requirements.

• Take joint action with other businesses, trade associations, or NGOs to raise environmental awareness.[45]

If the performance and value of environmentally improved products does not meet people's needs, the product is unlikely to sell. Procter & Gamble, for example, introduced Pump-n-Spray, a hairspray that used hand pumped air rather than an aerosol as the propellant. The result was much better environmental performance—but poor sales in the marketplace. P&G's conclusion was that customers were not willing to accept the inconvenience of hand pumping just to gain an environmental benefit. Eco-efficient products have to deliver environmental benefit and value and performance all together. P&G has developed its own tools to ensure that this happens.[46]

The medium-to-long term challenge of marketing is also to get closer to customers to form a view of their real needs and then to use the information to reconfigure products and services to meet them more eco-efficiently. The most interesting products from a business perspective are products that people need but cannot articulate that they need. 3M learned from hospital customer focus panels that existing methods of printing medical images were slow, inflexible, and environmentally polluting—so they produced a new technology, Dryview, which creates improvement on all fronts (see chapter 6). And the U.S. clothing retailer Patagonia decided that the large number of different styles and colors of clothing it sold created an adverse impact without fundamentally contributing to customers' real needs—and narrowed its range as a result.

Cleaner Production and Eco-efficiency in Tourism

Tourism is the largest and fastest-growing industry in the world, and its rapid growth is fueling the economy in many developing countries, especially Asia. The tourism industry's impact on the environment and the potential for change cannot be underestimated: in 1995 alone, tourism has produced close to 11% of world gross domestic product (GDP) and generated an estimated $3.4 trillion in gross output. Because of its "intangible" nature, the service sector such as tourism has traditionally been behind in embracing the concept of eco-efficiency and cleaner production. However, it has enormous environmental impact, ranging from transport to water consumption and waste generation. For this reason, it is a priority sector for the European Union's fifth environmental action program.

Experience suggests that there is much scope in all parts of the world for simple eco-efficient initiatives such as increased energy efficiency and waste minimization. UNEP, in partnership with the International Hotels Association (IHA) and the International Hotels Environment Initiative (IHEI), has published an environmental Action Pack for hotels that distills this experience and helps to identify opportunities for eco-efficiency.[43] This publication is intended to serve as a first-step guide for small and medium-sized hotels, which form a large part of the hotel industry, to set up and improve environmental management initiatives.

The Action Pack provides practical information, checklists, and examples concerning key issues such as environmental self-audits, priority action areas (energy, solid waste, water, effluent and emissions, choosing contracts and suppliers), the integration of environmental management in daily operations, and progress monitoring.

As a follow-up action to this document, the three organizations have begun to convene regional seminars to provide a showcase for good environmental practices. The first of these meetings, focusing on Asia, was held in Thailand in October 1995. As the resolution of the meeting, hotel business leaders agreed to push forward environmental action through their own hotel companies and to support the efforts of their national associations. At the international level, IHA has been entrusted with facilitating the exchange of experiences among national hotel associations. UNEP has pledged to support these efforts by providing technical and educational information through various UN units.

UNEP is now taking the Action Pack a step further by assessing the possibility of adapting its contents for the hotel school curriculum, and also by exploring the possibility of a project of identifying existing sources of "sustainable technologies" for tourism.

Procurement

Incorporating environmental considerations into procurement and purchasing policies can require suppliers to apply sustainable development practices to their products and services.

Some companies—such as those in the detergent industry—have done this for many years. Many more companies are now taking this action. In the United Kingdom, for example, the business association Business in the Environment has published guidelines on best practice and has a task force of leading companies who are introducing it.[47] The guidelines were influenced by two pioneers in the field, the telecommunications company BT, and B&Q, Europe's biggest do-it-yourself supplier. BT has an environment section in its procurement department and screens all major purchases. It also confers an Environmental Suppliers Award to recognize good practice among suppliers. B&Q conducts an annual questionnaire survey of its suppliers, which it uses to grade them on their production methods and source of materials. B&Q prefers to work with its suppliers to achieve improvement but at the end of the day will stop buying if poor performers do not mend their ways—four suppliers were delisted for this reason in 1994. The company also canceled a contract with a Finnish timber company that was producing from one of the few remaining areas of virgin forest in Finland.

Procurement policies are probably having the greatest impact on the forest products industry. As a recent WBCSD-commissioned study by the International Institute for Environment and Development (IIED) on the paper life cycle showed, environmental issues are shaping every stage of the product chain.[48] Tracking whether products are produced using sustainable forestry practices is now very much easier since independent certification is available. This is provided by the Forest Stewardship Council, a body created by the Worldwide Fund for Nature (WWF) and proactive timber users such as B&Q. The Scandinavian countries too are considering an independent certification scheme for boreal forests. To ensure that certification is adopted widely, the WWF has also organized the 1995 Club—of about 50 major companies—whose members are committed to ending purchases of forest products that have not been produced using sustainable foresting practices.

Aftersales Service and Disposal

Most companies recognize that their involvement in—and potential liability for—the environmental impact of product does not end with a
sale. They are adopting policies of *product stewardship* in which they
control or influence their use and disposal. Regulations—such as the
European Union Packaging and Packaging Waste Directive or takeback
requirements for electronic products—are also requiring or encouraging such policies.

The concept of product stewardship, so called, originated at Dow
Chemical in the early 1970s. Since then it has spread widely and today
multinational companies from many sectors have instituted their own
product stewardship or product responsibility programs. The list
includes electronics firms such as Hewlett-Packard, Intel, Xerox, and
Northern Telecom, and forest products companies such as International Paper, Noranda, and Avenor. In the chemicals sector, in order
to be a member of the U.S. Chemical Manufacturers Association
(CMA), companies must adhere to 10 guiding principles and six codes
of management practices outlined in the association's Responsible
Care initiative, many of which relate to product stewardship.

Product stewardship makes EH&S concerns a priority in all phases of
a product's life cycle. By way of illustration, the product responsibility
guidelines applied in companies such as Dow, SC Johnson Wax, and 3M
begin with research and development, when a product is first conceived,
and extend all the way through the product's design, manufacture, marketing, distribution, use, recycling, and disposal. The companies believe
that their product stewardship programs provide them with a competitive advantage because they involve lower operating costs, give greater
customer satisfaction, and mean reduced regulatory burdens and long-
term liability.

Product stewardship represents a significant shift in the mindset of
industry. It moves corporate thinking and action beyond the factory
walls and requires it to consider the upstream and downstream implications of its activities, and to take corrective action.

Of course, many companies have always had an involvement in
aftersales areas for purely business reasons. Provision of maintenance

and other services, for example, can often be more profitable than merely selling the product. Hence, there are likely to be many opportunities to create additional value for customers and the company and reduce environmental impact by becoming more involved in aftersales service and disposal. Moving in this direction also creates the more general eco-efficiency benefit of better knowledge of customers and their current and future needs.

Michael Braungart of the German Hamburger Umwelt Institut foresees an "intelligent products system" in which there are three classes of product—consumption products such as washing powders that are consumed during use, unmarketable products such as wastes (whose volume will gradually be reduced by pollution prevention and other measures), and service products, which remain substantially intact after their first use. A company would either lease or provide an end-of-life return system for all such service products. The industrial materials group Cookson provides an example, with its competitive strategy being built on renting or leasing its products and recycling them after use.[49]

Working with Others

Many of the measures discussed in this chapter work best when done in partnership with others. Taking products back at the end of their life, for example, often requires an infrastructure of agents who can collect them and return them to the manufacturer. Envisioning the future involves extensive interaction with the external agents such as think tanks, regulators, environmental groups, and others who are likely to set tomorrow's agendas. The next chapter provides more discussion of this issue.

Summary

There are many barriers, both internal and external, to the adoption of eco-efficiency. Nine key elements can help overcome them:

Leadership—the single most important requirement for eco-efficiency. If top management doesn't support it through words and action, change simply won't happen.

Foresight—looking into the future and translating this into a vision of sustainable business development and the competencies and technologies needed to achieve it.

Culture—individual employees make the difference between eco-efficiency happening or not so there must be a culture that creates commitment and action by everyone in the organization.

Management tools—such as environmental management systems, environmental performance measures, and environmental accounting techniques provide the data and incentives to drive eco-efficiency within the organization.

Life cycle management—understanding and improving the life cycle impact of products, particularly through eco-design.

R&D—to ensure that tomorrow's environmental challenges are dealt with as well as today's—sustainability means thinking in timescales of twenty or thirty years.

Production and operations—most companies begin their environmental actions in this area and much can be achieved through waste minimization and other initiatives.

Marketing—we need environmentally improved products, based on getting closer to customers to form a view of their real needs.

Procurement—can encourage suppliers to improve their own environmental performance and minimize buying-in waste or pollution problems.

Aftersales service and disposal—companies have a responsibility, and a business opportunity, to consider the environmental impacts created by use and disposal.

5	Partnership for Eco-efficiency

This chapter is about the value of partnership for achieving eco-efficiency, the ways partnership can be made successful and the organizations that business can partner with. We divide the latter into four main categories—those in the workplace and marketplace such as employees and customers; those in research and training; host communities and those in the public policy realm—and provide many examples of successful partnership for eco-efficiency in each. Later sections focus on those in an area that is particularly important to eco-efficiency, regulatory reform.

Of course, the value of partnership has not always been appreciated by business. The history of industry's response to environmental concerns has four main stages—denial, data, delivery, and dialogue, or the four D's. Back in the 1970s, most companies adopted the attitude that what went on within their fences was no one else's business. They shrouded themselves in a veil of secrecy, claiming the need to protect confidentiality and proprietary interests. They *denied* that they had problems. Not surprisingly, some outside of industry interpreted this as a sure sign that something was being hidden.

The second stage, roughly in the 1980s, was *data* collection and exchange—mainly "our facts are better than your facts." It was an improvement over the first stage in that people were at least communicating with each other. But the public was still unimpressed. One important piece of learning from this period was that people simply do not care about what companies know—they want to know how much they care.

Caring means taking action—and the 1990s message to business has been that fine words mean nothing if business cannot show continuous improvement of environmental performance and development of environmentally sound products and processes. Business leaders acknowledged this with the widely quoted maxim "don't trust us, track us." Of course, some companies and industries had been achieving such improvement for years but for many it was only in the late 1980s and early 1990s that corporate environmental performance became a real issue.

But experience shows that even *delivery* is not sufficient. There is a fourth (or, more accurately, a parallel third) stage of *dialogue.* Dialogue is essential to ensure that what is being delivered is what stakeholders want—and that what is being planned for delivery tomorrow is what they will want then too. It is also the key to getting recognition for success and tolerance for any temporary failures.

The best form of dialogue is when it is continuous, so that each party reacts over time to what others are saying and trust is established. Then there is a basis for real partnerships between business and its stakeholders—and with other businesses—which can greatly support moves toward eco-efficiency and sustainable development. One study has summarized the benefits of such partnerships in this way:

It can mobilize greater amounts, and a wider variety, of skills and resources than can be achieved by acting alone.

It can address problems in a more integrated, multidisciplinary, and comprehensive manner.

It can eliminate unnecessary duplication of cost and effort, which is especially important where there are shortages of financial resources or relevant skills.

It can help traditional adversaries, or organizations which have had little cause to interact in the past, to broaden their perspectives and to respect each other's needs and capabilities.

This in turn can facilitate the dialogue, creativity and mutual trust needed to work through diverse and apparently conflicting interests, toward common goals.

The multiple face-to-face interactions which occur between partners can also facilitate the flow of information and promote technology transfer.[1]

The same study identifies four main areas of activity where partnership can take place (see figure 5.1).

In the workplace and marketplace: during the course of its direct activities business can cooperate more closely with its employees (including trade unions), its customers, suppliers, financiers, and even its competitors and environmental

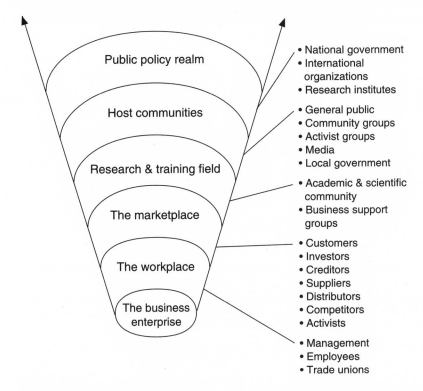

Figure 5.1
Potential partners for eco-efficiency.
Source: United Nations Environmental Programme, Prince of Wales Business Leaders Forum and Tufts University, *Partnerships for Sustainable Development: The Role of Business and Industry* (London, 1994), p. 10.

activists, to develop cleaner processes and products, to establish voluntary standards and policies, to market sustainably managed resources and to share experiences and burdens.

In the research and training field: business can forge partnerships with the academic and scientific community to develop new technology, new products, and new management styles.

In host communities: companies can work with non-governmental organizations, local government, and the public to add to the quality of life and to make social investments in the human and physical development of their neighbors.

In the public policy realm: the business community can collaborate more closely with government, at both a national and regional level, and with international organizations and research institutes, to develop incentives and regulatory frameworks that help business to improve its environmental performance, without undermining its economic performance. [2]

Building Partnerships

This excerpt from Monsanto's 1995 environmental report provides an example of the range of partnerships that one company is developing around the world:

Because the very foundation of our existence is good scientific research, Monsanto helps fund the Chemical Industry Institute of Toxicology (CIIT). CIIT is an independent research firm that scientifically studies the potential adverse side effects of chemicals, pharmaceuticals, and consumer products on human health.

With twenty eight other commercial enterprises, we also sponsor the Center for Waste Reduction Technologies, which works on innovative waste reduction technologies and methodologies. Monsanto is also one of several large industrial sponsors of the Environmental Solutions Program at the University of Texas, Austin, which focuses its research on water-treatment solutions.

Under the sponsorship of the Remediation Technologies Development Forum, which was established by the U.S. Environmental Protection Agency, Monsanto has joined five major corporations in a consortium to develop new technologies to clean up contaminated sites.

We provide funding for several research programs. One at Washington University's Chemical Reaction Engineering Laboratory in St. Louis, Missouri studies source reduction technologies. We also fund grants for studies of environmental solutions at the Center for Environmental Science and Technology at the University of Missouri–Rolla, and at the Center for Bioengineering and Pollution Control at the University of Notre Dame in South Bend, Indiana.

We realize that research is not the only way to find environmental solutions. Monsanto is working with organizations such as The Nature Conservancy, the World Bird Sanctuary and the Wildlife Habitat Council to help educate people about the environment and to foster improvements.

The Wildlife Habitat Council has already certified six U.S. Monsanto sites verifying that we are carrying out our pledge to "manage all corporate real estate, including plant sites, to benefit nature."

In 1995, we sponsored a World Bird Sanctuary student education program. Students in six of our plant communities saw—for the first time, in many cases—live eagles, owls, hawks and falcons. The students learned how they can help save endangered species.

Maintaining regular dialogue with our communities is critical to earning the trust and confidence of our neighbors. Many of our plants have established community advisory panels to promote two-way communication and to help educate community members on safety and environmental issues at manufacturing sites.

Our community partnerships have frequently developed useful ideas for solving environmental problems or providing educational tools for the local community. The Indian Orchard plant in Springfield, Massachusetts, teamed up with local citizens emergency personnel, and the Environmental Hazards Management Institute, a nonprofit organization experienced in designing learning aids, to develop an "Emergency Action Wheel." The wheel was designed to provide instructions for planning and dealing with various emergencies, ranging from fires to floods to chemical spills.

We are building partnerships throughout the world at the local, national, and international levels. As a member of organizations such as Business for Social Responsibility and the International Chamber of Commerce, we are better able to identify global issues that present opportunities for environmental and business improvements.

Monsanto sites with community advisory panels: Decatur, Alabama; Antwerp, Belgium; LaSalle, Canada; Pensacola, Florida; Augusta, Georgia; Soda Springs, Idaho; Sauget, Illinois; Fort Madison, Iowa; Muscatine, Iowa; Kungwon-Do, Korea; Luling, Louisiana; Springfield, Massachusetts; St. Louis, Missouri; Trenton, Michigan; Fayetteville, North Carolina; Addyston, Ohio; Greenwood, South Carolina; Alviri, Texas; Morpeth, United Kingdom; Ruabon, United Kingdom.

Many companies—for example, Monsanto (see box)—now operate partnerships in all of these areas to help them achieve eco-efficiency. The following sections provide selected examples of other partnerships for eco-efficiency in all four of the identified areas, and analyze the reasons for their success.

Partnering in the Workplace and Marketplace

There are many ways in which companies can achieve eco-efficiency through individual actions or partnerships. Often this will be a powerful source of competitive advantage. But there are also strong reasons for longer-term partnerships with a number of companies (commensurate with antitrust laws). Dave Buzzelli, vice president and corporate director, EH&S and public affairs at Dow, puts it this way:

Sometimes it's better to work together to improve the credibility of an entire industry and make it publicly accountable. When someone comes up with a great idea, the first question we ask is: Should we execute this alone, or should we get two or three other companies and execute it together?[3]

Buzzelli—when president of Dow Canada—was one of the founders of perhaps the most successful environmental initiative by an industry association, the chemical sector's Responsible Care program. This was originated by the Canadian Chemical Manufacturers Association in 1985 and has now been adopted by many national chemical associations around the world, including the U.S. Chemical Manufacturers Association (CMA) in 1988. Many of these associations have developed their own codes, guides, notes, and checklists to help member companies develop Responsible Care within the specific requirements and needs of their home country.

In the case of the CMA members and partners pledge to abide by 10 underlying principles, which include:

recognizing and responding to community concerns about chemicals and plant operation

developing and producing chemicals that can be manufactured, transported, and disposed of safely

making health, safety, and environmental considerations a planning priority

reporting promptly on health or environmental hazards and recommending protective measures

pursuing relevant research and communications activities

participating with government and others in creating responsible laws, regulations and standards to safeguard the community, workplace, and environment.

A public advisory panel composed of individuals from the public and private sectors meets four times a year and helps CMA identify public concerns and decide how to respond to them, reviews Responsible Care codes of management practices, and evaluates other features of the initiative. The CMA and its members also subject the scheme and its implementation to continuous critical appraisal. This creates strong peer pressures—on good performers to get even better and on poor performers to transform their EH&S practices.

According to Fred Webber, president of CMA:

Through Responsible Care, the chemical industry has taken a significant step towards satisfying the public's desire for both useful products and a safe and clean environment. The chemical industry's commitment to following through on performance improvement is unprecedented. In my opinion, Responsible Care is more than a good initiative—it's the industry's franchise to operate.[3]

It also contributes to eco-efficiency by helping to reduce toxic emissions—with an emphasis on pollution prevention—and reducing energy and material intensity through cutting wastes and maximizing recycling.

Responsible Care is so successful that it is now being replicated in many other sectors. In the United States, for example, the American Petroleum Institute, American Textile Manufacturers Association, and Printing Industries of America have all initiated similar programs for their members.[5] The International Hotels Environmental Initiative also shows that the ideas can be extended to a global service industry.[6]

Partnerships can also extend through the product chain, as with Fiat's F.A.RE (Fiat Auto Recycling) plan. This links car manufacturers and distributors, customers, recyclers, and materials suppliers. The plan in Italy involves customers returning their cars to specialist green centers at selected Fiat auto dealers. The centers ensure that the vehicle is prepared for safe disposal by recovering all polluting fluids—including oil and fuel—and the battery and sending them for recycling and disposal. The vehicle is then dispatched to one of around 100 dismantling centers around Italy. These were selected in collaboration with the Italian Association of Auto Demolition Companies. The dismantling centers remove nonmetallic components and materials and return them to their original manufacturers for reuse or recycling. As well as creating economic value, this removal also simplifies the next stage of shredding and melting the car frame to recycle the metal.

Fiat has also signed a collaboration agreement with BMW, Renault, and Rover to handle the recyling of one another's cars in their respective national territories. In the longer run the rate of reuse and recovery of components and materials from Fiat cars—and the economic return created by F.A.RE—will be further increased by the company's Design for Recycling program.

PET Container Recycling Europe (PETCORE) provides an example of partnership between producers and downstream users of polyethylene terephthalate (PET). Its founder members include Akzo, Constar International, Continental PET Europe, Eastman Chemical, Hoechst, ICI Chemicals and Polymers, Inca International, Johnson Controls International Europe, Shell International Chemicals, and the European Association of PET Convertors. PETCORE is a nonprofit-making association whose mission is to facilitate recyling of containers made from PET. This high-quality polymer can easily be recycled into a variety of uses, ranging from insulating fiber for bedding and clothing to nonfood containers. PETCORE supports such recycling by developing a collection-and-return infrastructure for end-of-life PET products across Europe. This avoids disposal costs, provides a low-cost raw material, and avoids the use of resources to produce the materials that recycled PET replaces. PETCORE also helps achieve eco-efficiency by developing new cost-effective uses for recycled PET and by giving converters advice on waste minimization.

Joint Implementation

Interbusiness partnership is especially valuable when it transfers know-how and technology from developed to developing countries. Such projects are encouraged, for example, under the joint implementation (JI) provisions of the Climate Change Convention as a valuable means of reducing emissions of carbon dioxide in the developing world. They are also supported and facilitated by the WBCSD's International Business Action on Climate Change (IBACC) initiative. The Canadian power and resources company TransAlta—whose senior vice president of sustainable development, Jim Leslie, is the chair of IBACC—is one company developing joint implementation with India's Andhra Pradesh State Electricity Board. The partnership will upgrade the distribution system to reduce power losses and therefore avoid the need for new generating capacity and the creation of additional carbon dioxide emissions. The environment will also benefit in other ways from this reduced energy intensity of power production while the board's revenues will be increased. TransAlta would make no immediate profit from the exercise itself, although any avoided carbon dioxide emissions might provide future emission credits for its Canadian operations.

National Business Initiatives

Many established business associations encourage eco-efficient action by their members. Japan's Keidanren, for example, has an environmental charter that its members are required to adopt—a very powerful commitment under the Japanese system. It stresses key eco-efficiency indicators such as reducing toxic dispersion and wastes and maximizing energy efficiency and recycling.

A number of specialist bodies have also been created. In the United Kingdom the Prince of Wales has been instrumental in establishing three linked business-led bodies that contribute to different facets of eco-efficiency both in the United Kingdom and elsewhere. Business in the community focuses on the need for companies to be involved in communities and contribute to their development. The Prince of Wales Business Leader's Forum develops awareness of environmental and corporate responsibility issues among top managers and stresses the opportunities for developing win-win solutions. Business in the Environment provides detailed advice and publications on business-related environmental topics such as environmental performance measurement, life cycle assessment, and environment-integrated procurement. Much of its work has focused on ways of reducing toxic emissions and wastes and improving energy and materials utilization while gaining business benefits such as reduced costs.

WBCSD—itself a global partnership of over 120 leading companies—has also been instrumental in establishing national business councils for sustainable development in developing and transitional economies, where good environmental information and assistance is often scarce. Their aim is to spread the message of eco-efficiency, to provide practical guidance on how it can be achieved, and to foster eco-efficient initiatives by local business. A case study provides details of this for BCSD Colombia (see chapter 6).

Asian Business Councils for Sustainable Development
Asia has some of the world's fastest growing economies. This growth creates both environmental problems and tremendous opportunities to achieve eco-efficiency by designing pollution out of, and energy and materials efficiency into, the new buildings and equipment that are

constantly being ordered. For these reasons, a number of national environmental associations have been created. Six are now affiliated with WBCSD—BCSD Indonesia, BCSD Malaysia, BCSD Taiwan, BCSD Thailand, BCSD Vietnam, and Philippine Business for the Environment. These bring together almost 200 corporate leaders to provide active leadership on key issues.

BCSD Malaysia is the largest of the five groups. It has become the main link between the government and business on the country's sustainable development agenda—encouraging the participation of business in, and providing a business perspective on, the decision-making process at the state and federal level.

BCSD Malaysia places great stress on helping Malaysian business to develop long-term mechanisms for achieving eco-efficiency. Environmental management systems are a top priority and a model framework has been developed for members to implement. Business sectors are also being encouraged to quantify the effect of their activities on the environment through assessment, monitoring, and auditing. Education and communication are also important parts of its work program. Courses, conferences, seminars, position papers,and reports are used to drive the message of sustainable development home to employees, customers, and the public—while BCSD Malaysia takes an active part in the environmental debate with governments and NGOs. It has also organized a number of successful environmental demonstration projects by local businesses.

BCSD Thailand has over 50 members. It too fosters eco-efficiency by providing a model framework for environmental management, fosters environmental quality circles among its members, and supports projects demonstrating distinctive business initiatives for environmental cleanup. One, the Pesticide-Free Agricultural Village project, aims to cut the use of chemical pesticides through the substitution of natural products. In its first eight months, the projects cut chemical use by half in the villages where it was applied. Another project involves renovating the historic Klong Lod's environment and landscape by transforming it into a pollution-free recreational area.

BCSD Indonesia, BCSD Taiwan, BCSD Vietnam, and Philippine Business for the Environment offer similar information and services to their members. In addition, BCSD Indonesia organizes a regional

Southeast Asian conference on eco-efficiency and cleaner production that brings together business leaders, policymakers, and production managers to discuss key policy options and practical methods of improving environmental performance. Philippine Business and the Environment also runs a highly successful Industrial Environmental Management Project (IEMP) that has helped members become more eco-efficient by catalyzing a number of highly successful energy and waste minimization projects.

Czech BCSD
In Eastern Europe, the post-Communist regimes inherited an inefficient economic system and a blighted environment. The concept of eco-efficiency therefore made perfect sense to many in government and industry. In the Czech Republic the ideas have been applied by three main bodies, the Czech Environmental Management Centre, the Czech Centre for Cleaner Production, and the Czech BCSD. Their work has contributed to substantial improvements in the overall performance of Czech industry. A Czech BCSD study of 10 enterprises found an aggregate 80% decrease in effluents to surface waters, a 63% fall in emissions of nitrogen oxides and a 47% reduction in emissions of sulphur dioxide between 1989 and 1994. These decreases were proportionately greater than the decline in production that also occurred during this period. Energy consumption also fell, contributing to an overall reduction in energy consumption per unit of Czech GDP of 11% between 1992 and 1994.

The work of the Czech BCSD in supporting these achievements and building a consensus on the new State Environmental Policy promulgated in 1995 has been recognized by the award of the Minister of Environment's Prize to its honorary chairman, Frantisek Hromek. Czech BCSD has also led a working group of WBCSD member companies in a study which looked at the way liability for past environmental damage is handled in the Czech Republic. Their report offered some trenchant and practical suggestions about what the Czech authorities and business should each do to achieve the most sensible apportionment of responsibility for historical environmental damage. Some of its recommendations have already been implemented and the results are now being extended to other countries in Central and Eastern Europe.

Supply Chain Partnerships

More and more businesses are also beginning to collaborate for eco-efficiency with their suppliers and customers. Chapter 4 explored instances
of companies doing this alone. There are also plans that bring together
a number of companies, both upstream and downstream, together with
NGOs and other stakeholders.

The Marine Stewardship Council was originated by a partnership of
foods producer Unilever and the Worldwide Fund for Nature (WWF) to
encourage sustainable fishing. It now encompasses a range of businesses and other organizations. The council has general guidelines on
what constitutes sustainable fishing and specific standards for major
fishing areas. Products made from fish that meet the standards—such as
U.K. Unilever's Bird's Eye fish fingers—gain a council logo. Unilever's
project manager for the initiative, Caroline Whitfield, believes that

It's in our commercial interest to secure our supplies for the future. If our business is to be sustainable, we must ensure that fish stocks are sustainable too.

Her equivalent at WWF, Mike Sutton, thinks the

initiative offers our best hope yet of reversing the worldwide crisis in marine
fisheries. By working together with progressive seafood companies, we can
enlist consumer power in favour of conservation goals.[7]

Partnering for Research and Training

The aim of partnership in this area is to develop ideas and equipment
for achieving eco-efficiency and disseminating best practice. This is
especially important in developing or transitional economies where the
knowledge base is often poor. Initiatives by individual companies and
multilateral agencies such as the UNEP Industry and Environment Programme or WBCSD are therefore crucial. Partnerships between agencies can also have advantages—UNEP and WBCSD are cooperating to
bring education and training in the ideas of cleaner production and eco-
efficiency to a large number of practitioners in developing countries
and economies in transition. Several of these are described below.

The best results occur when these activities go beyond one-off transfers and build a long-term capacity for eco-efficiency. Such capacity

building is very much the aim of the UNIDO-UNEP program to establish national centers for cleaner production (a concept having much in common with eco-efficiency).[8] The centers are hosted by a local nongovernmental institution that has committed its own resources to carry out training, information networking, industry demonstration projects, and policy analysis. They work with industry to show the economic and environmental benefits of cleaner production (the bottom up approach), while working with governments to set a policy framework to reward cleaner production (the top-down approach). There are now numerous national centers in such countries as Brazil, China, the Czech Republic, India, Mexico, the Slovak Republic, and Tanzania.

The National Cleaner Production Center in Zimbabwe provides an example of their work.[9] It was established in 1994 by the Environmental Forum of Zimbabwe, a group of leading local private industries. The center has already worked with six companies in sugar refining, breweries, packaging, and timber product manufacturing to conduct cleaner production audits and implement the conclusions. These are achieving reductions in such key eco-efficiency indicators as reduced toxic emissions and dispersion, energy intensity, and material intensity. It has also launched training programs for engineers and managers in partnership with local educational institutions.

The box provides further details of cleaner production initiatives in China, which requires much more eco-efficient businesses if it is to achieve its growth ambitions.

The WBCSD/WEC Industrial Eco-efficiency Program in Transitional Economies

The European countries in transition from communism to free market systems also face severe environmental problems. In partnership with the Swiss government, the WBCSD and the World Environment Center (WEC) have launched a joint initiative to provide training and advice on eco-efficiency in Bulgaria and Romania.[11]

The overall program objective is to bring an appreciation of the inherent economic value of eco-efficiency to selected sectors of industry by means of awareness workshops and the adoption of eco-efficiency principles through low-cost waste minimization demonstration projects.

Developing Eco-efficiency in China

Chinese policymakers know that environmental problems could be a major constraint on the country's economic development. A joint project of the National Environmental Protection Authority (NEPA), the United Nations Environmental Programme (UNEP), and the World Bank is demonstrating that even relatively poor Chinese companies can achieve environmental improvements and business benefits by increasing resource productivity.[10] The project's specific goals were to:

1. Adapt UNEP's cleaner production methodology to suit local Chinese needs
2. Develop training materials to educate Chinese professionals
3. Carry out several industry demonstration projects, such as that at the Yantai Second Distillery (see chapter 3), to show the economic and environmental benefits of improving resource productivity and the technological and managerial options for achieving them
4. Formulate recommendations for supportive government policies
5. Build a network to disseminate results to government and industry
6. Build expertise across China within a wide range of institutions.

Over 600 people participated in training sessions, with 150 staff officially qualified in cleaner production auditing. Approximately 10% of auditors underwent further training to become trainers, which resulted in second- and third-generation trainees. Twenty-nine cleaner production audits were also carried out in 27 enterprises, resulting in annual economic benefits of $2.9 million from the adoption of management or technology changes that required little or no investment. These produced an average pollution load reduction of 30% to 40%—and in some cases up to 95%. The audits also identified technology changes capable of saving more than $215 million a year on an investment of only $200 million.

With a sound capacity base, the next step for cleaner production and eco-efficiency in China is developing financial support for it. For example, the World Bank, UNEP, and the Chinese government have developed a revolving fund project in Yantai City and the Xiaoqing River basin in Shandong province. The fund has $20 million of capital and a twenty-year lifetime. Companies can submit loan applications by conducting a cleaner production assessment and putting together a one- to three-year plan, depending on the loan amount, for cleaner production implementation. The project is administered in partnership with local financial institutions and environmental protection bureaus. Technical assistance in conducting assessments will be provided in part by Chinese experts trained in the first stages of the initiative.

Existing pollution prevention centers (PPCs) will be strengthened by establishing a local PPC in regions of each country that will help spread waste minimization to other companies in the region.

The first year of the industrial eco-efficiency program focuses primarily on implementation of eco-efficiency workshops, waste minimization demonstration projects laying the foundation for local companies to initiate their own waste minimization programs, and the development and strengthening of a local PPC in Timisoara, Romania, and Pleven, Bulgaria.

Starting in the second year, a project identification and financing initiative develops the necessary information to train the industrial community to apply for and manage market-rate financing so as to be able to invest in the larger waste minimization opportunities and to introduce the Swiss financial community to potential new clients.

A group of companies, led by WBCSD members, has also developed a $10 million educational initiative in Russia, half of which is being funded by the Scandinavian governments and half by participating companies in the form of support "in kind." The venture, which will combine classroom-based training with practical company internships, is designed to expose tomorrow's business and state-enterprise leaders in the former Soviet Union to the latest and best of Western managerial practice and thinking, laying particular emphasis on sustainable economic development. Two centers, St. Petersburg and Moscow, have been selected to initiate the program, and as many as 600 managers will benefit from it in the first 3 years of the project's life.

Extending Awareness and Knowledge

Collaborations can also be a useful way of generating knowledge and developing consensus about eco-efficiency opportunities in the developed world. The U.S. National Biofuels Roundtable provides an example. Jointly coordinated by the Electric Power Research Institute and the conservation group, the National Audubon Society, and with financial support from the federal government, the Roundtable brings together business, science, and others to guide the development of a sustainable biomass energy resource.[12] The Roundtable has concluded that between 66 and 198 million hectares of land could be available for energy crops and that a potential 50,000MW of power could be generated from it—not a huge portion of U.S. demand but useful nonetheless. It believes that thoughtful management can avoid potentially negative environmental impacts and provide ecological benefits such as improved wildlife habitat, maintenance of biodiversity, improved soil quantities, and reduced erosion.

European Partners for the Environment (EPE) has even more ambitious objectives. EPE emerged from a series of roundtable discussions organized by the European Environmental Bureau (EEB), an umbrella organization representing 150 European NGOs. EPE was established in 1993, with a more specific mission of raising the awareness of industry, governments, NGOs, and others about sustainability issues and helping to achieve the targets of the European Union's Fifth Environmental Action Programme, *Towards Sustainability*, in as eco-efficient a manner as possible. Its council contains representatives of NGOs, business, professional associations, and public authorities—including the corporate founder members Dow Europe, Hunton & Williams, Oree, and Procter & Gamble. Its products have included scenarios for future interactions between environment and the European economy and educational and training materials.

Partnering with Communities

Community partnership is an important aspect of eco-efficiency not only because communities are important stakeholders but also because community views can be an important driver of improvement and a determinant of priorities. Many odors, for example, are nontoxic but may be much disliked by local residents. Community partnership can also be an important means of gaining new ideas about possible process or product improvements or even of opportunities for completely new ones. Dow, Monsanto, and other companies have created community advisory panels (CAPs) at all their plants to achieve such partnership.

Community advisory panels are a key part of the chemical industry's commitment to Responsible Care, which encourages companies to communicate directly with local citizens about their environmental, health, and safety performance. When forming a CAP, companies ask a cross-section of community neighbors to serve on a self-directed panel for a year or two, asking questions and sharing ideas and feedback from the rest of the community. The aim is to build trusting relationships between the company and the community and facilitate dialogue and constructive problem-solving.

CAP members volunteer their time and service and include teachers, homemakers, artists, volunteer leaders, clergy, and business owners. They have the freedom to discuss any issue of concern, company-related or otherwise, from the community's perspective. They are assisted by a trained nonpartisan facilitator. Company representatives participate in some meetings, but only at the discretion of CAP members, who control the agenda.

Even more than with other forms of collaboration, the precondition for community partnership is listening and being responsive to partner's concerns. The American forest products company Weyerhaeuser understands this. In the words of a *Seattle Times* editorial:

Weyerhaeuser's town meetings last week set an important example for companies whose private business inevitably affects the broader public agenda. In a bold break from tradition, top corporate executives spent three long evenings in Portland, Tacoma and Seattle, listening to harsh criticism and suggestions from the public. The public meetings drew hundreds of citizens who understand that Weyerhaeuser's corporate decisions affect the region's economy, environment, and quality of life. Jack Creighton, Weyerhaeuser's CEO, acknowledged this when he told local citizens: "We essentially operate with a franchise from the public."[13]

Canadian resources producer Noranda has a similar policy. In June 1991 a malfunction at its CCR copper refinery in Montreal released a selenium-containing mist that was of limited danger to health but damaged paint. As a result a local citizens' committee was formed with eleven community members—including the local fire chief—and six employees. CCR now explains its operating plans to the committee and reviews any issues, such as new projects, that might have an effect on the neighborhood. Committee members have visited other Noranda facilities and exchanged information with similar citizens' committees at other smelters. Jacques Pageau, CCR's superintendent of Environmental Service and committee member, believes that Noranda has "pretty well opened our doors and our books to the community."[14] Jim Duff, a community member agrees, and believes that "the process has been tremendously effective because of the co-operation of CCR. The people in this community have a real sense that the company cares."[15]

Community involvement was also the key to Syntex (now a subsidiary of the Swiss drug and fine chemical producer Roche) overcoming local opposition to its plant in Boulder, Colorado. The local authority and consultants ECA brokered a series of discussions that eventually produced an agreement. This allowed Syntex to introduce the changes it wanted but also met the concerns of community activists—and provided a framework for future partnership. Alison Peters, director of Boulder's Office of Environmental Affairs, feels that

each player took on the challenge of trying a new game. That meant creating new ground rules, hammering out common goals, and convincing skeptical audiences that coming to agreement could be a win-win proposition. In the process, the parties created a framework for cooperative problem solving that will make a difference in Boulder—and that holds promise for other communities as well.[16]

She suggests too that the Boulder experience demonstrates four key lessons for making business-community partnership successful.

1. *Get people talking*—directly, about the real issues.

2. *Be sensitive to timing*—sometimes time is needed for anger and frustrations to be expressed; at other times deadlines are vital to concentrate minds.

3. *Keep the process open*—so that any latecoming interests can be involved.

4. *Make flexible use of what each party has to offer*—while recognizing the situation's dynamics. This may sometimes involve bringing in third-party assistance or mediation to offset perceived power imbalances between companies and community representatives.

Public Policy Partnerships

Partnership in the public policy area can take a variety of forms—from partnerships with governments, NGOs, and others for specific purposes, to partnership with regulators to introduce new and more flexible forms of regulation.

Achieving eco-efficiency is very much easier when it is supported rather than hindered by government regulations. The traditional method of influencing business to take environmental action has been prescriptive "command and control" regulation. This can be a powerful driver of environmental improvement and will always be necessary to ensure that laggards meet minimum acceptable standards. But policymakers and regulators around the world are coming to see that it can create barriers to eco-efficiency, for example, by mandatory requirements for end-of-pipe control measures that provide no opportunity for utilizing pollution prevention or by providing little incentive for companies to go beyond minimal compliance. In the United States, for example, business, environmentalist, and other members of the President's Council on Sustainable Development all agreed that command and control regulation is becoming too inflexible and costly.[17] Their report suggested that more cost-effective environmental improvement—that is, eco-efficiency—can be created by further adoption of five policy principles, a number of which are based on partnership:

1. *Provide greater regulatory flexibility with accountability.* Society and business develop a bargain in which the latter commit to developing higher environmental standards than would be achieved by regulation in exchange for greater flexibility in achieving them. Accountability is essential to ensure that regulators are not "captured" by business and public health and the environment is genuinely protected.

2. *Extend product responsibility.* As an alternative to regulation, members of product chains—such as manufacturers, users, and disposers—take voluntary responsibility for managing such issues as end-of-life equipment or environmental impacts of raw material production.

3. *Make greater use of market forces.* Creating economic incentives and disincentives for companies to take action such as environmental taxes or creation of pollution trading rights.

4. *Use intergovernmental partnerships* to develop cooperation and synergy between key environmental stakeholders, including business, and to ensure that economic development, environmental quality, and social policymaking are integrated with one another.

5. *Encourage environmental technologies,* particularly "eco-efficient" technologies that create markets and jobs while also reducing impacts on human health and ecosystems.

These ideas were based on a number of United States and international innovations to reform regulatory systems. Many of these innovations have been developed in the Netherlands, whose government held a major conference on sustainable industrial development in early 1996. The environmental consultancy Arthur D. Little was asked to identify the policy instruments that could achieve it. Little identified four main forms of environmental policy, based on the extent of government control and whether the relationship between business and government is confrontational or cooperative (see figure 5.2).[18]

Category 1, or *regulated*, policies

Category 2, or *negotiated*, policies

Category 3, or *induced*, policies

Category 4, or *unconstrained*, policies

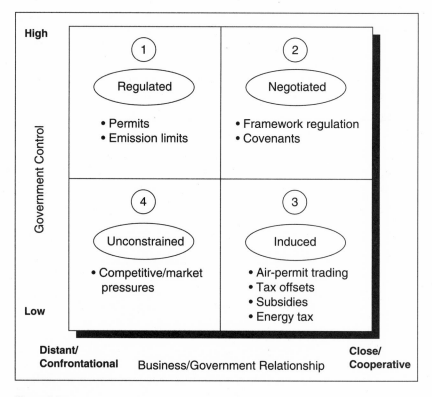

Figure 5.2
Four types of environmental policy for achieving eco-efficiency.
Source: Arthur D. Little, *Sustainable Industrial Development: Sharing Responsibilities in a Competitive World* (Den Haag: Netherlands Ministry of Housing, Spatial Planning and the Environment, 1996), p. 19.

Unconstrained Policies

These are both the beginning and end of environmental intervention. The beginning because this is the position prior to regulation. Some companies will take voluntary action—for example, because they have an environmental ethic, or because it is eco-efficient to do so, or are under pressure from suppliers or customers, or both—but most probably will not. Unconstrained policies are also the "ideal" end in that environmental considerations are fully internalized into corporate decision-making. In practice, however, there will always be a need for a broad framework established by some combination of the other three forms of policy.

Negotiated Policies

The strengths and weakness of category 1, *regulation*, have already been discussed in chapter 1. One vector of movement away from regulation is in the direction of *negotiated*, category 2, policies. Some countries, such as the United Kingdom, have always done this at the facility level. The Netherlands takes negotiation beyond facilities to the sectoral level. The foundation stones of that country's ambitious National Environment Policy Plan (NEPP) targets are agreements with leading industry associations about levels of environmental improvement over the next decade. That with the Dutch chemical industry association, VNCI, for instance, commits its members to:

- Reduce their emissions of a number of hazardous chemicals by 50% to 99% between 1985 and 2010
- Increase energy efficiency by 20% between 1989 and 2000
- Cut emissions of nitrogen oxides and sulfur dioxide by 90% between 1985 and 2000

The covenant requires companies to issue an annual report on their achievements and their plans for further progress.

One priority area for the Dutch government has been reducing carbon dioxide emissions. Over twenty sectors have signed agreements that they will increase their energy efficiency by approximately 20% during the course of the 1990s. An analysis of the first two years of the early agreements found an 8% average improvement in energy efficiency—more than twice the rate that was likely without the agreements.[19]

Germany is moving in a similar direction, with an agreement between the government and fifteen industry sectors to reduce their carbon dioxide emissions by approximately 20% between 1995 and 2005. It has also developed "loop closing" policies, which require reuse, remanufacturing, or recycling of products at the end of their lives. This approach was first applied in the area of packaging and has now been extended through a new act on waste management and product recycling. It will make many producers responsible for takeback of products at the end of their lives and require all to examine opportunities for reuse and recycling. However, such loop closing can be applied in a variety of ways and there has been much criticism of Germany's specific approach.

The EPA too is exploring negotiated policies under the Clinton administration's Reinventing Environmental Regulation plan. Its Common Sense Initiative brings together multistakeholder councils to drive environmental improvement in six pilot industries—auto manufacturing, computers and electronics, iron and steel, metal finishing, petroleum refining, and printing. These industries make up over 11% of the U.S. gross domestic product (GDP), employ nearly 4 million people, and account for 12% of all toxic releases reported by American industry.

Both the overall Common Sense Initiative Council and its subcommittees for the various sectors bring together representatives from federal, state, and local governments, community-based and national environmental groups, environmental justice groups, labor, and industry. The participants want solutions that achieve greater environmental gains at less cost, provide more flexible regulation and permitting, focus on industries and not specific pollutants, encourage pollution prevention, and are flexible.

The Pollution Prevention Pilot Project (4P) is a unique partnership led by a core group of experts from the Natural Resources Defense Council (NRDC), Amoco Petroleum, the Dow Chemical Company, Monsanto Company, Rayonier, and the New Jersey Department of Environmental Protection.[20] With a shared industry-environmentalist perspective, the group has begun to identify opportunities to cut production and environmental costs while reducing and preventing pollution at two chemical manufacturing facilities—a Dow Chemical plant in La Porte, Texas, and a Monsanto plant in Pensacola, Florida.

Through site-specific work, the group is exploring what internal, external, or regulatory barriers may have kept the plants involved from already practicing cost-saving pollution prevention. If these barriers were removed, projected cost savings for one project at the Dow Chemical plant alone would yield $500,000 each year and a projected return on capital of $2 for each dollar invested. There could be several additional projects at that site that could yield similar results. Moreover, early evaluations indicate that significant environmental improvements could be achieved by looking for creative ways to address environmental issues. Later, the group will craft policy proposals to be jointly advocated to state and federal government agencies in order to spur economic and environmental progress.

John Adams, the NRDC's executive director, believes that

What is exciting about this project is that it can produce tremendous environmental benefits by tapping the environmental strengths of business—its ability to build a better mousetrap, to find better and more efficient ways of producing a product.[21]

Of course, negotiated policies are often entered into because of the threat of regulation so the two approaches are interdependent rather than completely separate from each other. The success of negotiated policies is also dependent on contextual factors such as the topic area, national cultures, and legal traditions. Some companies operating in the Netherlands have argued that the covenant approach can be costly and time-consuming when used for inappropriate areas. They also work particularly well in the consensus-oriented Dutch context but can be more difficult to achieve in other societies.

Induced Policies

Regulation can also be substituted or enhanced by what Arthur D. Little terms *induced* policies. These create disincentives to negative environmental impacts and incentives to take positive environmental action through a variety of means. They work best when there is a simple relationship between environmental cause and effect, when the scale of action needed is relatively easy to define and when they are introduced in partnership with industry so that the inducements are ones that are synergistic with overall business objectives.

One form of induced policy is environmental taxes and levies, for example, carbon taxes or a levy on final product disposal. Norway and Sweden already have carbon taxes and it seems likely that other countries in Europe and elsewhere will follow their example. Ideally, such taxes would be set at a level that reflects the full environmental costs of the impacts so that these are internalized into the polluter's decision making. Leading companies and the WBCSD are broadly in favor of internalization. Change should be gradual so that business decisions are not unduly distorted and the proceeds are used to reduce taxes in other areas, resulting in no net increase in the tax burden.

A second form of induced policy is the creation of tradable rights to pollute. The American Clean Air Act, for example, specifies permissible levels of sulfur dioxide emissions from power plants. Companies reducing their emissions below this limit can sell surplus "pollution rights" to others that are emitting more than the limit. Environmental improvement is achieved by a reduction over time in the total amount of permitted emissions—to half the 1990 level by 2010. Utilities benefit from greater flexibility in reducing emissions, which allows more cost-effective strategies to be pursued. They can choose from such measures as energy conservation programs, increasing reliance on renewable energy, reducing usage, using pollution control technologies, switching to low-sulfur coal, or retiring fossil-fueled plants. Utilities that go beyond compliance are rewarded by the additional income from selling emission credits.

A third form of induced policy is requiring disclosure of environmental information. The U.S. Emergency Planning and Community Right-to-Know Act of 1986, for example, requires most large companies to prepare and publish an annual toxic release inventory (TRI) of their emissions of some 330 specified toxic chemicals. Many in industry first saw this as a negative—and there are many legitimate questions about the precise risk posed by some of the chemicals on the list—but it has prompted many firms to voluntarily reduce their emissions. Although prescriptive, the program has resulted in a win-win situation for industry and the public. Industry has reduced emissions and the public is now aware of what pollutants are being emitted.

Another form of inducement is providing recognition to good environmental performers. The EPA's 33/50 program built on TRI by targeting emissions of seventeen especially risky chemicals from the inventory. The scheme was voluntary and required participants to cut emissions of seventeen chemicals, initially by 33% and ultimately by 50%, between 1988 and 1995. The challenge was accepted by 1,300 companies and the vast majority succeeded in achieving the target.

Green Lights is another EPA voluntary program. Companies joining it commit to conducting energy surveys of all their facilities and upgrading 90% of the lighting that can be upgraded profitably without compromising quality. The EPA provides information, software, and other assistance. The program's initiatives have generated an average rate of return of 30% in industries where it is used.

The European Union has also developed two distinctive forms of recognition. One is the Eco-Management and Audit Scheme (EMAS), which provides public evidence that industrial sites are operating to high environmental standards. The other is an official "ecolabel" that is awarded to products judged to have superior environmental performance. Both initiatives have their deficiencies and critics but are indicative of the way policies are moving toward incentive-based approaches within Europe.

Of course, a mix of various forms of policy is necessary to achieve sustainable industrial development and each form will be more or less appropriate to different stages of environmental evolution. But the successful initiatives in negotiated and induced policies demonstrate that industry, regulators, and the environmental community can work together to achieve environmental improvements AND economic savings. They also highlight the value of collective as opposed to unilateral efforts.

This is certainly the conclusion of MIT professor Vicki Norberg-Bohm. She analyzed the effects of partnership-based and traditional environmental policies for promoting technology innovation—innovation that is vital if the environmental impacts of processes and products are to be reduced to a sustainable level.[22] She examined six alternatives: regulatory standards; market-based policies such as tradable permits; mandatory information disclosure, for example, the toxic release inventory (TRI); voluntary initiatives such as Green Lights; the Common Sense industry councils; and loop closing policies. For each she assessed its ability to stimulate generation and disclosure of information by business; to create incentives for investment in innovation; to reduce long-term uncertainties for business; to provide operational flexibility; and to encourage development of life cycle management and multimedia approaches by business. Her overall conclusion is that regulatory standards are the least and loop closing and mandatory information disclosure the most effective of the six (see figure 5.3). However, in practice much depends upon the way regulations are framed.

Design Criteria For Promoting Innovation	Policy Mechanisms					
	standards	market-based	information	voluntary	industry councils	loop-closing*
stimulate industry generated information	◧	◧	●	◧	●	●
incentive for investment in innovation	○	○	◧	○	○	●
reduce long-term uncertainties	○	○	○	◧	○	◧
provide flexibility	○	●	●	◧	◧	●
lifecycle and multi-media criteria	○	○	◧	○	◧	◧

IMPACTS:

● high   ◧ moderate   ○ low

*Based on German experience. No experience with this in the United States.

Figure 5.3
Effectiveness of alternative policies for promoting technology innovation (based on
current practice in the United States). (Courtesy of Professor Vicki Norberg-Bohm,
Massachusetts Institute of Technology, Cambridge, Mass.)

Partnering with NGOs

Many of our examples involve partnership between business and NGOs. This may seem surprising, for the two are often at odds. But while there will always be some areas of disagreement, experience shows that they can work together successfully as long as each side trusts and respects the other. Eastman Kodak and WWF, for example, have worked in partnership on an environmental education program. Hayes Bell, vice president and director of EH&S at Eastman Kodak, believes that

Even though the WWF and Kodak are partnering on an education program and not a program dealing directly with our operations, it was critical that WWF become familiar and comfortable with Kodak's past and current environmental issues. No company is perfect, and the environmental group needs to come to terms with that fact. However, they do need to believe that the company is giving environment (and health and safety) the proper level of attention. It is also important that the group is proud of their alliance with the company.[23]

One important factor in making such partnerships possible is the realization of many environmentalists that, while protest has its place, the growing acceptance of an eco-efficiency philosophy within business makes collaboration a more fruitful strategy than confrontation. Paul Gilding, former executive director of Greenpeace International, is

convinced that the real leadership in the 21st century will come from the business community. This may sound strange coming from someone who has spent most of his life facing down businesspeople . . . [but] . . . the environment has become a mainstream issue, from living rooms to corporate boardrooms. People's minds have been changed. The task now is to change their behaviour.[24]

WBCSD executive director Bjorn Stigson welcomes such changes of heart and believes that green NGOs

must get involved in helping to find solutions that work, and cooperate with industry in implementing them. The days when NGOs could remain on the outside looking in—like theatre critics on opening night—are gone. Now, they must join the cast of the play in helping to put on an award-winning performance.

The logical end of this process is partnership at the heart of the business, with the entry of environmentalists into the boardroom. This is starting to happen. The U.S. environmentalist John Sawhill is now a member of the Procter & Gamble board. The U.S. hydrocarbons and chemicals producer Ashland Oil has also appointed Pat Noonan, former president of The Nature Conservancy, as a nonexecutive director. Paul Chellgren, Ashland's president and CEO, believes that this represents

a major commitment by Ashland to consulting with and trusting those whose primary interests and expertise are in the environmental field. This example is being repeated throughout industry. What makes this partnership viable today is the emergence of the next generation of leaders in the environmental movement. They understand business strategy, budgets, resource allocations, priorities, and choices. Moreover, their knowledge and understanding of the environment is vital to industry's future. . . . In co-operating with industry this next generation of environmental leaders is taking a certain risk. They may be censured by their more ideological colleagues who may think it is a mistake for the head of an environmental organization to sit on an industry board. But the willingness to take that risk distinguishes those leaders who will see us into the next century—a century we trust will be cleaner and healthier for all.[25]

President's Council for Sustainable Development

This emerging rapprochement between at least some environmental NGOs and business is symbolized by a remarkable multistakeholder partnership in the United States—the previously mentioned President's Council on Sustainable Development. Their 1996 report, *Sustainable America*, stresses the need for America to meet Agenda 21—and to do so in a way that maximizes eco-efficiency.[26] In some respects the council's conclusions are merely importing to America concepts that are widely understood and beginning to be implemented in other countries. But it is distinctive for the breadth of its vision, its emphasis on the need for partnership between business and other elements in society—and the way in which it implemented this ideal in its own membership and processes.

The council was unusual, if not unique, in being co-chaired by a business leader and an environmentalist. The business leader was David Buzzelli, vice president and corporate director of EH&S, public affairs, and information systems at Dow Chemical. The environmentalist was Jonathan Lash, president of the World Resources Institute, a leading

NGO research and advisory body on poverty, development, natural resources, and environmental quality. Other members were from a wide spectrum of American society, including federal and state government, business, NGOs, unions, and minorities.

Remarkably, this diverse collection of Americans reached a consensus about the need for, and characteristics of, eco-efficiency and sustainable development in the United States. They identified ten goals for a sustainable America—most of which relate to broader social rather than narrowly environmental issues (see box). They also identified five practical ways of achieving them:

1. Building a new framework for environmental protection
2. Informing and educating U.S. citizens about sustainability
3. Strengthening communities
4. Developing an ethic of natural resources stewardship
5. Limiting U.S. population

The council also specifically endorsed the ideas of eco-efficiency and established an eco-efficiency task force to examine how they can be further encouraged in the future.

The Secrets of Successful Partnerships

The President's Council and the other examples discussed in this chapter all exhibit the four characteristics of successful partnership that have been identified in a study by the Management Institute for Environment and Business (now part of the World Resources Institute) and a previous President's Commission.[27]

Shared vision and individual leadership is crucial. Leadership, as distinct from management, proved to be the most critical ingredient in the success of a partnership effort. To be effective, a partnership should involve either senior-level people in positions of power within their own organizations or a chosen facilitator.

Participants must identify common interests and avoid issues where mutual interests do not exist and no compromise can be found. Interest-based discussions and negotiations allow people to establish the legitimacy of their interests in the eyes of others. People learn from one another's

The Goals of a Sustainable America

The President's Council on Sustainable Development identified ten inter-dependent goals for sustainable development in America.

Goal 1: Health and the Environment
Ensure that every person enjoys the benefits of clean air, clean water, and a healthy environment at home, at work, and at play.

Goal 2: Economic Prosperity
Sustain a healthy U.S. economy that grows sufficiently to create meaningful jobs, reduce poverty, and provide the opportunity for a high quality of life for all in an increasingly competitive world.

Goal 3: Equity
Ensure that all Americans are afforded justice and have the opportunity to achieve economic, environmental, and social well-being.

Goal 4: Conservation of Nature
Use, conserve, protect, and restore natural resources—land, air, water, and biodiversity—in ways that help ensure long social, economic, and environmental benefits for ourselves and future organizations.

Goal 5: Stewardship
Create a widely held ethic of stewardship that strongly encourages individuals, institutions, and corporations to take full responsibility for the economic, environmental, and social consequences of their actions.

Goal 6: Sustainable Communities
Encourage people to work together to create healthy communities where natural and historic resources are preserved, jobs are available, sprawl is contained, neighborhoods are secure, education is lifelong, transportation and health care are accessible, and all citizens have opportunities to improve the quality of their lives.

Goal 7: Civic Engagement
Create full opportunity for citizens, businesses, and communities to participate in and influence the natural resource, environmental, and economic decisions that affect them.

Goal 8: Population
Move toward stabilization of the U.S. population.

Goal 9: International Responsibility

Take a leadership role in the development and implementation of global sustainable development policies, standards of conduct, and trade and foreign policies that further the achievement of sustainability.

Goal 10: Education

Ensure that all Americans have equal access to education and lifelong learning opportunities that will prepare them for meaningful work, a high quality of life, and an understanding of the concepts involved in sustainable development.

---

perspectives of a problem. If a solution has to involve a significant shift in direction or organization, interaction can encourage those alterations over time. Time to work through issues to a position of mutual respect and trust is essential.

Stakeholders have something tangible to gain from partnership. Partnerships bestow a variety of benefits, including enhanced credibility, additional knowledge, and more effective or efficient solutions to problems.

Key stakeholders must be involved as equal parties in the partnership. Equity issues can be addressed even when participants have an unequal power base. Negotiations between individuals provide a basis for sharing legitimate concerns. Since other public policy approaches are characterized by power politics, this aspect of partnerships is particularly important.

These principles can be implemented for individual issues through a contact plan (see box). It is also important to recognize that there can be a disparity of resources and information between business stakeholder groups that makes trust difficult to develop. This may sometimes require action to redress the balance. Since the Brent Spar incident—when opposition prevented Shell from disposing of a large oil storage platform at sea—the company has made space available for environmental groups to explain their point of view in educational and other materials that it has prepared.

We've seen that partnership for eco-efficiency does work and can take a variety of forms and involve a range of different groups. It's also clear that different areas of partnership are at different stages of development.

WBCSD's director of development, Serge de Klebnikoff, is a strong advocate of partnerships, to achieve both specific eco-efficiency objectives and to gain early warning of—and opportunities to influence—emerging issues that are relevant to them. He believes that "When you've been handed the legal documents, you've already lost the debate. If you have to start lobbying about unsatisfactory proposals, you've already lost the game." To forestall this, he recommends that companies draw up a contact plan for each environmental issue or area of eco-efficiency. This, in his view, has four key steps.

1. Identify and prioritize the organizations with which you wish to interact. The more you research and find out about the organizations, the better you can tailor your contacts and interactions to achieve the goals required.

2. Identify the best channels to communicate with each group.

3. Identify who in the organization is responsible for dealing with which issues and who—because of his or her knowledge and expertise on the issue at hand—is best placed to work with you on building a partnership.

4. Create a separate strategy for each issue and apply this to all organizations you plan to contact on that issue. This may mean using different strategies for different issues when you are dealing with several issues simultaneously.

Those in communities, for example, are well developed while those in the area of regulation are much more recent.

We return to the issues of partnership and regulation in the final chapter but first present a number of case studies of eco-efficiency in practice.

Summary

Industry's response to environment has had four main stages—denial, provision of data, delivery of results and dialogue, and partnership with external stakeholders. Dialogue and partnership are essential:

- to ensure that what's being delivered is what stakeholders want—and that what is being planned for delivery tomorrow is what they will want then as well.
- to achieve recognition for success and tolerance for any temporary failures.
- to mobilize all available resources and any duplication of effort.
- to transfer know-how and technology to developing countries.

Partnership can take place in four main areas:

The workplace and marketplace—for example, between business and trade unions, customers, investors, creditors, suppliers, distributors, activists, and other businesses.

Research and training—usually involving cooperation between business and educational institutions, and sometimes governments and international agencies.

Host communities.

Public policy—especially partnerships between business and governments, regulators, nongovernmental organizations, and others to create new and more flexible forms of regulation.

One public policy partnership was the U.S. President's Council for Sustainable Development, which brought together business, environmentalists, policy makers, community representatives and others. It called for five policy changes:

Provide greater regulatory flexibility with accountability.

Extend product responsibility to members of product chains as an alternative to regulation.

Make greater use of market forces so that companies have more economic incentives and disincentives to take action.

Use intergovernmental partnerships to develop integrated and consensus solutions.

Encourage "eco-efficient" technologies that create markets and jobs while also reducing impacts on human health and ecosystems.

6   Case Studies

This chapter contains case studies of selected WBCSD member companies from a variety of continents and sectors—ABB, Andersen, EBARA, SC Johnson Wax, Kvaerner, Ontario Hydro, Philips, Roche, Statoil, Swiss Bank, Dow, and 3M. The final two are somewhat longer than the rest for they discuss the organizations we know best. There is also a case on eco-efficiency in Colombia.

The cases—which are based on material supplied by the organizations themselves—are not intended to summarize all of the organization's activities related to sustainable development. Rather they present examples of eco-efficient initiatives that illustrate one or more of the seven eco-efficiency guidelines discussed in chapter 3:

1. reduce the material intensity of goods and services
2. reduce the energy intensity of goods and services
3. reduce toxic dispersion
4. enhance material recyclability
5. maximize sustainable use of renewable resources
6. extend product durability
7. increase the service intensity of goods and services.

A summary at the beginning of each case identifies the main eco-efficiency guidelines that are highlighted in it. Some highlights worth emphasizing are:

Material intensity—the Philips case shows how a cross-functional team halved the weight of a medical imager and cut costs in the process. The SC Johnson Wax case also demonstrates the potential for reducing the use of materials in packaging and products.

Energy intensity—is a function not only of how much energy is used in their creation, use and disposal but also of how efficiently the energy is produced. The ABB case describes how its products improve efficiency in both these areas, thereby reducing the need for new power stations. The Statoil case also shows how determined efforts can halve the energy consumption of offices while that on 3M describes some of the products that can help achieve it.

Toxic dispersion—Dow and Roche are just two of the case companies that have greatly reduced process emissions. Statoil has cut emissions of toxic materials from underwater pipeline testing. SC Johnson Wax has also reduced the use of VOCs in many of its products.

Recycling—EBARA's activities have been built on providing technology "veins" to control and dispose of wastes and emissions—but as the case shows its philosophy is to become an "artery" business that recovers resources from the veins. Roche has also cut its raw materials purchases by 80% at one plant through recycling a process waste product.

Sustainable resources—Ontario Hydro has established a program to expand usage of renewable energy resources. Andersen works hard to ensure that its primary raw material of wood is grown in a sustainable manner.

Durability—Andersen's Fibrex composite—a high-value product made from waste sawdust—increases the lifetime of windows while reducing their price to consumers. Philips redesigned lighting tubes also last longer and need less maintenance than conventional ones.

Service intensity—Kvaerner's Ship of the Future reduces costs by using a single, multifunctional, engine and also extends the range of uses by providing greater maneuverability. The Colombian case study shows how a small tannery has achieved environmental improvement and also increased the suppleness of its leather, so that customers can put it to a wider range of uses.

Two of our cases are about organizations—CECODES and PROPEL in Colombia and Swiss Bank in Switzerland—which are using their influence to improve their client's performance in all seven eco-efficiency areas.

Several cases also address the economic and social dimensions of sustainability. Much of ABB's business is in helping developing and transitional economies generate more power from less resource input.

And the Colombian affiliate of WBCSD, CECODES, is working with the sugar cane producers in that country to improve working conditions and education and training and to further community development.

ABB

Summary: ABB's products—such as advanced turbines, high capacity trans-mission lines, and high-efficiency motors—reduce overall needs for power and thereby avoid the energy *and* mass *requirements associated with new power stations and transmission lines. By cutting emissions of sulfur and nitrogen oxides they also reduce* toxic dispersion.

The Swedish-Swiss ABB Asea Brown Boveri Group is a global $35 billion company serving electric power generation; transmission and distribution; industrial and building systems; and rail transportation customers worldwide. It often emerges from business surveys as Europe's most respected company. The accolades are given for many reasons—but one is a staunch commitment to corporate responsibility and eco-efficiency.

ABB is committed to sound environmental management in the way it operates its own business. It has audited over 3000 manufacturing processes in some 450 facilities in over thirty countries. This has resulted in the reduction or elimination of a number of chemicals, improved waste handling at many sites and the establishment of new recycling and cleanup programs.

Overall, however, ABB's greatest improvement to sustainable development is through improving the resource productivity of electricity generation, transmission, and utilization. It calculates that a 10% efficiency improvement in the new and reconstructed power generating capacity planned over the next twenty years worldwide would generate an additional 200,000MW of electricity—output equivalent to more than 300 large fossil fuel power plants.

Efficient Generation of Electricity

ABB supplies power generation equipment and power plants. The company's approach is to constantly improve power efficiency, reduce emissions and waste, and use less material in construction. ABB technologies also extend the lifetime and improve the performance of existing plants. All of these create considerable bottom line savings for utilities.

In the case of gas turbines, use of new high temperature-resistant materials in combination with optimized design has increased energy efficiency from 30% to close to 40% over the last decade. When waste heat from the gas turbine is used to drive a steam turbine in a so-called combined-cycle plant, the fuel efficiency of natural gas can be boosted to almost 60%. Utilizing warm cooling water from the steam turbine for industrial or domestic heating can increase peak efficiency to over 90%. Gas produces less carbon dioxide and minimal sulfur dioxide per unit of energy compared with other fossil fuels but its combustion emitted considerable quantities of nitrogen dioxide in the past. Now ABB's low-No_x burner has cut them to less than fifteen parts per million—under a third of the 1980s' level.

Coal is the most used fuel for power generation and—as it is abundant in developing countries with fast-growing power demands such as China and India—is likely to remain so. However, its combustion creates much greater amounts of carbon dioxide, sulfur dioxide, particulates, and heavy metals than other fossil fuels. Hence, clean coal technology is vital if cheap power is to be reconciled with low environmental impact. ABB's high-efficiency steam turbines help achieve this by increasing electricity output from a given quantity of coal. Innovative combustion technologies also result in very low levels of nitrogen dioxide and carbon monoxide. And sulfur dioxide can also be reduced by more than 90%, using ABB's fluidized bed technologies.

Transmission and Distribution

ABB's transmission and distribution businesses are also achieving eco-efficient improvements. On average, between 10% to 20% of the electricity generated in a power plant is lost during transmission to the end user. Overhead power lines are also visually intrusive and there is growing—although unsubstantiated—concern about electromagnetic radiation. ABB's reactive power compensation technology helps reduce the number of lines by providing a 30% increase in power line capacity. And ABB's high-voltage direct current transmission technology can transmit two to three times more power over a given line than traditional alternating current methods. ABB's converter technology also makes it easier for different systems to link to one another and share electricity demand when one system's demand is high and another's is low. This reduces the need to build additional peaking capacity and thereby reduces overall resource requirements.

Efficient Electricity Utilization

Electric motors consume about half of all electricity used in industry. Improvements in motor efficiency can therefore create substantial energy and financial savings: ABB's high-efficiency motors convert up to 96% of the incoming electrical energy into mechanical energy. Their most distinctive feature is variable-speed drives, in which motor speed is matched precisely to load conditions. This eliminates the need for gears, which in turn lowers wear and tear on equipment and the amount of electricity consumed.

By increasing motor efficiency, variable-speed drives also allow the development of new technologies to further reduce environmental impacts. For example, ABB's new-generation high-efficiency CFC-free chiller combined with ABB's new motors has very high overall efficiency, has low mass and energy consumption, and is quiet and flexible in operation.

ABB's process automation systems provide further efficiency gains. They monitor industrial processes, including key eco-efficiency parameters such as energy and raw material consumption, emissions, and product quality. Managers can then supervise and interact with the process more effectively—thereby increasing quality and productivity—and react quickly to any unexpected events, such as an increase in harmful by-products.

Environmental Management Systems and Life Cycle Assessment

ABB's formal environmental management program includes ABB products, processes, activities, and suppliers around the world. ISO14001 provides the framework to manage this program and the company has a target of achieving certification at all sites with significant environmental impacts by the end of 1998. Fifty ABB sites had been certified by the end of 1996 and implementation is happening or planned at a further 260.

Defining environmental impacts and setting environmental objectives and targets are core elements of ISO14001. ABB finds life cycle assessment (LCA) of products a useful tool for this process. To facilitate its use within the company, it has developed a comprehensive database on materials, energy sources, and transportation impacts and a software package to allow R&D staff, product developers, and others to quickly assess them. The database is linked to the newly established Centre for Environmental Assessment of Product and Material Systems (CPM) at Chalmers University of Technology in Gothenburg, Sweden. The software package is also being used to assess the environmental performance of suppliers.

One area where LCA has been especially valuable is in comparisons of different component or material alternatives. Their different environmental attributes are scored on a standard system to give an EPS (environmental points system) rating. One comparison was between copper and lead-sheathed high voltage cables. The EPS valuation showed that material manufacture, natural resource use, and the user phase (i.e., the heating of the cable) produced the greatest environmental impact. With 100% metal recycling there was no significant difference between the two cables. However, on more realistic assumptions of 70% to 80% recycling, the greater hazard created by lead in the environment means that copper is the environmentally preferable alternative.

ABB also made a comparison between a contactor with an aluminum base and one with a polyester plastic base. A contactor weighs about 8 kg and includes about twenty different materials. The LCA and EPS calculation showed that neither kind of base made much difference to the overall environmental impact. The two main elements in both instances were the use of silver, which is a scarce resource and energy intensive to produce, and the overall energy requirements of producing all the materials. The analysis therefore helped prioritize improvement actions in the areas where the greatest difference could be made—and which are also likely to offer significant cost-saving opportunities.

Transfer of Affordable and Low Environmental Impact Technology

More than almost any other Western company ABB has staked its future on providing eco-efficient technologies to meet the needs of newly industrialized, developing, and transitional economies. It encapsulates its contributions to sustainable development as follows:

• In Eastern Europe and the former Soviet Union, existing power generation and delivery need modernization to reduce emissions even further.

• In the newly industrialized countries, the need is for new power capacity to realize their full economic potential.

• In the developing world, affordable technology is required to fill many basic needs.

ABB also contributes more than most companies to local technological and managerial capacity. Its multidomestic structure gives it deep local roots in more than 100 countries on five continents.

Eco-efficiency in Colombia

Summary: Two organizations, CECODES and PROPEL, are helping small–medium-sized Colombian businesses to reduce their energy *and* materials *intensity and* toxic dispersion. *One company, Curtigran, has been enabled to increase the* service intensity *of its leather products. CECODES is also working with sugar cane producers to create* sustainable resource *use.*

Latin-American economies have been traditionally based upon agricultural exports, and have relied heavily upon the competitive advantage gained through access to cheap natural resources and inexpensive labor. However, many other countries now have one or both of these advantages. Latin-American companies are under pressure either to reduce labor costs still further and become more efficient. The pressures are particularly intense on the small and medium-sized enterprises that produce half of industrial output in most countries—and the bulk of industrial pollution. Many people believe that, given these economic conditions—and generally low per capita wealth—environmental and social investments are luxuries that Latin-American business cannot afford.

This case focuses on two not-for-profit organizations that provided an alternative view based on eco-efficiency—and put it into practice— in one Latin-American country, Colombia. The first organization is CECODES (Consejo Empresarial Colombiano para el Desarrollo Sostenible, or the Colombian Business Council for Sustainable Development), an affiliate of WBCSD. The second is PROPEL (Promocion de la Requelin Empresa Ecoefficiente Latinoamericana), which promotes eco-efficient management and technical solutions for small and medium-sized businesses in Colombia, Chile, Ecuador, and Bolivia (and ultimately other Latin-American countries). PROPEL was created by FUNDES Switzerland (Swiss Foundation for Sustainable Development in Latin America).

CECODES

CECODES began work in 1993 and now has twenty-three corporate affiliates. A number of these are agricultural growers and processors. CECODES director Maria Emilia Correa believes that this is one of two key differences between eco-efficiency in the rich North and the poorer South:

As agriculture in so important in our economy, and so much of industry is based upon it, it inevitably forms a large proportion of our work. And in countries with high levels of inequality and poverty we must put a lot of emphasis on social responsibility as well.

Both these points are illustrated by CECODES' work with Asocana, the industrial association for Colombian sugar growers and processors.

Asocana

Colombia contributes 3% of world sugar production and sugar cane is one of the country's most significant—and fastest expanding—industries. It is especially important in the Cauca River valley in the south-west of the country, where it provides direct and indirect employment for 33,000 people. The industry requires large amounts of water to operate and also generates waste material and air and water emissions from cane processing.

Asocana—the Colombian Association of the Cultivators of Sugar Cane—represents about 100 sugar cane growers and 11 cane processing mills. The association and most of its members have long had a view that the industry needs high productivity and labor stability and that social investment is an important part of achieving this. They have therefore, by Colombian standards, spent heavily on education and training, employee welfare, and community development programs. The result is an industry that is recognized as one of the world's most efficient and that expanded output by 18% between 1990 and 1994.

Asocana began addressing environmental issues in the 1980s, when it encouraged members to reduce water consumption and waste generation and minimize emissions to air and water. The results of this became apparent the following decade, when water inputs per ton of sugar fell by 34%, and land inputs by 12%, between 1990 and 1995. There is also much greater closure of loops through use of byproducts as fuel or raw materials. And during the 1990s voluntary initiatives—based on partnership between Asocana and its members and local authorities and communities—have been established to conserve and restore riverside habitat in the Cauca River valley. This scheme has been so successful that it is now being expanded to the national level.

PROPEL and Curtigran Tannery

Small and medium-sized businesses constitute 85% of manufacturing companies in Colombia and 90% of industrial companies in Latin America. Yet these same firms produce less than half of all the output for these sectors—and disproportionately account for the industrial pollution in the region.

The leather tanneries of San Benito, in the outskirts of Bogota, were just such polluters. Most had under twenty employees and were often dirty, smelly, and noisy—no surprise when their basic operation is curing, pressing, and cutting animal hides. However, in 1994 they produced

$60 million in leather products and employed thousands of people. Even in the current difficult period of increasing international competition, they are the strongest economic resource in the region.

PROPEL initiated an eco-efficiency project at a number of tanneries. Its engineers examined the many processes involved in tanning and suggested means of preventing pollution. These were first implemented in 1994 at the Curtigran tannery—a family business with thirteen employees. The company was facing regulatory and community pressure to comply with current and forthcoming environmental legislation—or be shut down. Environmental taxes on polluting industries were also being discussed.

However, Curtigran had financial difficulties. Raw materials were being wasted through inefficient processes. Competition was growing and marketing was poor. As a result the tannery was operating at only 60% of total capacity and profits were falling continuously. There was no money for pollution control equipment.

Fortunately for Curtigran, minor process and raw material changes produced substantial improvements in production and environmental performance. Its discharges of organic wastes fell by half while chrome concentrations in waste water were cut by two thirds. Water and energy consumption was also reduced by 30%. Cycle times have also fallen.

Curtigran's customers have also benefited from better quality. Its leather products are now more supple and can be used for a wider range of purposes. And a new by-product has been created, using waste animal hairs as a fertilizer. Conditions for workers are also much improved, consequently improving morale and commitment. All in all, the changes have reduced Curtigran's production costs by a minimum of $27,000 a year at virtually no capital cost. The company is now working at 100% capacity, is financially healthy, and is considered one of its industry's best environmental performers.

Andersen Corporation

Summary: Andersen has greatly reduced emissions and therefore toxic dispersion *from its processes, recycled waste sawdust, and used solvents and taken steps to ensure that its timber raw material is a* sustainable resource. *Its double glazed products also contribute to* energy *efficiency by consumers and a new wood-vinyl composite provides improvement on all the eco-efficiency guidelines—including* durability *—while lowering costs.*

Hans Jacob Andersen built a lumber business in the nineteenth century—and then saw an opportunity to use his raw material for window manufacture. At that time windows followed no standard design, so production costs were high and replacement parts difficult to obtain. Nine years before Henry Ford developed mass production of auto manufacturing, the Andersen Lumber Co. introduced standardized, precision-made window frames that were lower in costs, of better quality, and easier to maintain than existing windows.

The innovation—and others that kept Andersen growing in Bayport, Minnesota, even through the 1930s depression—followed one of Hans Andersen's three basic business principles:

1. Make a product that is different and better.
2. Hire the best people and pay top wages.
3. Provide steady employment as far as possible.

Following these principles has allowed Andersen to become a $1 billion corporation and the U.S. market leader in vinyl-clad wood windows and patio doors. With a product line of High-Performance windows and patio doors, eco-efficiency is the basis of Andersen's business. Its long-standing commitment to social responsibility—and the fact that Andersen's offices and manufacturing plant are on Minnesota's magnificent St. Croix River, a federally designated wild and scenic river—also means that the company has always respected nature and responded proactively to environmental concern.

Environmental Policy

Andersen Corporation's environmental policy is concise. It reads:

• Andersen Corporation, an environmentally responsible citizen of the global community, recognizes its perpetual duty to:
• Support the environmental goal to reduce pollution at the source.
• Conserve natural resources through reduction, reclamation, reuse and recycling of materials.

• Develop long-lasting products that have a minimal effect on the environment.

• Ensure that its facilities, processes and products meet or exceed all applicable governmental standards and regulations relating to environment.

Pollution Prevention

Andersen has a pollution prevention plan whose goal is zero emissions, with a specific target of no reportable TRI (toxic release inventory) emissions by 1998. The company participated in both the EPA 33/50 and Minnesota 50 programs to voluntarily reduce use of certain chemicals in manufacturing. The chemicals targeted in the voluntary program were reduced by 85% from 1988 to 1995, compared to the EPA target of 50%. Andersen's partnership with suppliers in the development of waterborne wood preservatives and the elimination of adhesives containing VOCs has also helped the company reduce total VOC emissions by over 50% since 1988. The net result of these and other initiatives was a 90% reduction in TRI emissions from 1988 through 1995.

Experienced people and state-of-the-art lumber cutting systems also reduce wood waste during manufacturing. Paint metering and mixing equipment creates the precise quantity of paint required, eliminating waste due to overblending.

Conserve Natural Resources

Andersen monitors its wood suppliers and encourages them to practice sustainable forestry to ensure renewable lumber supplies over the long term. The company is committed to buying lumber from suppliers who practice responsible forestry.

Wood is conserved in manufacturing by using wood veneers where appropriate and reusing wood by edge-gluing and finger-jointing in areas not exposed to view. Ninety-nine percent of sawdust is also collected. This has been used as a boiler fuel on site and at a nearby power plant, but growing quantities are now upgraded into Fibrex, a structural wood composite (see below). These and other recycling initiatives have reduced the amount of solid waste deposited in landfills by over 90% since 1988.

In addition, closed-loop cooling systems reuse process water so effectively that well-water usage dropped by 54% from 1988 through 1995. Large volumes of solvents have also been recovered for reuse since the 1970s, although solvent recovery is declining as water-based formulations are introduced.

Durable and Low Impact Products

Reducing energy intensity is a key eco-efficiency indicator. Through years of research investment Andersen's products achieve reduced energy intensity both through low embodied energy in the product and by conserving energy during use.

The embodied energy of a product is the amount of energy required to convert raw materials into their final form. Door and window cladding provides an example of Andersen's good performance on this measure. Installing Andersen vinyl-clad wood windows rather than aluminum-clad windows in a small commercial building in the U.S. Midwest saves energy equivalent to heating an average house for 6 to 7 years—and 67 less tons of carbon dioxide to contribute to global warming.

Andersen is the first window and patio door manufacturer to be accredited by Green Seal, the U.S. environmental certification body. Green Seal describes Andersen products as

among the most energy-efficient doors and windows available, offering considerable savings in heating and cooling costs, and reducing the air and water pollution associated with extracting and burning fossil fuels. . . . If all windows in the U.S. were as energy efficient as those made by Andersen, we would save up to 2.5% of the annual U.S. energy consumption—that's about 200 gallons of oil for every household in the country.

The benefits are particularly pronounced with Andersen High-Performance windows, which are 35% to 40% more efficient than ordinary double-glazed windows at preventing heat loss in winter and reflecting solar energy during summer (thereby reducing energy requirements for air conditioning).

Reinventing the Window

Like every product, there are opportunities to improve vinyl-clad wood windows. Vinyl, as a material, is an excellent insulator but expands and contracts with heat to a greater degree than aluminum or wood. As a single material, vinyl can, over time, bow, crack, and, eventually, leak air and water. Vinyl alone can also distort on exceptionally hot days. Wood contains natural variations such as grain, knots, and moisture content, which means that—to guarantee structural stability—more needs to be used than with alternative materials. And, unless properly preservative treated, it decays in the long term.

The two materials, if properly combined, can build on the strengths and overcome the weaknesses of each material used alone. An optimal combination is the basis of Andersen's current material. After years of intensive R&D—including twenty-eight patent applications—Andersen has created this solution in the form of Fibrex, a wood-vinyl composite. It has the strength and thermal stability of wood and the low variability and decay resistance of vinyl. The composite is made from waste sawdust and vinyl, which were previously either used for low-value purposes or sent to the landfill. In the longer term, the composite itself can be reclaimed as doors and windows made from Fibrex are replaced after decades of use. In this way, Andersen can actually consume its own wastes.

Fibrex can either be used to replace specific window components or to create entire custom windows—with the latter currently being marketed regionally in the United States for residential replacement windows under the Renewal by Andersen brand. Either provides improvements on almost all the seven eco-efficiency indicators. They are more durable than conventional wood-vinyl windows, are based on recycled materials, conserve natural resources (of timber and the oil used to make vinyl), have lower lifetime energy and material intensities, eliminate the need to treat or glue wood, and increase service intensity by requiring less maintenance and allowing a greater expanse of glass. Best of all, Fibrex also costs less than either wood or vinyl.

Andersen Benefits from Eco-efficiency

While Andersen has realized millions of dollars in savings from eco-efficient environmental programs, the savings to the company's customers from High-Performance Andersen windows and patio doors are even greater. Jerold W. Wulf, Andersen's president and CEO, puts it this way:

At Andersen, eco-efficiency is our business. Andersen people demonstrate eco-efficiency every day by developing and building ever more environmentally sound, energy efficient products, preventing pollution and providing real bottom line benefits. Our company's environmental ethic springs from a work philosophy based on a location since 1903 on the scenic St. Croix River. Eco-efficiency at Andersen is embodied in our Mission and corporate Environmental Policy. We take our Mission's objective of engaging "in responsible stewardship of the environment" very seriously.

EBARA

Summary: EBARA's business has been built on pollution control but the company is now developing technologies for recycling of wastes and recovery of energy. Many of these eliminate or reduce toxic dispersion by converting potentially harmful emissions such as nitrogen oxides into valuable resources.

EBARA is a multibillion-dollar Japanese environmental engineering company. Its activities have been built on what are called in Japan "vein" activities—dealing with the waste products of industry through pollution control equipment and other means. Now it is becoming an "artery" business—supplying industry with valuable energy or raw materials that are recovered from the veins and thereby close the material loop.

EBARA's long-term goal is to minimize external emissions in its own activities and those of its customers. As a result, it is a strong supporter of the Zero Emissions Initiative (ZERI) at Tokyo's United Nations University.

Creating Value from Waste

One of EBARA's "artery" technologies is fluidized bed gasification of mixed municipal or industrial wastes. This generates a fuel gas that can be burned either to provide heat or to drive a gas turbine. Energy recovery is far superior in this route to burning the waste directly. With additional treatment, valuable components such as ammonia and gasoline precursors can be separated from the gas before combustion. Metals such as iron, copper, aluminum, and nickel melt within the bed itself and can be recovered and separated for sale. Residual ash can be utilized as a construction material or as an input for cement manufacture. The process is very cost-effective, completely destroys hazardous materials such as dioxin and polychlorinated biphenyls (PCB), and has low emissions of pollutants. The only obstacle to it achieving EBARA's zero emissions is its carbon dioxide emissions—although the contribution to global warming that results is much less than if the waste were burned or landfilled (which would create emissions of the even more powerful greenhouse gas, methane).

Powerful Fertilizers

EBARA's Electron Beam Flue Gas Treatment System (EBA) is also based on the zero emission concept. It substitutes for the current flue gas desulfurization equipment—and to a lesser extent the nitrogen oxide control plant—which remove sulfur dioxide and nitrogen dioxide from the combustion gases emerging from fossil fuel boilers. These are classic end-of-pipe technologies that are costly to build and operate, reduce the overall energy efficiency of power generation and produce either waste products or low value industrial materials such as gypsum.

EBA involves injection of ammonia into the flue gases and irradiation of the mixture with an electron beam. Chemical reactions then create ammonium nitrate and ammonium sulfate—the main components of fertilizer.

EBARA sees the technology as being particularly well suited to China. China is already the world's largest producer and burner of coal and 80% of its power comes from fossil fuels. Its electricity demand is expected to at least double over the next decade—and will be largely supplied from new coal-fired power plants. It also has a large and growing population whose food supply requires large amounts of fertilizer—whose current production creates considerable environmental impacts. If EBA were to be installed at a third of China's plant it could produce 20 million tons of nitrogenous fertilizer a year—a fifth of the country's entire needs. According to Norio Takagi of EBARA's environmental staff:

It's a good example of how the zero emission concept can close material loops and help to achieve sustainability. The technology promotes economic development in China through more efficient power generation and lower cost fertilizer, while cleaning up harmful emissions at the same time. It also shows the importance of technological collaboration among the global community.

SC Johnson Wax

Summary: SC Johnson Wax has reduced its overall use of materials *for packaging and some products, and increased the proportion that are* recycled. *It has also cut* toxic emissions *of VOCs and other substances. Further improvements will be achieved through a Design-for-Eco-efficiency process.*

SC Johnson Wax, family owned and privately held, has a long history of responsible environmental management. Sam Johnson, owner and chairman, made history in 1975 by announcing his company's decision to eliminate CFC propellants from its aerosols worldwide—the first company to do so. It is not surprising that this $4 billion global manufacturer of products for the home and workplace, helped coin the term eco-efficiency and is one of the pioneers in practicing it. In 1990, the company formalized its environmental management program and set long-term goals to drive continuous action to improve the environmental performance of products and processes, setting specific measurable targets for progress worldwide.

These targets have been achieved. While the company enjoyed over a 50% increase in production from 1990 through 1995, significant progress was made in preventing and reducing waste to improve the environmental, financial, and efficacious performance of products and processes.

• Virgin packaging as a ratio to total formula was cut by 26.8% between 1990 and 1995, exceeding the 20% target. The main contribution came from increased use of recycled materials and progress with light-weighting containers.

• The ratio of volatile organic compounds (VOCs) to finished formula weight was down 16.4% between 1990 and 1995, more than halfway to SC Johnson's long-term goal of a 25% reduction by the end of 2000.

• Worldwide manufacturing operations reduced combined air emissions, water effluents, and solid waste disposal as a ratio to total production by 46.7%, slightly short of SC Johnson's reduction target of 50%.
• North American manufacturing and office facilities achieved 90% miscellaneous waste recycling.

The company continues to monitor and update environmental and safety data profiles of ingredients in new and existing products to identify and eliminate those deemed to pose more risk than benefit.

Integrating Environment into the Business

SC Johnson Wax attributes its significant progress toward meeting environmental goals to a combination of a green ethic, good business sense and enlightened and dedicated employees. By translating waste prevention and reduction efforts into traditional cost-savings measurements, the company has built eco-efficiency into the product development process and is driving the integration of environment into new product development programs. From product concept, to research and development, to packaging design, from manufacturing to marketing, multifunctional teams work to continuously improve product, package, and process design to meet both business and environmental goals.

While corporate and employee green philosophies are generally synchronized, reaching this stage has not come without its challenges. Key among these is the deeply held attitude among some executives—as at other companies—that the environment represents all cost and no gain. Early in 1991, SC Johnson Wax vice president of Environment and Safety Jane M. Hutterly coined the term *green wall* to identify management thinking and decisions that reflected and foster that misperception. According to Hutterly:

This corporate "green wall" attitude may well result from working within inflexible command and control regulatory frameworks which dictate and penalize versus motivate and reward progressive, innovative waste-eliminating technologies. We knew that real progress would only be made if we were to climb over that wall and get the other side involved in helping us break it down. To begin that process, we launched an aggressive, broad-based program designed to build our business' understanding of the financial value and contribution to long-term competitiveness that comes from more and better eco-efficient decision-making.

Design-for-Eco-efficiency (DFEE) workshops play an important part in breaking down the wall. A core component of SC Johnson's management education program, the workshops provide a highly effective experiential learning curriculum that has made good progress toward the company's long-term eco-efficiency goals. They bring together SC Johnson's product development teams to identify formulation and packaging alternatives that help cut waste in manufacture, use, and disposal, and save money. Many focus on VOC and packaging waste reductions with emphasis on materials substitution, lightweighting, and increased recycled content. Multifunctional teams learn the basics and then set to work on real products and processes. In many cases, the result is reduced manufacturing costs, added value for consumers and customers, and sometimes a regulatory advantage.

RAID Ant 'n Roach

A reformulation of the RAID Ant'n Roach insecticide achieved all these benefits. This insecticide aerosol was based on a VOC solvent. The RAID brand team knew that this was unsustainable and—although there was at that time no relevant legislation—spent much of the 1980s and 1990s in trying to find a water-based alternative. The breakthrough came in 1993, with a new formulation that cut the VOC content in half. The product now meets all anticipated regulatory developments with time to spare—unlike competitors who have had to initiate crash programs to catch up. SC Johnson Wax estimates that the result of the reformulation will be an annual reduction of 15 million lb of VOC emissions across the United States and 2 million lb in California alone.

Customers also prefer the smell of the new product and appreciate the decreased residue use. Distributors are happy they no longer have to warehouse a flammable, solvent-based product. And SC Johnson Wax is delighted both at these benefits and the $2 million per annum reduction in manufacturing costs.

Continuous Product Improvement

This same process of implementing eco-efficient strategies up-front and adding new scientific learning for continuous product improvement is successfully applied to other products and processes. For example, a newly designed flea control trap was given a different geometry that required 35% less plastic by weight and cut unit costs by $2. Superconcentrate technology applied to professional cleaning product lines reduces energy and material intensity, cuts packaging and other costs, and increases customer value through less bulky packages. In Australia, products are packaged in bottles made from recycled plastic milk jugs and in collapsible ultralightweight refill containers. And in Brazil, industrial cleaners were concentrated to go from a 20-liter to 5-liter package that is also lightweighted with 50% recycled content.

Meeting Consumers' Real Needs

Joe Mallof, president of North American Consumer Products, believes that SC Johnson Wax can continue along this path by considering customer's real needs:

In my experience, very few consumers come out and say, "I want products that help the environment." But if we listen hard, we might hear them say, "I want to do more with less. I want my life to be more simple. I don't want to waste." Those words have strong eco-efficiency undertones—and give us the incentive to keep delivering more value with less resource.

New specific targets are now in place to drive even more eco-efficient decision-making by the company. By the year 2000, SC Johnson Wax seeks to maximize operational eco-efficiency by further minimizing waste, risk, and costs in the formulation, manufacturing, use, and disposal of products and services. Success will be measured against the following actionable goals:

Product Stewardship

Expand the company's database on ingredient toxicity for improved product and process risk assessment.

Reduce VOC use as a ratio to formula weight by 25% compared with the 1990 level.

Reduce virgin packaging as a ratio to formula weight by 30% compared with the 1990 level.

Process Stewardship

Reduce combined air emissions, water effluents, and solid waste disposal by an additional 25% as a ratio to production while cutting manufacturing waste loss by 25% compared with the 1995 level.

Reduce energy usage as a ratio to production volume by 15% compared with the 1995 level.

Organizational Effectiveness

Establish new financial and product eco-efficient measurement systems.

Stakeholder Outreach

Maintain open dialogue on local and global fronts with community neighbors, business partners, environmentalists, and consumers and end-users in continual pursuit of new and enhanced partnerships for sustainable development.

Kvaerner

Summary: Kvaerner has reduced the energy *consumption and* toxic emissions *of both its own processes and its products. The latter include oil platforms and ships that use fewer* materials *and are easily* recyclable. *Kvaerner has also designed new ships and floating oil production platforms to provide improvements on all the eco-efficiency guidelines, including* durability *and* service intensity.

Kvaerner is a Norwegian-based international technology group with interests in shipbuilding, oil and gas equipment, mechanical engineering, and pulp and paper machinery. It gives high priority to preventive environmental protection and resource productivity. This is reflected in the company's environmental policy, which accepts an obligation to promote sustainable development based on an awareness of product life cycles. The environmental achievements of its four main business areas between 1993 and 1995 include (per unit of revenue):

A 34% decrease in energy use

A 23% decrease in waste generation

A 47% decrease in carbon dioxide emissions

A 28% decrease in nitrogen oxide and sulfur emissions

Kvaerner's products, services, and technologies also help increase the eco-efficiency of its customers in the transportation and natural resource and processing extraction industries, as the following examples illustrate.

Ship for the Future

Kvaerner is Europe's largest developer and builder of specialist ships and an international leader in the field. Ship for the Future is a joint $100 million R&D project of Kvaerner group companies in a number of countries. It embraces development of vessels, systems, and equipment for the next century with the aim of cutting construction and operating costs and reducing environmental impacts. The project addresses all aspects of a ship's life cycle, from raw materials used, to eventual recycling of scrapped vessels, and involves cooperation with customers, suppliers, and academic institutions.

Hull design is the key to a ship's speed, load capacity, seaworthiness, and efficiency. The goal for the Ship of the Future is to increase service intensity by providing a 15% improvement in vessel maneuverability and seakeeping with a 10% cut in required engine power. This is being achieved with lighter materials, improved hull and propeller design, use of multifunctionality—with a single, highly efficient and clean power plant replacing the main and auxiliary engines of current designs—and the Kvaerner Ship Management System, an integrated maneuvering, steering, and control system. The outcome will be cheaper construction, reduced emissions, a cut in energy requirements of about 20%, and lower risk of accidents and oil spills in the world's increasingly congested sea-lanes.

Vapor Recycling

Several Kvaerner companies have been collaborating with oil companies, shipowners, and the Norwegian Oil Pollution Control Authority to reduce emissions of VOCs from tankers carrying oil and gas. Recycling systems are being developed to capture the vapor and either return it to the cargo or burn it in the ship's engines. The value of reduced vaporization alone should be enough to pay for the investment in 3 to 5 years.

Making Marginal Oil Fields Profitable

Oil and gas producers and Kvaerner's engineering and manufacturing companies have been collaborating for thirty years on developing technologies that ensure the best possible utilization of resources and reduced environmental impact. For offshore oil, the traditional production technology has been fixed platforms made from concrete or steel. Large platforms are the world's heaviest manmade objects and all are extremely mass- and energy-intensive. As Brent Spar showed, they are also difficult to recycle and dispose of.

Kvaerner companies are working to make fixed platforms lighter and more recyclable and to develop more eco-efficient substitutes. These are floating production, storage, and offloading facilities (FPSOs), that is, purpose-designed ships that fill up with oil and then ferry it to nearby terminals. They can substitute for fixed platforms in many smaller fields. Evaluation of the financial and ecological impact of the FPSO throughout its life cycle shows that it offers substantial improvements over fixed platforms in both areas.

FPSOs are lighter than fixed platforms and can be built to standard designs. For these and other reasons they are cheaper and faster to build. Unlike platforms, FPSOs are also highly mobile. The cost of moving or reusing them once a field is depleted is relatively low. Moving a ship from the North Sea to Southeast Asia, for example, would cost something like 100 to 200 million Norwegian kroner ($15–30 million) when process modifications are taken into account. FPSOs can also be modified for other purposes, such as oil storage, and—when their life is finally over—can easily be scrapped and the material recycled. All these attributes make the product more durable and increase its secondhand value.

Reduced Emissions and Greater Energy Recovery in Pulp Production

Kvaerner Pulping's technology for wood pulp production has made a major contribution to cutting emissions and energy consumption and increasing the material utilization. The achievements are particularly striking for chemical pulp, where the company's fabrication systems have improved by orders of magnitude:

• Emissions of organic chlorine compounds have been reduced from 3 lb per ton of pulp in 1970 to less than 0.1 today and will soon approach zero.

• The chemical oxygen demand of wastewater has declined from 180 to 220 lb per ton in 1970 to less than 50 today and should be down to roughly 20 by 1998.

• Water consumption has declined from about 4,500 cubic feet per ton of pulp in 1970 to less than 450 today and should be under 150 cubic feet by the end of the century.

Kvaerner Pulping has also developed technology for gasifying wastes from the pulp making process and using the gas to drive high-efficiency gas turbines. This more than doubles the energy recovery rate compared with traditional alternatives and creates considerable cost savings. Emissions of nitrogen oxides, sulfur, and noxious odors are insignificant and carbon dioxide emissions are much reduced.

Environment as Core Competence

Erik Tonseth, Kvaerner's president and CEO, wants to build on these achievements. He believes that

The natural environment is a place to seek inspiration and resources for growth. Growth without limit in a closed system like the Earth is against nature. We have to create more value from less environmental impact. This means more responsibilities and duties for companies—but also opportunities. Kvaerner's products, solutions and technological developments already get more out of fewer resources and therefore benefit users and the environment.

Our aim is to continue to develop our environmental core competence to improve both our own eco-efficiency and that of our customers. We believe this will make us a preferred supplier in international markets as well as an attractive and meaningful place to work.

Ontario Hydro

Summary: Ontario Hydro has reduced its use of energy *and increased the recycling of waste products, such as gypsum and warm cooling water. It has*

also reduced its use and emissions of toxic substances *and is encouraging the development of* renewable *energy resources.*

Ontario Hydro faces many environmental challenges as the largest electrical utility in a country—Canada—that is one of the staunchest supporters of sustainable development. The company is convinced, in the words of Brian Kelly, head of its Environment and Sustainable Development division, that

sustainable energy development is not just an environmental issue but a forceful influence on the bottom line. Decreased remediation and pollution control costs, reduced maintenance and energy resource expenditures, and rapidly increasing international markets for energy efficiency and environmental technologies are three examples of where business and sustainable energy development principles regularly converge.

While Ontario Hydro takes a number of actions—such as forestry and wildlife management—because it is the responsible thing to do rather than a self-serving economic calculation, the main business drivers for its sustainable energy development programs are the following:

- Reducing operating costs through resource use efficiency
- Reducing costs or generating revenue through improved business practices
- Proactively responding to environmental regulation
- Reducing the risk of future environmental liabilities
- Using strategic partnerships to achieve business objectives
- Developing new business opportunities
- Retaining and attracting customers

Reducing Operating Costs through Resource Efficiency

During 1995 Ontario Hydro saved 680 Gigawatt hours (GWh) of electricity through energy and process conversion efficiency improvements. These had a corporate value of about $37 million. One example was fitting energy-efficient lighting—and using motion sensors to ensure it is on only when people need it—at its Toronto head office. This reduced the building's electricity consumption by 29%, creating savings of over

$500,000 a year. The sensors also helped security, as intruders can no longer creep around in the dark.

Reducing Costs and Generating Revenues Through Improved Business Practices

Ontario Hydro has put great effort into recycling or reusing materials previously viewed as wastes. Gypsum from a flue gas desulfurization plant is now sold to a wallboard producer. Fly ash from the Thunder Bay plant is also sold as cement replacement for mine backfill and ready-mix production—saving landfill space and avoiding 1 ton of carbon dioxide emissions for every ton of cement replaced. On a smaller scale, 17,000 tons of wood chips generated from line clearing or tree-trimming are now sold or given to customers and nurseries rather than being landfilled—creating cost savings from reduced tipping fees of over $850,000 a year.

Proactively Responding to Environmental Regulation

The laundry facility at Ontario Hydro's Bruce nuclear power station used CFCs to thoroughly dry-clean radioactive protective clothing. Canadian legislation required that CFCs for this use be phased out by 1995—a target that was originally costed as needing $32 million of equipment to achieve. In the early 1990s staff adopted a proactive approach to the problem and identified a two-part solution. One was to reduce the volume of cleaning by more careful checking of whether clothing was contaminated. The second was to switch to water-based methods utilizing existing liquid waste systems within the station. The result was a 99% reduction in the amount of clothing undergoing dry cleaning, and total elimination of CFCs. This has saved $350,000 a year at a capital cost of only $1.4 million. The employee involvement in the exercise has also meant tremendous improvements in the function, ergonomics, and efficiency of the facilities, which has improved morale and worker safety.

Ontario Hydro is being similarly proactive in exploring emissions trading with other utilities as a means of achieving Canadian government targets for reductions in nitrogen oxides and VOCs. By aggressively pursuing a market-based approach to emissions management,

Ontario Hydro may be successful in preempting rigid command and control regulations while still achieving desired results.

Reducing the Risk of Future Environmental Liabilities

Ontario Hydro is a pioneer in undertaking research on the costs that its emissions impose on society (externalities). The trend toward internalizing external costs—either through taxes or creation of legal liability for damages—could mean that these ultimately appear on every company's balance sheet. By calculating them now, the company is able to take them into account when making new investment decisions.

Using Strategic Partnerships to Achieve Business Objectives

Cooling water from Ontario Hydro's power stations contain considerable residual heat. Ontario Hydro has instigated several partnerships with food companies to utilize the warm water for fish farms, where it encourages rapid growth.

Developing New Business Opportunities

Ontario Hydro has a major program to upgrade long-established hydro stations so that more power can be generated with the same amount of water throughput. For example, renewal work at its 78-year-old Merrickville station more than doubled its power- and revenue-generating capacity to 1.8MW.

The Renewable Energy Technologies (RET) program is a long-term project to promote the development and marketplace acceptance of solar, wind, biomass, landfill gas, and microhydro energy sources. Stage 1, to the year 2000, involves technology development and demonstration, gaining operating experience, and establishing niche markets. Thereafter the technologies should be cost-effective and a source of considerable business development opportunities. The program is already creating economic benefit for the province of Ontario. A German wind turbine manufacturer has established a plant near London, Ontario, while Ontario Hydro Technologies' acquisition of Texas Instruments' solar cell technology could eventually create an Ontario-based solar industry.

Ontario Hydro is also developing a program whereby environmentally minded customers can support renewable energy directly by buying Green$shares. The proceeds will go into a fund to support development of renewable technology. Green$shareholders will receive no income from the shares but do have the satisfaction of putting into practice their wishes to reshape the power system.

Retaining and Attracting Customers

Electrotechnologies can reduce overall energy consumption by substituting electricity—which can be precisely applied and controlled—for combustion-based techniques (even after the energy losses from producing the electricity are taken into account). Frequently, the result is also reduced emissions. For example, a steel company in southern Ontario has built an electric arc furnace. Although the process is electricity-intensive when compared with alternative methods, it reduces overall energy consumption, allows greater recycling and reuse of scrap steel, less water consumption and pollution, and reduced emissions to air.

Synergy Between Competitiveness and Sustainability

Ontario Hydro takes the view that the companies that will be setting the competitive standard in future will be those who see environmental requirements as business opportunities rather than added costs. For Brian Kelly of the company's Environment and Sustainable Development division,

it's become clear that there's a synergistic relationship between competitiveness and sustainability. Our customers' wish that we continuously control and reduce costs compels us to look for greater efficiencies in resource use and reuse through innovation. At the same time, the commitment to sustainable development and the window it opens to new business opportunities enhances the development of vital business skills that contribute to innovation and customer satisfaction and profitability.

Philips

Summary: Philips has reduced the materials *requirements of a number of products and their packaging. Its also reduced the* energy *consumption of its processes and many of its products, eliminated many* toxic substances *and increased the* recyclability *—and use of recycled materials in—products such as television sets. Lighting has been redesigned to be more* durable *—an outcome of the company's sophisticated eco-design processes.*

Dutch-based Philips is one of the world's producers of industrial and consumer electronics. It is a highly decentralized company that expects every division to have high levels of environmental performance and prioritize eco-efficiency. Environment is one of the few areas where it has central targets. These are:

- Implementation of certifiable environmental management systems (ISO14001/EMAS) throughout the company
- A 25% reduction in energy consumption by the year 2000
- A 15% reduction in packaging material used by the year 2000

The targets were based on pilot projects and general experience at leading sites and businesses within Philips and other companies in the Netherlands and elsewhere.

It also spends a considerable amount of time in considering future environmental trends so that these can be incorporated into today's decisions about product development and investment.

Eco-design

Philips puts great emphasis on designing environmental problems out of its products. Stefano Marzano, senior director of Philips Corporate Design, believes there is a

new industrial renaissance—a revaluation within our high-tech society of the human experience in the broadest sense, with genuinely relevant products meeting our true needs and aspirations.[1]

Part of this relevance is ensuring minimal environmental impact. The Corporate Environmental and Energy Office has developed a number of environmental assessment methods to increase awareness among product designers and developers. Some of these are simple and qualitative, such as a set of "five fast questions," that are used to give quick insights into important issues and the best directions in which to go (see chapter

4). Others are in the form of checklists, such as the one on chemicals and materials that highlights those that are banned or discouraged. Philips has also developed several quantitative tools, such as a costing model to consider end-of-life product issues and an eco-indicator approach. The latter is based on research sponsored by the Dutch government that calculated environmental impact points for a given level of emission of potentially harmful substances. Hence, the aggregate points from all emissions for one product or product option can be calculated and compared with others (see chapter 3).

The eco-design methodology has helped create a number of products, including eco-efficient televisions, a new design of magnetic resonance imaging equipment, edgeless packaging, and new lighting models.

Compact Green TV

Philips Sound and Vision has a long history of minimizing the environmental impact of the televisions and other consumer electronic products it manufactures. It was the first major manufacturer, for example, to eliminate bromide flame retardants from its sets.

In the mid 1990s the division's Eindhoven laboratory developed a 14-inch compact Green TV, with the aim of testing out eco-efficient ideas for gradual application into the existing model range. The design has eliminated almost all hazardous materials, makes extensive use of lighter and recycled materials, uses 30% fewer components and requires less power in operation than previous models, and can easily be disassembled and separated for recycling at the end of its life than previous models. Overall the model reduces lifetime energy consumption by 40% and mass by 11%, with corresponding cost savings to consumers and in manufacture. End-of-life disposal costs are also reduced by a third.

Eco-efficient Imaging

Philips Medical Systems wanted to improve the design of its magnetic resonance imaging equipment to cut costs, increase value, and reduce environmental impact. A life cycle assessment of its existing product found the main environmental impact to be manufacturing the hydraulic and mechanical components, air transport of materials required during the use stage, and disposal of the equipment at the end of its life. The last was necessary because the product contained mixed materials and could not be disassembled easily.

A cross-functional development team then considered how these impacts could be reduced while reducing manufacturing and use costs and enhancing customer value in other ways. The team brought together representatives from the different components of the product chain, including purchasing, product development and design, process development, production, marketing, and sales. It also made use of the previously mentioned eco-design tools.

The result has been a simplification of the product's mechanics and replacement of the hydraulics system with two small electric motors so that the mass of the new design is almost half that of its predecessor. Energy consumption is also lower. Easier disassembly and other design-for-environment (DFE) features mean that the equipment is easier to recycle. The next step is to find environmentally friendlier logistics methods.

Edgeless Packaging

As one of the world's largest manufacturers of appliances and consumer electronics, Philips uses a great deal of packaging material—although much less than in the past. One innovation that has contributed to this are the edgeless boxes developed by the Philips Domestic Appliances division to package vacuum cleaners. The design criteria were maintenance of, or enhanced, product protection; "stackability" and transport stability; a recognizable identity; reduced material content; optimal use of recycled materials; and full and easy recyclability.

The outcome is a box with beveled rather than straight edges. This is both distinctive and requires 14% less material. This reduces purchase costs, as does a reduction of the previous variety of sizes to just two. The cardboard used is made from 90% recycled fiber and the box is easily stacked and recycled.

Lighting

The eco-design process has also allowed Philips to reduce the length and diameter of small lighting tubes—to only 16 millimeters compared to a standard 26-millimeter tube. As a result, it offers far greater design freedom. At the same time, the use of glass, phosphor coatings, and mercury is reduced. Lighting standards are maintained through use of new Super/80 Phosphor technology that provides higher light efficiency. The tubes are also more durable and require less maintenance than conventional models.

Next Steps
Philips intends to continue improving its eco-design tools. But it also wants to find out more about what makes people more environmentally conscious and interested in eco-designed products. Its Corporate Energy and Environmental Office is working with other sections of the group to answer this question, with the ultimate aim of making highly eco-efficient products a core part of the company's future business.

Roche

Summary: Roche has greatly improved the energy *efficiency of its processes, reduced the level of* toxic dispersion *from them and increased its* recycling *of process wastes. The company is also a leader in developing measures of eco-efficiency.*

Roche is a $14 billion Swiss-based producer of pharmaceuticals, vitamins and fine chemicals, diagnostics, and fragrances and flavors. It has a long-standing commitment to high environmental standards, which are implemented and audited in a similar way in all its worldwide operations. Its recent achievements include:

• A reduction in air emissions of inorganic and organic pollutants by over 40% since 1991

• Discharges of heavy metals to water down two thirds (from an already low level) since 1991

• A decrease in carbon dioxide emissions below their 1990 level, despite an increase in sales

A more local but still significant improvement is diminution of smells from the fragrances and flavors plant in Dubendorf, Switzerland. Dubendorfers were not impressed by some of the scents that came wafting their way, so in 1992 the division installed a new biofilter plant based partially on natural materials. The filter is a substrate of humus, tree bark, and polystyrene beads. These provide a home to microorganisms that break down the odor components naturally and efficiently. Since these tiny creatures eliminate strongly smelling substances without a trace, there is practically no chance of anything being discharged subsequently to the air outside.

Eco-Efficiency and Pollution Prevention

Fritz Gerber states that Roche's

main thrust is no longer to eliminate pollutants. Instead, modern process research takes eco-efficiency as its yardstick, i.e., the best possible conversion of energy and raw materials into high-quality products with a minimum of environmental impact. The ecological and economic objectives are harnessed to produce efficient processes that are not only environmentally compatible but also lower costs. All told then, the primary goal of safety and environmental protection is no longer remediation but prevention of damage.

One example of this is the redesign of a process step for producing cough medicine. The original process emitted chlorinated VOC solvents and created large quantities of waste phosphate. The latter imposed a serious, and costly, burden on the site's wastewater plant. However, since the redesign 90% of the phosphate wastes have been avoided by in-process recycling of the phosphoric acid that is their precursor. The chlorinated VOCs have also been eliminated and emissions of all VOCs reduced by over 80% per pound of product. The overall result is significant cost savings from a 75% reduction in raw material consumption and lower waste disposal expenses from an 80% cut in the total amount of emissions and wastes per unit of product.

Increasing Energy Efficiency

Since energy consumption affects the costs of manufactured goods as well as impacting on the environment, Roche pays great attention to energy efficiency. Its Dalry, Scotland, plant recently won a U.K. Energy Management Award for a cogeneration plant that cut fuel bills and reduced pollution. Emissions of nitrogen and sulfur oxides have been cut by 74% and there has been a marked decrease in solid particulate and carbon dioxide emissions, even though production was increased at the same time.

Roche Basel also uses waste heat from cooling water to preheat incoming air to its laboratories. This enables 1200 tons of heating oil to be saved and prevents almost 4000 tons of carbon dioxide and 4 tons of nitrogen oxides from reaching the atmosphere. There is a financial bonus too. Investments totaling 3 million Swiss francs ($2.4 million) have reduced Roche's energy bill by 650,000 Swiss francs ($500,000) annually.

Roche monitors its energy efficiency in a uniform way at all sites. The Roche energy rate (RER) divides total site energy consumption by the number of employees and the tonnage of end products (with different weightings for products produced by chemical synthesis than for those produced in less energy-intensive pharmaceutical production or mixing processes). The lower the RER, the more efficiently energy is used. The measure is especially useful at tracking process step, production plant, and site energy performance and benchmarking the sites against one another.

Measuring Eco-efficiency

Roche has also put great emphasis on measuring its overall eco-efficiency. To do this, it has developed a new ratio: the EER or eco-efficiency rate. This divides corporate sales by expenditure on environmental protection and environmental damage created (expressed in environmental damage units). The EER can be improved either by doing more (generating more sales from a constant level of expenditure and damage) or by using or impacting less (e.g., reducing environmental damage while keeping sales and environmental expenditure constant). The environmental damage units are based on the mass of pollutants emitted and their degree of impact.

The EER is important less for its absolute level (which is heavily site- or sector-related) than for monitoring trends over time. It shows clearly that Roche became much more eco-efficient between 1990 and 1994, when the EER rose by 85%, from 0.79 to 1.46. However, it declined by almost 20%, to 1.17, in 1995, mainly because of outlays for site remediation and higher environmental damage due to the integration of the Syntex Group since the end of 1994.

Conclusion

Fritz Gerber summarizes his company's position in this way:

We continue to feel committed to the accepted goal of sustainable development. For us, safety and an intact environment are values closely allied with the concept of health. That's why we won't let up in our efforts to reduce environmental pollution. The principle of eco-efficiency is also a prerequisite for survival in markets characterized by fierce international competition. The prefix "eco" stands for both economics and ecology. Products and services must be supplied to the market not only at the lowest possible cost but also with efficient use of raw materials and energy. In the field of environmental protection, government and the business community must deploy the limited resources at their disposal where they will have the greatest impact.

Statoil

Summary: Statoil has gained economic and production benefits by recycling *gas that was previously flared. It has also reduced* toxic dispersion *from its operations in the North Sea and greatly improved the* energy *efficiency of its offices.*

Statoil is a state-owned, Norway-based oil and gas company with a 1995 operating revenue of 87 billion kroner ($14 billion). It is the leading player on the Norwegian continental shelf and the biggest petrol retailer in Scandinavia. It also ranks as one of the world's largest net sellers of crude oil and is a substantial supplier of natural gas to continental Europe.

Statoil aspires to be an environmental leader and statistics suggest that the Norwegian oil industry—of which it is by far the largest component—has higher resource utilization, better energy efficiency, and lower emissions to water and air per unit produced than comparable industry in other countries or regions. The company has also been a key player in the Kalundborg industrial ecology plant, in which a number of plants—including its oil refinery—utilize one another's wastes as raw materials.

Environmental considerations are assumed to be a prerequisite for competitiveness and are integrated into all parts of the management system, stretching from long-term business scenario analyses to control of daily operations. Improvement activities are documented in a 4-year corporate rolling plan and reported in the annual external environmental report.

All employees are involved through a health, environment and safety committee structure. Top management support has been critical. One way it has been manifested is through Statoil's CEO heading a joint-industry government to identify new strategies and tools for even more environment friendly oil and gas production on the Norwegian continental shelf.

Maximizing Flaring

One eco-efficient innovation is a new vessel that is able to store and process hydrocarbons that were previously flared during the initial stages of oil exploration and well testing. This flaring emitted about 80,000 tons a year of carbon dioxide—about 1% of the Norwegian off-shore total—and some unburned hydrocarbons. It also wasted a potentially valuable resource, created significant liabilities because of Norway's offshore carbon tax, and—because of the heat created—limited the test flows so that some key data was difficult to obtain.

The *Crystal Sea* support ship overcomes some of these problems. The vessel is linked to platforms by a long flexible hose. The test production is transferred through this at a rate of up to 31,000 barrels a day. Water and gas are then separated out and the valuable oil is stored in tanks. The gas is flared and the water cleaned until there are only low levels of residual oil, when it is discharged to sea. After a few days the ship sails to an oil terminal to discharge its cargo.

The concept of recovering oil with a dedicated processing vessel was developed jointly by Solco, Halliburton, Brovig, and Statoil. Construction of the ship, which is owned by Green Sea Operations, was backed by a long-term contract from Statoil. The first two uses of the ship on the Statfjord North oil field in 1994–95 saved 62,500 barrels of oil and reduced carbon dioxide emissions by 24,000 tons. The value of the oil recovered alone was greater than the cost of chartering the vessels, with additional savings in carbon tax and the faster well testing that was made possible by reduced flaring on the platform.

Gas flaring when platforms are in production represents a further 20% of Norwegian offshore carbon dioxide emissions. It is also a very visible symbol of waste. Flaring is sometimes necessary to deal with sudden gas surges, but much of the time it is carried out at a low level simply to provide a reliable and instantaneous source of ignition when a major surge happens. By providing an alternative source of ignition, and also taking other measures, Statoil engineers have managed to greatly reduce the amount of flaring carried out at its production platforms. The developments at one field, Gullfaks, will pay for themselves in three years just on the basis of carbon tax savings, with additional income coming from sales of the gas that would otherwise have been flared.

Environmental Gains in Pipeline Commissioning

Once developed, many oil fields transport their output to shore via undersea pipelines. Once built, new pipelines have traditionally had construction materials flushed out with chemically treated seawater and tested for leakage by pumping dyed water through them. They are then protected from internal corrosion until the oil is ready to flow by filling them with seawater containing chemical additives. Once ready for operation the chemicals are discharged into the sea and the pipeline is dried by pumping diesel, methanol, or natural gas through it and flaring it at the exit.

These procedures are expensive and have an environmental impact. Leakage during testing and discharge of chemically treated seawater can have potentially adverse effects on local ecosystems. Although studies suggest that any damage is minor, Statoil's goal is to reduce all forms of emissions wherever possible. Flaring is also wasteful and creates a carbon tax liability.

Statoil therefore initiated research into more eco-efficient means of providing protection. This has resulted in a number of new measures. Substitutes have been found for some of the most toxic—and costly— chemicals and the use of diesel has been eliminated. In addition, compressed air is now used for flushing and drying, eliminating flaring or the need for costly gas-drying equipment.

Energy-efficient Offices

Norway's northern latitude means that heating buildings requires large amounts of energy. Statoil puts great emphasis on energy efficient offices and almost halved energy consumption per square meter between 1978 and 1994.

A new research center near Trondheim offered opportunities for further improvements. In addition to maximum insulation and advanced energy management systems, the building uses a natural and renewable energy source—seawater. Although cold to humans, seawater contains a great deal of low grade heat on an absolute scale. This energy can be tapped through heat pumps, which transform the low-temperature heat into higher-grade heat in the form of hot water. (Refrigerators operate on the same principle and pump heat from their interior to the exterior.)

The heat pumps require electricity but are nonetheless a cost-effective means of providing 70% of the building's heating requirements. Supplementary heating is provided by a very-high-efficiency (90%) propane gas boiler with an exhaust gas heat exchanger. This use of clean fuels and the low overall consumption mean that emissions of carbon dioxide and pollutants are very small. And Statoil estimates the cost of the scheme will be recovered over 7 years, even if energy has a low price.

Swiss Bank Corporation

Summary: Swiss Bank has improved its own energy efficiency and recycling rates and is developing methods of assessing the eco-efficiency of its clients as a means of reducing its exposure of environmental-related risks.

Swiss Bank Corporation is one of Switzerland's main retail banks and a large international lender. It has also played a leading role in developing awareness of environmental issues within the financial sector.

In 1991 the bank developed an environmental mission statement that acknowledged its responsibility to develop an ecologically aware approach to its business. This was interpreted not only as minimizing the impact of its internal activities but also examining and adapting the products and services it offers. Swiss Bank has therefore been a leader in introducing environment into the credit ratings of its customers.

Energy

An initial environmental review revealed that energy consumption of buildings and equipment is one of Swiss Bank's principal environmental impacts. A more detailed review of its Zurich offices found that consumption could be immediately reduced by 15% through improved "housekeeping." A further 10% to 15% reduction was obtained by minimal investment, for example, by stopping leaks. More impressive gains of 30% to 35% were available cost-effectively from improved insulation and other straightforward engineering modifications.

The bank now has a target of reducing its fossil fuel consumption to 1990 levels by 2000 and of stabilizing its electricity consumption.

Swiss Bank is also taking measures to reduce consumption of transportation fuel in its operations and by commuting employees. These include installation of covered parking and showers to encourage use of bicycles, construction of an underground rail link between its head offices and the main post office in Basel, subsidization of public transportation season tickets, and introduction of parking fees at some of its employee car parks. The fees are not high enough to lead to use of other car parks but do generate funds for a staff ecology committee. The money is applied toward ecology-related transportation issues that will benefit employees.

Waste Minimization and Recycling

Swiss Bank has targets of reducing paper consumption by 10% by the year 2000 and increasing the proportion of recycled paper used by 40% by the same year. The bank calculates that if all its copying paper was 100% recycled, it would require ten times less freshwater and three times less energy than if made from 100% virgin wood pulp. It is also 10% cheaper to purchase.

To help achieve these targets Swiss Bank has initiated a regional scheme for collecting and recycling wastepaper from banks, insurance companies, lawyers, and other organizations in the Basel region.

Credit Risk Assessment

Swiss Bank has created a new position—environmental credit risk specialist—and an environmental credit risk committee to develop its capabilities in this area. These are supported by new procedures and tools.

The most formal procedures are conducted for real-estate lending, which is a substantial part of Swiss Bank's business. This involves a three-step approach:

1. Information provided by the customer
2. Screening carried out by bank internal specialists
3. Independent risk evaluations by external consultants

As chapter 3 discusses, evaluation of the overall environmental performance of a company is difficult. Nor does a company with high environmental expenditures necessarily have a good environmental performance because its efforts might be focused on end-of-pipe technology. Conversely, companies with integrated pollution control systems may have low environment-specific expenditures. Swiss Bank is now developing the tools to overcome these difficulties and assess the overall environmental performance of a company. They aggregate indicators like environmental strategy and policy, environmental and risk management systems, efficiency of resource usage, emissions, communications to stakeholders, and environmental expenditures.

Swiss Bank vice president and head of environmental management services Franz Knecht, believes that financial bodies that successfully develop and use such tools will gain competitive advantage. He argues that

those who are able to rate the eco-integrated economical risks of a customer will have two important trump cards in their hands. First, lower costs by owning a credit portfolio with more high quality customers and therefore with lower loan provisions. Second, the ability to offer very competitive conditions by knowing the customer's risks and managing the art of risk-adjusted pricing. To a borrower this means nothing less than "Documenting my eco-efficiency can be one of the ways not only to get money from a bank, but also to get it on better terms."

Dow Chemical

Summary: Dow has made great strides—and set further ambitious goals—in improving energy *efficiency and reducing* toxic dispersion. *Its WRAP (waste reduction always pays) program continues to find win-win investments through such means as improved* materials *utilization and* recycling.

In 1992 Dow became one of the first companies to base its environmental policies on the concept of sustainable development. It stated:

The following 10 principles will guide the company toward sustainability. We recognize that the public's understanding of the concept continues to evolve; so, too, will these principles as Dow strives to meet and exceed society's expectations. In doing so, we will periodically report our progress.

The ten principles are:

1. We will integrate environmental considerations into all business decisions, including the strategic planning of new and existing products, processes, and business opportunities.

2. We will design or modify our products to minimize their environmental impact by encouraging their prudent use so as to reduce the amount of material requiring ultimate disposal; and prolonging their useful life through reuse, recycle and recovery.

3. We will continuously improve the efficiencies of our current and future manufacturing processes to better preserve energy and natural resources.

4. We will emphasize pollution prevention in our processes and use a hierarchical approach to waste management, with source reduction as the preferred option, followed by recycling, treatment and destruction, and secure landfills to be used only as a last resort.

5. We will transfer and utilize the best available technology throughout the Dow world so as to build the most environmentally sound facilities.

6. We will adhere to the Responsible Care guiding principles and codes of management practice through our global operations.

7. We will work closely with our customers and distributors to ensure they use and dispose of our products in a safe and environmentally responsible manner.

8. We will be open and responsive to the public concerns through thoughtful listening and meaningful action, and assume a leadership role in promoting partnerships between industry, government, the environmental community and other key stakeholders in an effort to develop solutions to common problems.

9. We will participate in conservation projects on or near our properties so as to leave the land and its ecosystem as we found it—if not better.

10. We will use our resources and expertise to support education initiatives at all levels to help improve the public's scientific and environmental literacy.

During the 1990s these principles are being implemented through a number of initiatives. In 1991 Dow set ambitious performance goals to reduce global emissions of priority compounds by 50% from a 1988 baseline by the end of 1995. This target was achieved by 1994, when emissions were down 53% from their 1988 level notwithstanding an increase in output over the period. In 1996 Dow developed these further by announcing aggressive 10-year performance goals and targets in three areas of special emphasis: responsibility and accountability, preventing EH&S incidents, and increasing resource productivity.

Responsibility and Accountability

Dow Canada was closely involved in the original development of Responsible Care in Canada and has since taken a leading role in extending it around the world. In Hong Kong, for instance, Dow chairs the Responsible Care Leadership Team of the Association of International Chemical Manufacturers of Hong Kong (AICM) and helps lead efforts to train companies to raise distribution standards and embrace product stewardship. Two of its three targets under this head therefore relate to the program:

1. Fully implement the Responsible Care Codes of Management Practices globally by 1997.

2. Promote the Responsible Care ethic among major associations, customers, suppliers, and policymakers to advocate global regulatory harmonization.

3. Incorporate principles of sustainable development and eco-efficiency into business strategies.

One important aspect of Responsible Care is listening to and learning from communities. Dow does this by means of twenty two community advisory panels (CAPs) around the world. CAP participants represent a cross-section of the community—from political and educational leaders to homemakers and retirees. These participants volunteer their time and service to identify community concerns and to facilitate problem-solving.

Dow's CAP in Altona, Australia, is a good example of what the interaction of community and company can achieve. Here, the CAP is helping Dow to identify, prioritize, and focus on key issues and develop an Environmental Improvement Plan (EIP). The public EIP aims at improving environmental performance and is supported and endorsed by the regulatory authority and the CAP.

Meanwhile, in Guaruja, Brazil, another Dow CAP has done much in the area of community awareness and emergency response. After extensive research and information gathering, this CAP created an educational program for seven-to-fourteen year-old schoolchildren. The program, entitled "Prevention Is the Best Solution," teaches children how to avoid and prevent accidents at home, as well as how to behave in an emergency situation.

Together, Dow representatives and CAP members in Guaruja also mapped out potential risks and resources within the community to help develop a community-wide emergency response system. And, with help from municipal civil defense and fire brigade departments, the CAP has conducted fire and emergency drills. Through such drills, residents gain knowledge of and confidence in how to react properly in the event of an emergency.

Dow also has a high-level Corporate Environmental Advisory Council with a membership of environmental opinion formers from around the world. The council advises Dow management on key EH&S issues that impact its businesses, products, and processes.

How Dow Set Its 10-Year Environment, Health, and Safety Goals

Dow's new goals were triggered by the completion of the emission reduction targets that were established in early 1990 and achieved in 1994, one year ahead of schedule. The company felt it had taken significant steps toward sustainability but needed a more comprehensive set of goals, reflecting the concept of sustainable development and the interdependence of economic growth, environmental protection, and social issues. It also wanted to continuously improve its products and manufacturing processes to increase operating efficiency, reduce costs, and lessen impacts on the environment.

To begin the process of identifying areas of emphasis and 10-year targets, a global team of experts from many disciplines and functions was formed. It first agreed on three areas of emphasis relating to sustainable development—responsibility and accounting, preventing EH&S incidences, and increasing resource productivity—and then defined key objectives for each. The next step was defining specific goals and targets to reach these objectives, with specific reduction targets for each item worldwide over the 10-year period of 1995–2005.

Having established the goals and target levels, emphasis was placed on establishing projected return on investment as well as cost savings of ongoing operations. This persuaded business leaders not only of the contribution to environmental protection and the health and safety of our employees and neighbors but also the bottom line contribution to long-term business viability and shareholder value.

Having completed this analysis, EH&S staff then set about achieving senior management approval and commitment to achieve the 10-year targets. The proposals were reviewed with the global vice presidents of functions such as manufacturing, R&D and distribution and with the leaders of Dow's global business units and approved by the CEO, William S. Stavropoulos, and the Board-level EH&S Committee. At a number of stages progress was reported to, and reviewed by, the Corporate Environmental Advisory Council (made up of scientists, government officials, environmentalists and business leaders) and also with a number of community advisory panels in various locations, both inside and outside of the United States. The program was launched internally through a worldwide television satellite broadcast involving the CEO and the vice president and corporate director of EH&S, David T. Buzzelli. It was announced externally at a national press conference in Washington, D.C., and simultaneously in all the key Dow locations around the world.

David Buzzelli is optimistic that the goals will be accomplished, believing that:

Each of them will have a sponsor from the Corporate Management Board, and we will be tracking not only the performance against the goals but also the value that achieving them returns to the businesses' bottom line and to shareholder value. At present we see a projected 30–40 percent return on our $1 billion investment over the next decade. Because reduction of accidents, spills, and emissions offers a safer, cleaner work environment for employees I also expect that all our staff will be committed to achieving the goals.

We will also work to ensure there is a good management system in place within EH&S to support the Dow businesses. This will include well-defined roles, responsibilities, and processes to continually drive performance improvement.

A final driver will be the periodic reporting of progress to employees and key external stakeholders, including the media, communities, governments, environmentalists, shareholders, and analysts. We know they'll have something to say if we can't demonstrate our progress.

Of course, incorporating the concept of eco-efficiency into a corporate culture can be difficult in successful companies such as Dow with tried-and-true product development records. The EH&S function at Dow Europe overcomes this through an "eco-efficiency campus," which introduces the concept to the leaders of the organization's fifteen business units. Vice president Claude Fussler has also written a book, *Driving Eco-Innovation*, which is used both internally and externally to sell the concept.[2] He believes that

incorporating eco-efficiency into any culture is a process rather than an event. It takes a long-term commitment and a willingness to go beyond a business-as-usual approach and work more closely with customers and stakeholders.

Preventing EH&S Incidents

Dow already has a low rate of EH&S incidents but seeks to reduce them further toward zero. Its 10-year goals in this area are therefore the ambitious ones of reducing

- Injuries and illness per 200,000 work hours by 90%
- Loss of primary containment incidents (leaks, breaks, and spills) by 90%

- Transportation incidents per 100,000 shipments by 90%
- Process safety incidents by 90%
- Motor vehicle incidents per 1 million miles by 50%.

It also wants a substantial reduction in incidents with Dow products at customer facilities, although a goal has not yet been set for this.

Resource Productivity

Dow's 10-year goals in this area are to:

- Reduce emissions of dioxin by 90%
- Reduce emissions of priority compounds by 75%
- Reduce the amount of waste and water generated per pound of production by 50%
- Reduce energy use per pound of production by 20%

Priority compounds are those that pose the greatest risk to human and ecological health. They include persistent, toxic, and bioaccumulative compounds, known human carcinogens and selected ozone depletors.

Reducing the amount of waste and wastewater generated in manufacturing—preferably by source reduction—is a top priority for Dow. This is the idea behind the company's WRAP (waste reduction always pays) program, which began formally in 1986. Through WRAP, employees are encouraged to generate ideas about how to reduce manufacturing wastes and save money. Each year, top WRAP project teams are recognized for their efforts. In North America alone, WRAP projects reduced waste by around 45 million lbs a year and saved Dow more than $20 million a year in both 1993 and 1994.

WRAP projects take many forms. Dow's Terneuzen, Netherlands, polyurethanes plant reduced waste by more than 1500 tons between 1992 and 1994 through changes in operational procedures. Improved operating discipline resulted in 50% fewer spills, while efficiency improvements were made in cleaning both pumps and filters. The cost savings amounted to $1.4 million.

A waste reduction team at Dow's Pittsburg, California, site for manufacturing agricultural products achieved similar savings as a result of careful experimentation. Their goal was to recycle a reactant that was

How Dow's WRAP Program Works

Each of Dow's manufacturing divisions is responsible for the development and implementation of the WRAP program within its own operations. This allows each division the flexibility to tailor the program to specific needs. Their efforts are driven by a combination of Environmental Affairs personnel, site minimization champions, and operational plant and project staff.

Many methods of implementing WRAP have been used: idea-generating contests, utilization of quality performance techniques, plant waste reduction reviews, recognition programs, and even the development and communication of top ten generator lists for waste and emissions at a division.

Waste data—which includes emissions—is collected across all media, by process, at a facility. A ratio of waste versus production is then calculated to account for production variances. The waste ratio or index can be tracked and evaluated by each facility. The program flow chart lists the steps taken in the WRAP process to achieve continuous improvement.

Each plant is asked to develop an inventory of its waste streams that may impact the air, water, or land. Specific waste streams are identified and researched as to how they are produced by the process. They are then prioritized for further investigation and action based on volume and toxicity concerns, and individual targets are established for reduction projects. Tracking progress toward these targets is fundamental in monitoring the impact of the plant's efforts. It also allows the facility to communicate its performance to employees and the community.

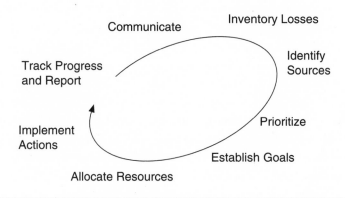

Source: Courtesy of the Dow Chemical Company.

being incinerated after a single use. Doing this required changing its residence time in the process. The team needed to find the optimal point for reactant injection, so that yields were maximized without significantly changing the reactant composition. This was achieved in part through the development of computer models to permit the monitoring of a number of variables, such as pressure, temperature, rate of feed and weight. The result has been a reduction in consumption of fresh reactant of 80%. This has cut wastes by 2.5 million lbs annually and achieved cost savings of over $750,000 a year. It is estimated that, at capacity production rates, total costs will be reduced by $8 million as a result of savings in yield, raw materials, and costs associated with environmental management and labor.

Another way Dow reduces waste is by using new technology to recycle process byproducts. Byproduct chlorinated hydrocarbons from Dow's manufacturing processes have always been recycled for the production of chlorinated solvents and CFCs. Demand for these products, however, has declined in recent years. Dow has now introduced selective hydrogenation technology to convert the byproducts into valuable feedstocks for other processes.

In many cases Dow plants combine a number of individual WRAP projects to obtain continual improvements in eco-efficiency. This has been the case at Dow's latex plant in Midland, Michigan. In 1989 this was one of the biggest contributors to Dow's landfill, sending more than 1000 cubic yards a month. The plant also sent more than three dozen tank trucks of organic wastes to Dow's incinerator each year and accounted for a significant proportion of the site's air emissions.

Plant workers looked at the volume of waste their plant generated and saw an opportunity to reduce it—one step at a time. Employee teams evaluated every aspect of latex production—every piece of equipment and every procedural step. The improvements they introduced ranged from complex chemical engineering changes, such as improving the performance of raw materials, to simple, commonsense measures like building a roof over the solid waste collection area to keep rain out and reduce the material required to solidify the waste. Some ideas came from individuals and some from teams; none involved major capital investments and several actually lowered the plant's operating costs.

Together, these "small" steps have resulted over a 5-year period in a 93% reduction in air emissions, a substantial reduction in waste sent to landfill, and a 48% increase in production capacity. The projects were all completed without investing capital funds and resulted in total savings of approximately $770,000 a year in environmental costs and improved yield. The impact of the waste reduction measures has also reached far beyond Midland. Dow's Latex Technology Center has analyzed the lessons and implemented them into the design of new facilities, such as one recently built in Thailand.

Dow also works with its customers to improve their resource productivity, for example, by enabling them to include more recycled material in their products. In 1991, for example, Dow researchers developed a process for the recycling of reaction injection molded (RIM) scrap, incorporating it into the same application with virtually no loss of performance or appearance. Today, some Dodge Caravan and Plymouth Voyager minivans have bumpers containing 10% in-plant recycled RIM material.

Dow expects WRAP investments to continue creating environmental benefit and 30–40% returns on capital for the foreseeable future.

Developing New Eco-efficient Products

Dow is also developing new products and businesses based on eco-efficient solutions to unmet needs. Hence discovering new products or redesigning existing ones to make them more sensitive to the environment is a major focus for research and development. An example of this ongoing research effort is Broadstrike, a new herbicide developed by DowElanco (a joint venture of Dow and Eli Lilly). This is highly effective and essentially nontoxic and is applied in ounces instead of pounds per acre. In addition, the compound can be used on both corn and soybeans, which allows flexibility in crop rotation. It also offers less risk to humans and other animals because it works against weeds by affecting those amino acids found only in plants.

In order to fully integrate environmental imperatives into product development processes, Dow Europe has developed an eco-compass that maps product performance in the main eco-efficiency dimensions identified by the WBCSD (see figure 3.3 in chapter 3).

Conclusions

Dow's commitment to continuous improvement has a long history. It's founder, H. H. Dow, was fond of saying, "if you can't do it better, why do it?" Now continual improvement in environmental performance is seen not only as a prerequisite for survival but as a major source of cost savings and new product opportunities. In the words of its president and CEO, William Stavropoulos,

We at Dow must meet the needs of our four stakeholders: employees, customers, shareholders and society. All of these want high standards for environment, health and safety. Achieving these standards is part of Dow's culture. Rather than being isolated in a separate function, these issues are increasingly integrated into our business decisions processes. At every level, teams of people are focusing on business opportunities and practices that sustain our economic and environmental performance. We believe, as we have for many years, that the factor likely to have the greatest impact on Dow's future will be our environmental, health, and safety performance.

3M

Summary: 3M has greatly reduced its toxic emissions *and improved its utilization of* energy *and both* recycled *and* virgin materials. *It has a long-running pollution prevention pays (3P) program that continues to identify win-win opportunities and is developing many eco-efficient products; for example, Scotchtint reduces energy consumption in buildings, makes windows more* durable *and increases* service intensity *through protecting fabrics from ultraviolet radiation.*

For more than 90 years 3M has invented products that solve problems—innovations like Post-it notes that change the way people communicate and high-technology products like the 3M-developed laser imager (now marketed by Imation), which produces sharper images of computed tomography (CT) scans, so doctors can make better diagnoses. These innovations call upon 3M's twenty core technologies, which range from coating substances and techniques to microreplication. The result is a 50,000-plus product range and over $12 billion turnover.

However, the scale and nature of 3M's business creates environmental challenges. It uses large quantities of energy and materials. And coating processes are used in the manufacture of approximately 75% of its products. Most of these processes have used petroleum-based solvents and emitted VOCs. Eliminating these requires development of substitute processes that do not compromise product quality.

3M's Environmental Policy

The company's formal environmental strategy, goals, and achievements span almost three decades. The two broad goals are to achieve zero emissions and to make 3M a sustainable growth company. Eco-efficient helps accomplish both of these. The formal environmental policy states that 3M will continue to recognize and exercise its responsibility to:

- Solve its own environmental pollution and conservation problems
- Prevent pollution at the source wherever and whenever possible
- Develop products that will have a minimum effect on the environment
- Conserve natural resources through the use of reclamation and other appropriate methods
- Assure that its facilities and products meet and sustain the regulations of all federal, state, and local environmental agencies
- Assist, wherever possible, governmental agencies and other official organizations engaged in environmental activities

3M today has a long experience of action in all these areas.

Solving Its Own Environmental Problems
The policy recognizes that 3M is committed to minimize any environmental impact from its products and processes. It has moved 3M from a reactive position based on what has to be done toward a proactive policy of moving beyond compliance with legislation and focusing on what should be done. As a result 3M's corporate financial commitment is extensive. The company invests $100 million a year on environmentally related R&D and an estimated $200 million on environmental operations worldwide. Since 1990, 3M also has invested $175 million worldwide on pollution control equipment to reduce air emissions. In addition, individual business units invest millions of dollars meeting environmental goals.

Pollution Prevention

3M established the world's first pollution prevention program, known as Pollution Prevention Pays (3P), in 1975 (see below).

Minimizing Product Impacts

3M devotes a substantial proportion of its $1.5 billion annual R&D budget to reducing the environmental impact of new and existing products and improving manufacturing processes. This has led to the environmental improvement of more than 100 major new or improved products. Some examples follow.

To ensure that products are reviewed in a systematic way, 3M has developed life cycle management guidelines. These address the EH&S and energy impact of each stage of the product life cycle, from development through manufacturing, use, and disposal. Implementation of life cycle management is the primary task of the corporate product responsibility group, working with product responsibility coordinators in each business unit. Product responsibility staff also work to ameliorate the environmental effects of suppliers and customers, often in association with their trade associations. For example, 3M has worked with the American Furniture Manufacturers Association to develop guidelines on use of coatings and other materials so that member companies can comply with environmental regulations.

Conservation of Natural Resources

Many 3P projects have involved reuse, remanufacturing, or recycling of wastes, thereby conserving materials and energy. 3M's energy efficiency programs have also reduced consumption of energy by 58% per unit of product since base year 1973. A current goal for manufacturing sites is to reduce energy per unit of production by 3% per annum. Non-manufacturing sites have a target of reducing energy consumption per square foot by the same amount.

Compliance with Regulations

3M's Environmental Technology & Safety Services department has over 100 employees working with business units to ensure compliance with both legislative and 3M requirements, for example, through regular audits.

Assisting Government and Other External Bodies

3M also assists business to achieve environmental improvements in developing or transitional economies, either alone or in collaboration with others. Currently, for example, it is working—together with other companies and the World Environmental Center—to provide environmental advice to cement and oil refinery facilities in Kazakhstan and Uzbekistan.

Stretch Goals

Moving beyond compliance also involves setting "stretch goals"— goals that can be reached only by finding new and better ways of doing things. They are difficult to accomplish but also create more progress than relying on easily achieved objectives. 3M's ultimate goal is zero discharges from its plants and minimal impact from its products. But it also sets nearer term targets. In 1988, for example, it set a target of reducing air emissions by 70%, which was accomplished by 1993. Current targets include the following:

Air emissions—reducing process air emissions by 90% by the year 2000, using 1990 as the base year. This is 3M's greatest environmental challenge, as meeting it requires replacement of many solvent-based processes.

Water—3M is also well ahead of schedule on its similar target of reducing releases to water by 90% over the period 1990–2000.

Waste—3M's target was to reduce all waste generation by 35% by 1995 and by 50% by 2000. By the end of 1995 it had almost achieved its goal.

Energy—the goal was to improve energy efficiency 20% per unit of production or per square foot of office and warehouse space between 1990 and 1995. This target was not met, largely because of changing activity patterns and installation of energy-intensive air pollution control equipment.

Pollution Prevention Pays

The 3P program is an approach that prevents pollution at the source—in manufacturing processes and products—rather than removing it after it has been created. While the idea itself was not new when 3P was started in 1975, the concept of applying pollution prevention on a company-wide basis and documenting the results had not been done before.

The program's success has been widely acknowledged. In its first twenty years 3M employees originated 4,450 projects. These have eliminated more than 1.2 billion lbs of pollution to the air, land, and water and significantly cut pollution per unit of production. 3M's first-year savings alone from these projects totaled more than $750 million. These achievements were recognized in 1996 when the 3P program received the President's Award for Sustainable Development.

Pollution can be prevented in four main ways:

1. Product reformulation
2. Process modification
3. Equipment redesign
4. Recycling and reuse of raw materials

Some examples of how these have been accomplished include:

A resin spray booth had been producing about 500,000 lbs annually of overspray that required special incineration disposal. New equipment was installed to eliminate excessive overspray. The new design reduced the amount of resin used, saving more than $125,000 a year on a $45,000 investment in equipment.

A 3M plant developed a new product from the waste stream of an existing product at the plant. The new product is used in industry to contain and absorb hazardous waste spills. The new product has provided revenue, cut landfill costs, and helped the environment.

Other 3P projects worldwide have ranged from improved control of coating weight at a facility in Wales and the recycling of wastewater in a plant in Germany, to a variety of combustion control and heat recovery processes in Japan.

The box provides details of how 3P was implemented

Environmental Management System

3P is complemented by two other mechanisms that help to achieve eco-efficiency—an environmental management system (EMS) and life cycle management. The objective of the EMS is to "ensure compliance to

Implementing Pollution Prevention

In 1974 3M was faced with a torrent of new environment legislation and regulation. At the same time economic growth had been halted by the oil crisis, which sent energy bills soaring. Ray Herzog, 3M's president, asked Dr. Joseph Ling, the head of the environmental group, if he could develop a program to comply with regulations but at a low capital and operating cost and with minimal additional requirements for energy.

Ling and his staff believed that preventing pollution at its source—in products and manufacturing processes—was the answer. The idea of this was not new but the concept of applying pollution prevention on a permanent and company wide basis was. The first stage in its introduction was clarifying the ways in which it could be achieved—product reformulation, equipment redesign, process modification, and recycling and reuse of waste materials—and developing reference and guidance material.

This was relatively easy, compared to the second stage of making a then almost unknown concept into something that could be understood and supported by staff and could win vital support from senior management. The approach was to demonstrate the financial and environmental benefits that could be obtained from pollution prevention and to reward employees for successful projects (commonplace now but unusual at that time). A formula was worked out—only first year savings were recognized. This was deliberately conservative—ignoring any savings in subsequent years—to build credibility for the measure. The program was also unusual within 3M for being open-ended. Most programs in 3M have set time frames to accomplish goals. But Dr. Ling realized that, for the foreseeable future, any new product or process would create some pollution, so the message of prevention needs to be timeless.

An award program was also introduced. Employees from qualifying projects receive a certificate or wooden plaque, which is usually presented by a divisional vice president or country managing director at a special lunch.

The third stage involved promoting the concept to all the 60,000 staff on six continents, using employee publications, meetings, and every other means of communication available to us. Separate videotapes—then a new communications medium—were produced for three target audiences: science, engineering and manufacturing, and International Operations. Each began with an appearance by 3M's board chairman, who gave the program his enthusiastic support. Then, the vice president of R&D spoke to his people. The head of engineering and manufacturing talked to his people. And the head of International addressed all 3M locations outside the United States.

The program took two to three years to gain momentum and overcome a number of challenges. One was its voluntary nature, which can require a significant commitment from already busy employees. A second factor is reluctance to change a manufacturing process that is running smoothly. When changes are made, new "bugs" may be introduced, decreasing production and product quality until the process is refined. Even if product quality can be maintained, the time and cost for development of a product or process changes can create difficulties. A final challenge can be limited availability of capital.

Ling himself ties the success of 3P to five factors:

1. Top management support—which has been present at all times from CEOs and other top managers.

2. Employee involvement—by all staff. While the bulk of the ideas have come from process engineers, we have had some great ideas from clerical staff, maintenance personnel, sales people, and others.

3. Simplicity—applying for a 3P designation is done on a one-page application form.

4. A reward system—all employees like recognition by their peers and bosses. It makes them feel good about themselves, reinforces reputations, and contributes to career growth.

5. Promotion—we did this both internally and externally. It means that new employees are exposed early in their careers, that for older staff it becomes a way of life, and that external recognition builds internal motivation.

global regulations and 3M policies and facilitate continuous improvement of environmental performance." It has 5 key elements:

1. Regulations and Policies: Identify all regulatory and 3M policy requirements that affect products and operations.

2. Environmental Management Plan: Establish and maintain an environmental project plan that defines goals, action plans, and assignment of responsibilities.

3. Environmental Operating Procedures: Document operating procedures that achieve and maintain compliance objectives.

4. Environmental Assessment: Conduct compliance and system audits to verify performance and identify improvement opportunities.

5. Continuous Improvement: Measure and target reductions of waste and emissions, exceed environmental performance expectations, and employ life cycle management in the identification and satisfaction of customer needs, from product design and manufacture through final use and disposition.

A Life Cycle Approach

3M has always paid attention to the environmental impact of its products. We are now looking to do this more systematically with the piloting of life cycle management. The idea behind this is to consider, during product development, the impacts of choices in materials and manufacturing processes on safety, health, and environment at all stages of the product life cycle. The LCM process highlights opportunities for incorporating the WBCSD eco-efficiency criteria into product design and using them for market advantage. The process will also involve closer interaction with suppliers and customers to find ways of reducing upstream and/or downstream environmental impacts.

3M Pharmaceuticals used this approach in developing the world's first CFC-free metered dose inhaler (MDI) for the treatment of asthma. Observing growing pressure for a phase-out of CFCs in 1987 researchers began evaluating alternative propellants to deliver the medication. They eventually settled on the hydrofluoroalkane HFA-134A, which has no ozone-depleting potential. Later, with several other pharmaceutical companies, 3M funded toxicology testing that led to approval of the propellant by the U.S. Food and Drug Administration.

But developing the new CFC-free MDI required far more than exchanging one propellant for another. In comparison to CFCs, HRAs have very different physical properties. Every component of the MDI system, as well as the manufacturing and quality assurance processes, had to be reassessed and in many cases, redesigned.

The following sections demonstrate that this is already being accomplished by many existing 3M products. The more systematic processes for life cycle management that are now being introduced will ensure that even more do so in the future.

3M Scotchtint Window Film

In 1966 3M invented a film that can be attached to windows to increase their energy efficiency. The invention—which is based on thin metal coatings on translucent polyester or other substrates—drew on 3M's core competencies of coatings and tapes. Its complexity—involving up to ten layers of materials within a total thickness of a piece of paper—and the need for completely uniform distribution to ensure optical clarity make its manufacture one of the most difficult in the company. Over the last three decades the products have been constantly improved and the global market for window films in cars and buildings has grown to $300 million.

Scotchtint provides eco-efficiency by reducing building energy consumption. By reflecting sunlight, Scotchtint films can reduce solar heat gain in buildings by 55%-76%, depending on the film chosen. At the 249,000-sq ft Hitachi America headquarters, application of Scotchtint film cut heat gain through the windows by 72%. The reduced need for air conditioning translates into electricity savings of $25,000 a year. This gave Hitachi a three year payback period. In addition, there was a 41% reduction in complaints about the air conditioning in the building.

New designs of Scotchtint film can also reflect heat back into buildings during the winter, cutting heat losses through windows by up to 30% while still providing all the other benefits of standard sun control films.

Scotchtint films not only save electricity, but they also create additional benefits for the customer. They use abrasion-resistance to allow windows to better withstand washing and day-to-day abuse. This makes them more durable—thereby minimizing replacement costs as well as creating another form of eco-efficiency. Buildings that use these films are also more comfortable, with reduced temperature imbalances and less solar glare. In addition, Scotchtint films block a high percentage of the sun's harmful ultraviolet (UV) radiation, thus improving protection for carpets, curtains, and other furnishings and extending their life; reduce flying glass if windows shatter; and put less strain on air-conditioning systems, with consequent reductions in maintenance costs and complaints and extension of service life.

3M Silverlux Reflective Film

The creation of new U.S. markets for Scotchtint-type reflective tape was far from 3M researcher John Roche's thoughts in the 1980s when he tackled the problem of designing low-cost solar heating panels for developing countries. Roche's Christian beliefs created a personal drive to help the world's poor—while 3M's system of allowing researchers 15% of their time to pursue personal projects provided the opportunity to implement it. Roche used metalized film to create a reflective surface to concentrate the sun's rays on areas to be heated. His work sparked a thought—if reflective tape could allow solar energy to be more precisely directed, why could this concept not be adapted to make fluorescent lighting more efficient?

Roche knew that conventional fluorescent lighting fixtures absorb a lot of the light energy, converting it to heat. This is not only inefficient but also adds to air-conditioning loads unnecessarily. Placing a highly reflective surface behind the lamps could greatly reduce the energy being wasted.

Roche's idea came to market in the mid-1980s as Silverlux reflective film. The product reflects 95% of the light that touches it and has minimal absorption of heat. The reflective film is formed into lighting reflectors by converters that retrofit them to existing fluorescent light fixtures. The efficiency of the reflective surface provided by the Silverlux film allows removal of up to half of the lamps while still providing optimal lighting levels.

The eco-efficiency result of installing reflectors made with Silverlux film is a substantial reduction not only in the energy used for lighting but also in the energy consumption of air conditioning equipment. Heat absorbed by lighting fixtures can account for 15% of nighttime air-conditioning loads. These energy savings translate into reduced environmental impact from electricity generation. For example, every 92Ws of fluorescent lamps and ballasts that can be removed from the lighting system by use of Silverlux film translates—if lighting is used for 7 hours daily—into annual avoided emissions of 383 lbs of carbon dioxide, 3 lbs of sulfur dioxide, and 1.5 lbs of nitrogen dioxide if the electricity is generated from coal.

Safest Stripper

In the mid-1980s 3M's Do-it-Yourself division was running consumer focus groups to discuss the problems of painting and varnishing—and to find new product opportunities. The panelists were especially unhappy about the fumes, potential skin burns, and other problems of stripping away old paint and varnish. 3M staff knew that these difficulties were due to the active ingredient of the strippers, methylene chloride. They also knew that the chemical was a VOC—and therefore a contributor to air pollution—and had other health and environmental question marks that might lead to its banning.

After much development work, the consumer feedback led to a new water-based stripper, Safest Stripper Paint and Varnish Remover. This eliminates the potential toxic risks of methylene chloride and other caustic ingredients, is readily biodegradable, can be disposed of in drains, and is nonflammable.

The product has captured a small portion of the U.S. market for paint and varnish removers. A useful slice—but not as much as originally hoped. One reason is that there are as yet no restrictions on the use of methylene chloride. Because Safest Stripper has higher production costs, it has to be sold at a price premium over the cheaper methylene chloride-based products. Although the product takes longer to remove paint and varnish, it does so in a safe and effective manner. Most customers will put up with the problems of conventional products in order to get the job done quickly. But for some, Safest Stripper provides additional nonenvironmental advantages. It allows greater flexibility in doing work—stripper can be applied and left (even overnight) while other tasks are carried out. It has high "vertical cling," so that there is little running or dripping, and better penetration of materials, so that even deep stains can be removed. The slowness also makes it easier to remove surface layers of paint and varnish while leaving base coats untouched—a boon for activities as varied as restoring paintings and removing temporary camouflage paint from military vehicles. The U.S. Marine Corps used it for the last-named purpose at its San Diego base—

not only to avoid complete repainting but also because it is the only stripper compatible with the county's exacting requirements on discharges to water.

But if Safest Stripper is, absent new regulation, the tortoise of the paint and varnish remover market, it is the hare of wallpaper removal. 3M wallpaper and paste remover was only launched in 1994. But it already has substantial market share and sales continue to grow rapidly. The main reason is its water-based formulation, which allows it to penetrate paper more easily. Hence, stripping is twice as fast as with conventional solvent-based products. The high vertical cling creates another advantage.

Safest Stripper shows how eco-efficient actions can create a marketing and technological platform that, even if not dramatically successful at first, provides a platform for future new or second generation projects. Randy Taylor, a product marketer, certainly believes that the wallpaper removal story shows that "our water-based formulation can provide increased customer service as well as environment benefit. We're hoping to use its unique properties to extend the range into other new products in the future."

Dryview Laser Imaging
Unique properties, positive environmental impact, and great future potential are also the characteristics of Dryview laser imaging systems. This was the outcome of one of the most complex ever 3M R&D programs and, when launched in 1994, achieved one of the fastest ever rates of sales growth. The product is now owned and marketed by Imation, the imaging and printing company spun off from 3M in 1996.

The Dryview system originated in 3M Health Care's market research into medical radiography. At that time images from equipment such as CAT scans were printed using a wet chemical process. As with photography, the image was printed on light-sensitive silver-coated film and then developed and fixed with chemical rinses. The problem for users is that the process generates large amounts of wastewater, which is contaminated with a number of hazardous chemicals contained in developer and fixer, and also contains silver. The user must therefore operate waste water treatment and silver recovery equipment and ensure it is in compliance with relevant regulation. This usually requires two treatment facilities to ensure that input water is of the high quality that the process requires. The need for extensive plumbing also limits the location of image printers within hospitals. As well as increasing costs, these requirements create special problems for medical facilities in areas of water shortage or poor water quality, as is often the case in developing countries.

Market research demonstrated that these problems were important in themselves but also contributed to customers' number one concern —containing costs. The opportunity was clear—could a dry image process be found that completely eliminated the need for wet chemical processing?

The Dryview laser imaging system does just this. Its centerpiece is a new film that develops with precise application of heat. No chemicals are required to produce an image of equivalent quality to wet processing. The system creates operating cost reductions of 10% to 20% and capital savings of 25% to 50% compared with conventional systems. As no water inputs are required—or wastewater generated—it can be located anywhere in a hospital.

Each replacement of a wet processing system with the Dryview process saves the annual equivalent of 3,380 liters of developing and fixing chemicals and 182,000 liters of rinse water. If all the approximately 11,000 medical imaging lasers in the United States were converted to the Dryview process the result would be a reduction in chemical inputs of over 37 million liters and savings of 2 billion liters of rinse water. All the components used in the Dryview process are also recyclable. The overall system is also more durable than conventional equivalents because it can be more easily upgraded, whereas the wet chemical equipment requires frequent replacement.

Recycled Post-it Notes
No survey of 3M is complete without a reference to one of its best known products, Post-it notes. These are eco-efficient when recycled and by avoiding heavy metal based dyes and pigments. Also, Post-it dispensers are made from recycled plastic.

Recycled Post-its, made from 100% recycled paper (with a minimum of 20% postconsumer waste), have been available since 1990, and now account for about 10% of the range's total sales.

Toward Sustainable Business

3M's stretch goals, 3P program, and product process innovations show that, in the words of David Sonstegard, vice president for 3M Environmental Technologies and Safety Services

3M is moving beyond an era of compliance with environmental regulations toward one focused on sustainable development. We are convinced that, in the future, the most competitive companies also will be the most environmentally responsible companies. Long-term, 3M's goals embrace the concepts of eco-efficiency and sustainable development, with a focus on life cycle management. Continuous improvement of environmental performance has benefited, and will benefit, our employees, investors, and customers, and the communities in which we operate.

7   A Leadership Role
for Business

Sustainable development is not a stable state, a plateau we reach and say, "We've made it, now we can turn to something else." It is a process whose central aim is leaving future generations with an array of choices. Achieving this requires the bringing together of economic, environmental, and social imperatives. The economic imperative is to manage our resources efficiently while contributing to the prosperity of all by adding value. The environmental imperative is not to exceed what the earth, the oceans, and the atmosphere are capable of providing and absorbing and to remedy already damaged systems. The social imperative is to put humanity at the center of our concern, with its value of equal opportunity, social justice and freedom.

We have shown that many businesses are already making positive responses to these imperatives. They are thinking of the world beyond today and adopting eco-efficiency and eco-innovation to improve the prospects for tomorrow.

To some degree, these changes are a result of continuing pressures from customers, investors, employees, legislators, and, increasingly, from banks and insurance companies. Companies adopting a strategy of eco-efficiency know that simply responding to pressure is not enough. Not enough to achieve sustainable development. Not enough to retain the social legitimacy of business. And not enough to prosper in the sustainability-shaped markets of tomorrow.

They know the importance of proactively pursuing resource productivity. This not only delivers more to society from less but also catalyzes more general innovation. Achieving it will become even more critical as the world becomes increasingly crowded and runs out of acceptable sinks for wastes and pollution, and as valuable resources become scarcer and increasingly costly.

They know too the importance and value of creating an eco-efficiency mindset. This means, first, understanding the needs of sustainable development and secondly, envisioning them as unmet market opportunities.

The companies that are leading the way to eco-efficiency also recognize business's responsibility to provide *leadership* for sustainable development in other ways. After all, business is best placed to

Understand fundamental customer needs and how these can be delivered through much more eco-efficient services and products that create step improvements in environmental performance

Create the core technologies that are critical to sustainable development

Transfer technologies and ideas around the world

Use its marketing skills to inform consumers who may sometimes be unaware of the urgency and requirements of sustainable production and consumption about the opportunities for eco-efficient products and processes.

Technology, while not always perfect, and not the only element in achieving sustainable development, is nonetheless important. A recent report by the U.S. National Council of Science and Technology has highlighted its overall contributions and also demonstrated that we need to change the balance between avoidance, control, monitoring, and assessment and remediation (see figure 7.1). At present, many of our actions are focused on remedying past impacts and control of current emissions and wastes. In the future, we need more development and application of technologies for complete avoidance of environmental impacts, for example, by pollution prevention or product design. Monitoring and assessment will also become more important, both to gain a better understanding of their ultimate impact on natural systems. If this is done, then, during the early decades of the next century

intensified expenditures to minimize environmental harm will begin to pay off. Agricultural practices will be less wasteful and more sustainable, manufacturing processes will be more efficient in the use of resources, consumer products will be designed with the environment in mind, and the infrastructures that supply energy, transportation services, and water supplies will be more resource efficient and environmentally benign. Investments in cost-effective remediation will have cleaned up a large portion of existing hazardous waste sites. Our ability to respond to existing environmental problems will be aided

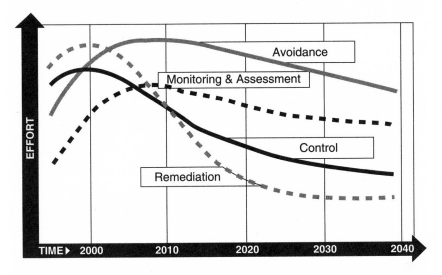

Figure 7.1
Future Balance Between Different Environmental Strategies
Source: National Science and Technology Council, *Bridge to a Sustainable Future*
(Washington, D.C., 1995), p. 5.

by more advanced monitoring systems, microsensors, and data analysis tools that continually assess the state of the environment locally, regionally, and globally. Finally, we will have developed effective ways of restoring or recreating severely damaged ecosystems to improve the long-term health and productivity of our natural resource base.[2]

Technology requires investment. This makes fundamental change in resource productivity possible as new, cleaner plants and products replace or improve upon older ones.

Continued, eco-efficient, growth is vital if the necessary scale of investment to achieve sustainable development is to occur.

Industry's marketing and communicating strengths are also vital. Sustainable production practices need to be matched by changes in the consumption and usage patterns of millions of individuals and businesses. However, environmental improvement alone does not sell products—it has to be combined with value and performance. Only intimate, day to day, contact with customers can create the understanding of real needs that is the basis of providing such a combination—and of informing and educating customers about the importance of the environmental component of the product's use.

Criticisms of Eco-efficiency

Of course, not everyone agrees with our views. Some in business say that the vision of eco-efficiency exaggerates the practical opportunities that are available. As chapter 2 discussed, this can be true in the short term but is less valid in the long term when the dynamics of regulation and changing social expectations constantly reshape opportunity spaces.

Others in business believe that eco-efficiency is only for large companies in the rich North. We hope that the many examples we have described from small and medium-sized companies and from Africa, Asia, and Latin America demonstrate that this is not the case. The greatest benefits from resource productivity can often be gained in small companies that have paid little attention to it in the past. Small players may also have an advantage in developing eco-efficient products over large companies who are wedded to established ways of doing things.

Some outside businesses argue that examples from a few innovative companies give a misleading picture of business as a whole, and mask generally poor performance. Although we think industry's general record and influence have been positive, we acknowledge that the companies we describe are pioneers. There are still too many businesses that are content to merely comply with legislation—or, worse, evade it. We firmly believe that their numbers should diminish through natural selection—the companies that do not increase their resource productivity and follow other tenets of eco-efficiency will be handicapped financially and in other ways and may disappear from the marketplace as a result.

Some environmentalists and many business people have difficulty in believing that industry can adopt the tenets of sustainable consumption, which they interpret as meaning that some products should not be made or sold even if people want them. We do not deny that this is an especially difficult challenge. Business has to meet the needs of its customers. Experience shows that, at least at present, many of those customers—including final consumers—don't want to pay more for "green" products and services. As chapter 1 discussed, we do not believe that this means they are uninterested in or do not value environment. Rather it creates a challenge for business to develop more eco-efficient offerings that either do not require or greatly reduce the extent of trade-offs between cost and environmental performance.

In the meantime, there is much that can be done in informing them about the implications of their choices—and designing and marketing more eco-efficient services and goods that make consumers change their minds about what they really want. And, of course, public agencies and NGOs have an important role in shaping customer expectations.

Many environmentalists also argue that eco-efficiency ignores the existence of global inequalities and other social dimensions of sustainable development. It is true that these issues are dauntingly large and complex and that it's sometimes difficult for individual companies and employees to see how they can impact upon them. At the same time they are an intrinsic part of an eco-efficiency approach—which says we have to create value for a company *and* society by doing more with less—and need to be addressed. The practical actions that can be taken include transfer of technology and know how to less-developed countries and the creation of eco-efficient products for their consumers. Progressive businesses have already done much in these areas—and there is no question that more is necessary if, as a minimum, basic needs are to be met in all parts of the globe. However, any measures taken should not unduly reduce democratic and economic freedom, which is also important.

Of course, some critics have no problem with the ideas of eco-efficiency but believe that the size and wealth of large corporations are inimical to some of the basic features of sustainable development, such as commitment to community and place. For example, Stephen Viederman, president of the Jessie Noyes Smith Foundation, argues that the "sustainable corporation" is an oxymoron. He believes that there needs to be

a rethinking and re-creating of a new capitalism, or something beyond capitalism that we cannot now envision. With the demise of communism this should be easier.

That re-envisioning will require us to go back to first principles. What is it that we want for ourselves, our children and their children? For all children? What then is the role of corporations in this new economy to create healthy, sustainable communities and places?[3]

We agree that these are important questions to ask. And we believe that the answer is that the proven wealth creation and management abilities of corporations makes them essential to achieving these goals.

The Next Steps for Eco-Efficiency

Eco-efficiency has come a long way since its entry to the public arena in 1992. Companies are applying it, bodies such as the WBCSD and UNEP are spreading their experience around the world, and governments are incorporating it into their policies. But there is still more to be done in both deepening and extending it.

Extension means:

doing even more to show that eco-efficiency is relevant and valuable to small–medium-sized enterprises and provide practical guidance on how they can best approach it

building on current initiatives to help developing and transitional economies achieve eco-efficiency

provide more examples of how eco-efficiency can be relevant to service organizations, whose individual environmental impacts are often relatively minor but that account for a large proportion of economic activity in developed economies.

Extending eco-efficiency means:

building on the work of the WBCSD's task force on sustainable consumption to develop more examples of what business can realistically do to contribute to the difficult issues of sustainable consumption.

building the evidence for linkages between eco-efficiency and shareholder value and devising new accounting techniques to enable organizations to assess it more effectively

developing better metrics for assessing eco-efficiency.

Of course, a healthy and vibrant small business sector with strong roots in local communities is important. A large part of the reason for this book is to help such small companies to prosper by introducing them to the ideas of eco-efficiency. But there are some things that only larger enterprises can accomplish. In the long run, too, consumers and citizens will decide what the role of large corporations should be. We certainly believe that they will make judgments about companies that have neglected the communities they operate in—and also that they'll recognize the economic contribution and sincerity and community and environmental commitment of companies like Dow, 3M, and others that are putting the ideas of eco-efficiency into action.

The box summarizes the next steps we believe that business, and representative bodies such as WBCSD, need to take to respond to these points and build on their progress to date.

Barriers to Eco-efficiency

Achieving sustainable development is not just up to business, however. All sectors share a responsibility to work together—business, government, environmental organizations, and private citizens. One sector simply cannot hope to do the world's work alone.

As chapter 5 showed, there are many encouraging examples of partnership between these different elements to create favorable conditions for eco-efficiency. However, there are still many areas where the framework conditions are more like barriers than supports. If the full potential of eco-efficiency is to be unleashed, governments and others will need to take action to remove these barriers.

Costly and inflexible environmental regulation is one of the main barriers. Of course, regulation is necessary. We certainly do not advocate a complete rollback, but rather seek constructive change. We envision a new paradigm for regulatory oversight that fosters a spirit of innovation and responsibility rather than merely an obligation to comply. This paradigm involves regulation that is more inspiring and less prescriptive than that on the books today. The best results will come from overarching performance-based goals, backed by flexible implementation and market incentives to stimulate innovation.

Overcoming these barriers requires reform at the national and international levels. The reform agenda has been spelled out for the United States by an eco-efficiency task force of the President's Council on Sustainable Development, whose conclusions we strongly endorse.[4] The task force brought together the same mix of industrialists, policymakers, and environmentalists as the council itself to study opportunities for, and barriers to, eco-efficiency in the U.S. economy. It also conducted hands-on studies of selected industries such as auto manufacture, chemicals, and lithographic printing.

The task force envisaged a sustainable U.S. economy distinguished by six characteristics: (1) a sense of Responsibility throughout society for eco-efficiency; (2) continued economic growth; (3) sustainable resource utilization; (4) protection of environmental quality; (5) flexible, cost-effective government regulatory policy; and (6) increased social well-being. It made nine policy recommendations as to how these can be achieved:

1. *Environmental management system.* Establish a new environmental management system that uses participatory decision making to set verifiable and enforceable performance goals and allows regulated utilities operational flexibility to meet those goals.

2. *Extended product responsibility.* Encourage the practice of shared responsibility for the environmental impact of products among the designers, suppliers, manufacturers, distributors, users, and disposers of those products.

3. *Market incentives.* Market incentives, such as tradable permits and environmental fees, should be used to achieve environmental goals and stimulate technological innovation.

4. *Information collection and dissemination.* Collect and disseminate high-quality information efficiently to allow verification of progress toward sustainable development goals and to improve the capacity for decision making required for successful extended product responsibility.

5. *Integrated accounting.* Augment accounting of the GNP by implementing a satellite system of national accounts that measures sustainable development through integrated tracking of the environment, the economy, and the natural resource base.

6. *Sustainable development indicators.* Develop a full set of national sustainable development indicators to highlight and enable monitoring of the nation's economic, environmental, and social trends.

7. *Access to capital.* Develop innovative financing programs to improve and facilitate access to capital for small businesses and communities so that they may more easily invest in eco-efficient practices.

8. *Subsidy reform.* Redesign or eliminate federal subsidies that fail to incorporate the economic value of natural, environmental, and social resources into the marketplace and into government policies.

9. *Revenue-neutral tax shift.* Shift taxes away from activities that promote economic progress—such as work, savings, and investment— toward activities that lead to excessive environmental damage.

While some of these conclusions are of specific relevance to the United States context their general spirit is relevant to all parts of the world. Indeed, organizations and individuals in many other countries have reached similar conclusions and begun to implement them. Denmark, Finland, and Norway, for example, have begun to introduce incentive-based policies, have developed integrated accounts and are encouraging producer responsibility. The recommendations of the United Nations Environmental Programme (UNEP) on how to make policies supportive of cleaner production also encompass many of the same points (see box).

Environment and Trade

There is one important "framework" condition that is not covered by these various recommendations, which is trade barriers and eco-efficiency. Many importers have claimed, for example, that German packaging recycling legislation is more difficult for them to meet than for local companies and therefore constitutes a trade barrier. A number see similar dangers in eco-labels.

Some environmentalists are supportive of environment-based trade barriers as a means of ensuring high standards in their own country. But we believe that free trade is the best means of achieving environmental improvement. In the words of a WBCSD report on the topic:

Trade and environment are neither mutually exclusive nor areas that must be in conflict with one another. Trade can help optimize the efficiency with which resources are used, a key requirement in achieving sustainable development. It can also provide higher levels of wealth to support environmental activities, and open trade enables the flow of technology which, in turn, encourages new environmentally beneficial technologies.[5]

In many respects, the solution to resolving potential conflicts between trade and the environment lies in business' own hands. A crucial step is to make environmental management a priority within each company's structure, taking that responsibility right up to the chief executive. Companies should also consider the environmental performance of all their trading partners. In other words, the concept of product stewardship should be applied to traded as well as to domestically

UNEP's Recommendations to Governments

While it is industry that implements cleaner production and eco-effi-ciency, the government plays a crucial role in providing the environment that will encourage industry to move ahead. The following policy "instru-ments" that have been successfully implemented in various countries can help governments create this cleaner production-friendly environment:

1. Regulatory Reform

The task of government is to continue and improve the existing regulations that include requirements for enhanced environmental performance and implementation of cleaner technology. Therefore, governments need to
• Encourage "negotiated compliance" with industry, use general and flexible guidelines, and open dialogue between the regulators (govern-ment) and the regulated (industry).
• Assign priority to cleaner production over pollution control by phasing out regulations that may lock industry into the use of specific technologies.
• Set new and integrated industrial and environmental regulations that reward industries that are serious about cleaner production.

2. Use Economic Instruments

• Include cleaner production in the development of new instruments, such as environmental duties, subsidies, and support programs.
• Eliminate unsustainable underpricing of water, energy, and other nat-ural resources.
• Establish management and technology assistance for small and medium-sized enterprises.
• Assist R&D in cleaner processes, products, and services.

3. Provide Support Measures

Two elements inhibit the spread of cleaner production: the concept is not familiar to industry, in particular to SMEs, and when the concept is known, its commercial benefits have not been communicated or appreci-ated. The following elements can help reverse this trend:

• Provide information to industry in the technical and managerial aspects of applying cleaner production.
• Support cleaner production programs that can help in building awareness, R&D, and improving capacity within government and industry.
• Assist in adaptation of educational curricula of business and engineering programs to incorporate preventive measures.
• Establish technology transfer assistance plans.

4. Obtain External Assistance

Countries with little cleaner production expertise can benefit from external assistance to enhance their own ability to manage technological and managerial changes. These can come in the form of financial aid, transfer of information, technology transfer, education, and training. There is a need to
• Urge international financial institutions to integrate cleaner production into their lending practices.
• Commit national resources (financial and in-kind) to match assistance provided by development and technical cooperation plans.

produced and consumed goods. There is also a strong case for applying the same environmental criteria to all investment, whether at home or abroad.[6]

Where government action is thought necessary, voluntary measures are to be preferred to legislation.

Financial Markets

The WBCSD study, *Financing Change*, concluded that financial markets are beginning to take the environment seriously. However, it also concluded that they need to become even more prominent, probably by means of putting prices on it. Many in the financial community are looking to the accounting profession to devise systems that "put a number on" the environment, in other words, that put a price on things that current accounting practices and regulations exclude from the accounts. Accountants should strive to help eco-efficient companies communicate their progress—and the business benefits that flow from them—to the financial markets. *Financing Change* also suggests that shareholders should be supplied with as much information as possible about their company's environmental performance and risks and encouraged to make known their views on investment decisions. Again, some of these measures can be taken by business itself, but they also require action by financial institutions and policymakers.

The New Contract

The rising costs and inefficiency of traditional command-and-control regulation and the spread of an eco-efficiency philosophy in business create the conditions for a "new contract" between society, government, and industry. Under it corporate leaders pledge to invest in eco-efficient innovation and move toward sustainable business—that is, to achieve radical rather than incremental environmental improvement over the long term, to work to reduce global inequalities and to be responsible employers and community members. They accept that, to allay inevitable suspicion among NGOs and others, this requires governments to establish a framework of regulation and information disclosure to encourage long-term progress and penalize free riders without damaging competition. They accept too that companies that cannot adapt may go out of business.

In return, societies and governments accept that moving to sustainability needs to be done cost-effectively and in a way that enables progressive companies to gain some reward for their initiative. Eco-efficient products will fail if there is no market for them.

Achieving this new contract will be far from easy. We are proud of the achievements of 3M, Dow, and other WBCSD members to date but we also know that, like every other organization and individual, our companies have much to do to be sustainable. Business in general has to ensure that the long-term issues of sustainability are not driven out by short-term pressures, that it builds a life cycle approach into all of its activities and makes constructive responses to the dilemma of products that might be unsustainable in the longer term, even though customers want them. Large corporations also have an obligation to ensure that the concept of eco-efficiency is not elitist but is understood and adopted by small and medium-sized companies in every country.

More generally, the challenges of the new contract have been well summarized—and the practical implications analyzed—by Rodney Chase, managing director of British Petroleum and a past WBCSD chairman. His words to a Malaysian audience provides a fitting conclusion to our journey:

We must be conscious that society may ask us to change the way we do things, the products we make, or how they perform. We do not question this right, but we do ask for society's understanding of what we need to respond constructively.

We may need time to make some of the changes. This is not an excuse for delay, but to ensure we get the right results. We need a well-considered and durable framework of rules and guidelines. And let us not be obstructive in this: let's work with others to find the right approach. We need a level playing field that allows us to compete on the same terms as others. And we do need to be understood if we are to deliver successfully. This means that we must be prepared to put our case forward constructively, and show an understanding of the priorities and concerns which others may have.

We have brains: let's put them to good use. We have imagination: let's think differently. We can innovate: let's do so. We will succeed if we can manage change, so let us build an agenda for this. We are leaders: let us show the way to others.

We should thrive on the ability to compete: let us show what we can do. We have a persuasive case: let us talk to others—our governments, our customers, our shareholders, the communities in which we live and work.

So for business, the message in planning or sustainable development is: "Let us do what we do best." Let us set our strategies, develop our plans, and achieve our targets. Let us ensure our business is well run and renewable, and we will be rewarded.[7]

Summary

Business can provide leadership in the move toward sustainable production and consumption through:

understanding fundamental customer needs and how these can be delivered through much more eco-efficient services and products that create step improvements in environmental performance

creating the core technologies that are critical to sustainable development.

transferring technologies and ideas around the world

using its marketing skills to inform consumers who may sometimes be unaware of the urgency and requirements of sustainable production and consumption about the opportunities of eco-efficient products and processes.

There are many criticisms that can be leveled at eco-efficiency. It is certainly a young concept with much scope for improvement. But it is creating practical environmental improvement and can do so to an even greater degree in the future—particularly if there are supportive "framework conditions,"

more flexible and incentive-based regulation.

a free trade regime to optimize the efficiency with which resources are used, provide higher levels of wealth to support environmental activities, and enable flows of environmentally beneficial technologies.

more supportive financial markets.

The rising costs and inefficiency of traditional command and control regulation, and the spread of an eco-efficiency philosophy in business, can create the conditions for a "new contract" in which:

• progressive business invests in eco-efficient innovation and moves toward sustainable business.

• societies and governments accept that moving to sustainability needs to be done cost-effectively and in a way that enables progressive companies to gain some reward for their initiative.

Business is already providing leadership for sustainable development in these and other ways. It can and will do even more in the future.

Notes

Introduction

1. Stephan Schmidheiny, *Changing Course* (Cambridge, MA: The MIT Press, 1992).

2. Jan-Olaf Willums and Ulrich Goluke, *From Ideas to Action* (Oslo: ICC Publishing and Ad Notam Gyldendal, 1992).

3. World Business Council for Sustainable Development, *Sustainable Production and Consumption: A Business Perspective* (Geneva: WBCSD, 1996).

4. World Business Council for Sustainable Development, *Trade and Environment: A Business Perspective* (Geneva: WBCSD, 1996).

5. International Institute for Environment and Development, *Towards a Sustainable Paper Cycle*, London, 1996. Summary available from World Business Council for Sustainable Development, Geneva.

6. World Business Council for Sustainable Development, *Environmental Performance and the Bottom Line: A New Competitive Advantage?* (Geneva: WBCSD, 1997).

7. Stephan Schmidheiny, *Financing Change* (Cambridge, MA: The MIT Press, 1996).

8. World Business Council for Sustainable Development and United Nations Environmental Programme, *Eco-Efficiency and Cleaner Production* (Geneva: WBCSD and UNEP, 1996).

9. World Business Council for Sustainable Development, *Eco-Efficient Leadership* (Geneva: WBCSD, 1996); World Business Council for Sustainable Development, *Environmental Assessment* (Geneva: WBCSD, 1996).

Chapter 1

1. Quoted in Arthur D. Little, *Sustainable Industrial Development: Sharing Responsibilities in a Competitive World*, conference paper prepared for the Dutch Ministries of Housing, Spatial Planning and the Environment and Economic Affairs, Brussels, 1996.

2. World Commission on Environment and Development (WCED), *Our Common Future* (Oxford: Oxford University Press, 1987).

3. United Nations Centre for Human Settlements (HABITAT), *An Urbanizing World: Global Report on Human Settlements 1996* (Oxford: Oxford University Press, 1996), p. 107.

4. Edward Wilson, *The Diversity of Life* (Boston: Belknap Harvard, 1994).

5. Richard Leakey and Roger Lewin, *The Sixth Extinction* (London: Wiedenfeld & Nicholson, 1996).

6. Food and Agriculture Organization of the United Nations, *The State of World Fisheries and Aquaculture* (Rome: FAO, 1995).

7. Intergovernmental Panel on Climate Change, *Climate Change 1995* (Cambridge: Cambridge University Press, 1996).

8. World Resources Institute, United Nations Environmental Programme, United Nations Development Programme and World Bank, *World Resources 1996–97: The Urban Environment* (Oxford: Oxford University Press, 1996).

9. Clyde Hertzmann, *Environment and Health in Eastern Europe* (Washington, D.C.: World Bank, 1994).

10. United Nations Centre for Urban Settlements, *An Urbanizing World: Global Report on Human Settlements 1996* (Oxford: Oxford University Press, 1996).

11. Ernst von Weizsäcker, Amory Lovins and Hunter Lovins, *Faktor Vier: doppelter Wohlstand und halbieter Naturverbrauch* (Munich: Droemer Knaur, 1995).

12. Roper Starch and S.C. Johnson & Son, Inc., *Sustainable Development: The New American Dream, A National Survey of American Attitudes and Actions for Economic, Environmental and Social Progress* (Racine: S.C. Johnson and Son, 1996).

13. Roper Starch and S.C. Johnson & Son, Inc., *The Environment: Public Attitudes and Individual Behaviours North America* (Racine: S.C. Johnson & Son, 1993).

14. Quoted in "Polled South Koreans Disdain Economy," *Tomorrow,* May–June 1996.

15. Laurie Morse, "Global Companies' Most Pressing Cause," *Financial Times,* 2 February 1996.

16. Daryl Ditz, Janet Ranganathan, and R. Darryl Banks (eds.), *Green Ledgers: Case Studies in Corporate Environmental Accounting* (Washington, D.C.: World Resources Institute, 1995).

17. See World Business Council for Sustainable Development and United Nations Environmental Programmme, *Eco-Efficiency and Cleaner Production* (Geneva: WBCSD and UNEP, 1996) for a discussion of the relationship between cleaner production and eco-efficiency.

18. World Business Council for Sustainable Development, *Eco-efficient Leadership* (Geneva: WBCSD, 1996).

19. See, for example, the President's Commission on Environmental Quality, *Total Quality Management: A Framework for Pollution Prevention* (Washington, D.C.: U.S. Government Printing Office, 1993); see also annual conference reports of the Global Environmental Management Institute, Washington, D.C.

20. United Nations Environmental Programme, *Cleaner Production in the Asia Pacific Economic Cooperation Region* (Paris: UNEP, 1996).

21. Richard Schonberger, "Strategic Collaboration: Breaching the Castle Walls," *Business Horizons,* March–April 1996.

22. World Business Council for Sustainable Development, *Sustainable Production and Consumption: A Business Perspective* (Geneva: WBCSD, 1996).

23. World Business Council for Sustainable Development, *Eco-efficient Leadership.*

24. President's Commission on Sustainable Development, *Sustainable America: A New Consensus* (Washington, D.C.: U.S. Government Printing Office, 1996), p. 28.

25. The President's Council on Sustainable Development, *Eco-Efficiency: The Task Force Report* (Washington, D.C.: U.S. Government Printing Office, 1996), pp. 23–24.

26. "State Air Emission Permit Boasts Exceptional Flexibility," *The Air Pollution Consultant*, May–June 1994.

Chapter 2

1. Noah Walley and Bradley Whitehead, "It's Not Easy Being Green," *Harvard Business Review*, May–June 1994, pp. 46–47.

2. Michael Porter and Claas van der Linde, "Green and Competitive: Ending the Stalemate," *Harvard Business Review*, September–October 1995, p. 120.

3. Daryl Ditz, Janet Ranganathan, and R. Darryl Banks (eds.), *Green Ledgers: Case Studies in Corporate Environmental Accounting* (Washington, D.C.: World Resources Institute, 1995).

4. Ronald McLean and Jonathan Shopley, "Green Light Shows Corporate Gains," *Financial Times*, 3 July 1996.

5. See Daryl Ditz et al. (eds.), *Green Ledgers*.

6. Quoted in Chris Tuppen (ed.), *Environmental Accounting in Industry: A Practical Review* (London: BT, 1996), p. 71.

7. Peter James and Martin Bennett, *Environment-related Performance Measurement in Business* (Berkhamsted, U.K.: Ashridge Management Research Group, 1994).

8. Neil Johnston, *Waste Minimisation: A Route to Profit and Cleaner Production* (London: Centre for Exploitation of Science and Technology, 1994).

9. Quoted in "Big Savings at Allied Colloids Confirm "3Es" Success," *ENDS Report*, April 1996, p. 7.

10. Business in the Environment and Environment Agency, *Profiting from Pollution Prevention: The 3Es Methodology* (Leeds, U.K.: Environment Agency, 1996).

11. United Nations Environment Programme, Industry and Environment, *Cleaner Production in the Asia Pacific Economic Region* (Paris: UNEP, 1995).

12. Quoted in Ian Anderson, "Polluter Pays Up in Papua," *New Scientist*, 22 June 1996, p. 9.

13. Procter & Gamble, *1995 Environmental Progress Report* (Cincinnati, 1995).

14. Stephan Schmidheiny, *Financing Change* (Cambridge, MA: The MIT Press, 1996).

15. Jeremy Leggett (ed.), *Climate Change and the Financial Sector: The Emerging Threat, The Solar Solution* (Munich: Gerling Akademie Verlag, 1996).

16. Mark Mansley, *Long-Term Financial Risks to the Carbon Fuel Industry from Climate Change* (London: Delphi Group, 1994), p. 20.

17. World Business Council for Sustainable Development, *Environmental Performance and the Bottom Line* (Geneva: WBCSD, 1997), Martin Bennett and Peter James (eds.), Environmental Management Accounting, special issue of *Greener Management International*, Spring 1997.

18. Claude Fussler with Peter James, *Driving Eco-Innovation* (London: Financial Times Pitman, 1996).

19. See Claude Fussler with Peter James, *Driving Eco-Innovation*, for details.

20. Volkswagen, *The Volkswagen Environmental Report* (Wolfsburg, 1996).

21. Ann Goodman, "Reinsurance Reacts," *Tomorrow,* May–June 1996.

Chapter 3

1. World Business Council for Sustainable Development, *Eco-Efficient Leadership* (Geneva: WBCSD, 1996).

2. Frederick Webster, "The New Marketing Concept," *Financial Times*, 21 June 1996.

3. Theresa Waldrop, "Getting Clean in the Process," *Tomorrow*, July–September 1995, p. 17.

4. Carl Frankel, "A Sustainable Sea Change," *Tomorrow*, July–August 1996.

5. Fiat Auto, *The Environmental Challenge* (Turin, 1995).

6. World Business Council for Sustainable Development, *Sustainable Production and Consumption: A Business Perspective* (Geneva: WBCSD, 1996), pp. 13–14.

7. Ibid., p. 22.

8. "The Natural Step: Where Science and Business Meet Sustainability," *Business and the Environment*, July 1996.

9. Ernst von Weizsäcker, Amory Lovins, and Hunter Lovins, *Faktor Vier: doppelter Wohlstand und halbieter Naturverbrauch* (Munich: Droemer Knaur, 1995).

10. World Business Council for Sustainable Development, *Sustainable Production and Consumption*, pp. 16–17.

11. Ibid., p. 15.

12. Ibid., p. 18.

13. Ibid., p. 17.

14. Ibid., p. 16.

15. P. White, B. De Smet, J. Owens, and P. Hindle, "Environmental Management in an International Consumer Goods Company," *Resources, Conservation and Recyling* 14 (1995).

16. World Business Council for Sustainable Development, *Sustainable Production and Consumption*, p. 15.

17. United Nations Environmental Programme, *Cleaner Production in the Asia Pacific Economic Cooperation Region* (Paris: UNEP, 1994).

18. UNEP Industry and Environment Programme, *Cleaner Production Worldwide*, vol. 2 (Paris: UNEP, 1995).

19. Joseph Romm and William Browning, *Greening the Building and the Bottom Line* (Snowmass, CO: Rocky Mountain Institute, 1994).

20. Ibid.

21. Ecomed in cooperation with UNEP and Impresa Ambiente, *Cleaner Production in the Mediterranean Region* (Paris: UNEP Industry and Environment Programme, 1995).

22. United Nations Environmental Programme, *Cleaner Production in the Asia Pacific Economic Cooperation Region*.

23. World Business Council for Sustainable Development, *Sustainable Production and Consumption*, p. 21.

24. Lester Brown et al., *State of the World 1995* (New York: Norton/ Worldwatch Institute, 1995).

25. World Business Council for Sustainable Development, *Sustainable Production and Consumption*, pp. 21–22.

26. Ecomed in cooperation with UNEP and Impresa Ambiente, *Cleaner Production in the Mediterranean Region* (Paris: UNEP Industry and Environment Programme, 1995).

27. Paul Harris, "At DuPont, Aiming for Zero is an Environmental Calling," *Environmental Management Today*, July–August 1996.

28. World Business Council for Sustainable Development, *Sustainable Production and Consumption*, p. 20.

29. Ibid., p. 21.

30. Dwight Holing, "Sustainable Skyscrapers," *Tomorrow*, October–December 1995, p. 66.

31. United Nations Environmental Programme, *Cleaner Production Worldwide*, vol. 2 (Paris: UNEP, 1995).

32. Ian Hamilton Fazey, "Old Bugs Learn New Tricks," *Financial Times*, 7 June 1994.

33. World Business Council for Sustainable Development, *Sustainable Production and Consumption*, p. 17.

34. UNEP Industry and Environment Programme, *Cleaner Production Worldwide*, vol. 2.

35. Ibid.

36. World Business Council for Sustainable Development, *Sustainable Production and Consumption*, p. 18.

37. Ibid.

38. Ibid.

39. Ibid.

40. Ibid., p. 17.

41. John Douglas, "New Markets for Heat Pumps," *EPRI Journal*, May–June 1996.

42. Neil Bayley, *Making the Most of Life: Upgradeability* (Cambridge, U.K.: UK Centre for Environment and Economic Development, 1995).

43. World Business Council for Sustainable Development, *Sustainable Production and Consumption*, p. 17.

44. Ibid.

45. This section draws on the comments of an anonymous MIT reviewer and the discussion in M. Bennett and P. James, *Environment-Related Performance Measurement*, London: Chartered Association of Certified Accountants (ACCA), 1997.

46. Virve Tulenheimo, Rabbe Thun, and Mikael Backman, *Tools and Methods for Environmental Decision-Making in Energy Production Companies*, Lund, Sweden: International Institute for Industrial Environmental Economics, 1996.

47. World Business Council for Sustainable Development and United Nations Environmental Programme, *Eco-efficiency and Cleaner Production* (Geneva: WBCSD and UNEP, 1996), p. 7.

48. Claude Fussler with Peter James, *Driving Eco-innovation* (London: FT Pitman, 1996).

49. Ernst von Weizsäcker, Amory Lovins, and Hunter Lovins, *Faktor Vier: doppelter Wohlstand und halbieter Naturverbrauch*.

50. Claude Fussler with Peter James, *Driving Eco-innovation*, p. 303.

51. Based on Peter James, *Achieving Eco-Innovation* (Congleton, U.K.: Sustainable Business Centre, 1997).

Chapter 4

1. President's Commission on Environmental Quality, *Total Quality Management: A Framework for Pollution Prevention* (Washington, D.C.: Government Printing Office, 1993).

2. World Business Council for Sustainable Development, *Eco-efficient Leadership* (Geneva: WBCSD, 1996), p. 8.

3. Personal communication.

4. Paul Harris, "At Du Pont, Aiming for Zero Is an Environmental Calling," *Environmental Management Today*, July–August 1996, p. 1.

5. Quoted in "Du Pont's Environmental Management Training Programs," *Environmental Manager,* September 1992.

6. Paul Harris, "At Du Pont, Aiming for Zero is an Environmental Calling," *Environmental Management Today,* July–August 1996, p. 11.

7. Peter James and Stephanie Stewart, "The European Environmental Executive: Technical Specialist or Corporate Change Agent?," *Journal of Corporate Environmental Strategy,* December 1994.

8. Personal communication.

9. Quoted in Kim Loughrin, "Hybrid Future," *Tomorrow,* January–February 1996.

10. Ernst von Weizsäcker, Amory Lovins, and Hunter Lovins, *Faktor Vier: doppelter Wohlstand, und halbieter Naturverbrauch* (Munich: Droemer Knaur, 1995).

11. Quoted in Carl Frankel, "We've Been Wrong Before," *Tomorrow,* July–August 1996.

12. Quoted in Carl Frankel, "Calm Progress," *Tomorrow,* January– February 1996.

13. A. L. N Stevels, *A Roadmap for Eco-Efficient Take-Back of Consumer Electronic Products,* presented to Globec'96/Recycle 96 Global Environmental Technology Conference, Davos, Switzerland, 18–22 March, 1996; obtainable from Philips Sound & Vision, Eindhoven, Netherlands.

14. S. Noble Robinson, Ralph Earle III, and Ronald A. N. McLean, "Transnational Corporations and Global Environmental Policy," *Prism,* First Quarter 1994.

15. Quoted in The Conference Board, *TQM and Environmental Management,* New York, 1995.

16. Roger Segelken, "Employees Boost Toxic Reduction Plans, Study Says," *Cornell Chronicle,* 18 May 1995.

17. Quoted in "Du Pont's Environmental Management Training Programs," *Environmental Manager,* September 1992.

18. Volkswagen, The Environmental Report (Wolfsburg, 1996).

19. Quoted in The Conference Board, *TQM and Environmental Management.*

20. Quoted in Joseph Avila and Bradley Whitehead, "What is Environmental Strategy?" *McKinsey Quarterly*, No. 4, 1993.

21. Noranda, *1995 Summary Environment, Health and Safety Report* (Toronto, 1995).

22. A. Goodman, "Philips Goes to School,"

23. Julie Hill, Peter James, and Bob Kenyon, *Environmental Management: Costs and Benefits*, Croner's Environmental Policy and Procedures: Special Report (London: May 1995).

24. Matthias Gelber, Bernard Hanf, and Sven Huther, "EMAS Implementation at Hipp in Germany," *Greener Management International*, April 1996.

25. World Business Council for Sustainable Development, *Environmental Assessment — A Business Perspective*, Geneva: WBCSD, 1996.

26. Ibid.

27. Rodney Chase, *Sustainable Development: Business Perspectives and Opportunities*, speech to The Global 500 Forum: Towards Corporate Environmental Excellence, Kuala Lumpur, October 1995 (London: British Petroleum, 1995).

28. Martin Bennett and Peter James, *Environment-Related Performance Measurement in Business*, (London: Chartered Association of Certified Accountants, 1997); Mark Epstein, *Measuring Corporate Environmental Performance* (Chicago: Irwin, 1996).

29. M. Bennett and P. James (eds.), Environmental Management Accounting, special issue of *Greener Management International*, Spring 1997.

30. A. White, M. Becker, and J. Goldstein, *Total Cost Assessment — Accelerating Industrial Pollution Prevention through Innovative Project Financial Analysis* (Washington, D.C.: Environment Protection Agency / Tellus Institute, 1991).

31. Robert J. Kainz, Monica H. Prokopyshen, and Susan A. Yester, "Life Cycle Management at Chrysler," *Pollution Prevention Review*, Spring 1996.

32. UNEP Industry and Environment Programme, *Cleaner Production Worldwide*, Vol. 2 (Paris: UNEP, 1995).

33. Joseph Fiksel (ed.), *Design for Environment: Creating Eco-Efficient Products and Processes* (New York: McGraw-Hill, 1996) p. 3.

34. Source: Hans Brezet et al., *PROMISE Manual* (Den Haag: Rathenau Institute; Netherlands Ministry for Housing, Spatial Planning and Environment and UNEP Industry and Environment and National Research Programme on Reusing Waste Materials, 1996), p. 35.

35. Robert D. Shelton and Jonathan Shopley, "Improved Products Through Design-for-Environment Tools," *Prism*, First Quarter 1996.

36. Braden Allenby, "The Conceptual Framework for DFE at AT&T," in Joseph Fiksel (ed.), *Design for Environment*.

37. Theresa Waldrop, "Luxury Testcars," *Tomorrow*, January–February 1996.

38. Theresa Waldrop, "Getting Clean in the Process," *Tomorrow*, July–September 1995.

39. Goran Leijonhufvud, "Supercritical Chinese," *Tomorrow*, July–August 1996.

40. World Business Council for Sustainable Development and United Nations Environmental Programme, *Eco-Efficiency and Cleaner Production* (Geneva: WBCSD and UNED, 1996).

41. Personal communication.

42. International Council on Metals and the Environment and United Nations Environmental Programme, *Case Studies Illustrating Environmental Practices in Mining and Metallurgy* (Paris: International Council and UNEP, 1996).

43. World Business Council for Sustainable Development and United Nations Environmental Programme, *Eco-efficiency and Cleaner Production*, p. 9.

44. *Sustainability, Who Needs It?* (London: Sustainability, 1995).

45. World Business Council for Sustainable Development, *Sustainable Production and Consumption: A Business Perspective* (Geneva: WBCSD, 1996).

46. Peter Hindle, Peter White, and Kate Mannnion, "Achieving Real Environmental Improvements Using Value: Impact Assessment," *Long Range Planning*, June 1993.

47. Business in the Environment, *Buying into the Environment—Guidelines for Integrating the Environment into Purchasing and Supply* (London: 1994).

48. International Institute for Environment and Development, *Towards a Sustainable Paper Cycle*, London, 1996. Summary available from World Business Council for Sustainable Development, Geneva.

49. World Business Council for Sustainable Development, *Sustainable Production and Consumption: A Business Perspective* (Geneva: WCBSD, 1996), p. 23.

Chapter 5

1. United Nations Environmental Programme, Prince of Wales Business Leaders Forum, and Tufts University, *Partnerships for Sustainable Development: The Role of Business and Industry* (London: Prince of Wales Business Leaders Forum, 1994) p. 16.

2. Ibid., p. 10.

3. Quoted in Joseph Avila and Bradley Whitehead, "What is Environmental Strategy?," *McKinsey Quarterly*, Number 4, 1993.

4. Quoted in The President's Council for Sustainable Development, *Sustainable America: A New Consensus* (Washington, D.C.: Government Printing Office, 1996), p. 43.

5. Andrew Hoffman, "Faces of Environmental Stewardship," *Chemical Week*, 5–12 July 1995.

6. Rappaport and Flaherty, *Corporate Response to Environmental Management: Initiatives by Multinational Management* (New York: Quorum Books/Greenwood, 1992), pp. 117–122.

7. Quoted in "Sustainable Fish Sticks," *Tomorrow*, May–June 1996.

8. See World Business Council for Sustainable Development and United Nations Environment Programme, *Eco-Efficiency and Cleaner Production* (Geneva: WBCSD and UNEP, 1996) for a discussion of the linkages.

9. World Business Council for Sustainable Development and United Nations Environmental Programme, *Eco-efficiency and Cleaner Production* (Geneva: WBCSD and UNEP, 1996), p. 12.

10. World Business Council for Sustainable Development and United Nations Environmental Programme, *Eco-efficiency and Cleaner Production*, p. 13.

11. Ibid., p. 11.

12. Taylor Moore, "Harvesting the Benefits of Biomass," *EPRI Journal*, May–June 1996.

13. *The Seattle Times*, 27 June 1994, as quoted in Weyerhaeuser's 1994 environmental report.

14. Quoted in Noranda, *Environmental Report* (Toronto, 1995).

15. Ibid.

16. Alison Peters, "Cooperative Pollution Prevention: The Syntex Chemicals Agreement," *Pollution Prevention*, Spring 1996.

17. The President's Council on Sustainable Development, *Sustainable America: A New Consensus* (Washington, D.C.: Government Printing Office, 1996).

18. Arthur D. Little, *Sustainable Industrial Development: Sharing Responsibilities in a Competitive World*, conference paper prepared for the Dutch Ministries of Housing, Spatial Planning and the Environment and Economic Affairs, Den Haag, 1996, p. 19.

19. "German Industries Follow Dutch in Volunteering CO_2 Reductions," *ENDS Report*, May 1995.

20. World Business Council for Sustainable Development and United Nations Environmental Programme, *Eco-efficiency and Cleaner Production*, p. 11.

21. Personal communication.

22. Paper presented to MIT conference on Proactive Environmental Strategies for Industry, Cambridge, Mass., 8–9 May 1996.

23. Quoted in The Conference Board, *Environmental Alliances: Critical Factors for Success* (New York, 1996).

24. Quoted in James Geary, "Environmentalism's Second Wave," *Tomorrow*, January–February 1996.

25. Paul Chellgren and Patrick Noonan, "Finding Common Ground Through Alliances and Partnerships," *Prism*, Third Quarter 1993.

26. The President's Council on Sustainable Development, *Sustainable America: A New Consensus* (Washington, D.C.: Government Printing Office, 1996).

27. The President's Commission on Environmental Quality, *Partnerships to Progress* (Washington D.C.: U.S. Government Printing Office, 1993).

Chapter 6

1. "Philips: Integrating Eco-design into Product Development," *ENDS Report,* September 1993, p. 22.

2. Claude Fussler with Peter James, *Driving Eco-Innovation* (London: Financial Times Pitman, 1996).

Chapter 7

1. Claude Fussler with Peter James, *Driving Eco-Innovation* (London: Financial Times Pitman, 1996).

2. National Science and Technology Council, *A Bridge to a Sustainable Future* (Washington, D.C.: U.S. Government Printing Office, 1995), p. 4.

3. Stephen Viederman, "Sustainable Corporations?" *Tomorrow,* July–August 1996.

4. The President's Council on Sustainable Development, *Eco-Efficiency: Task Force Report* (Washington, D.C.: General Printing Office, 1996).

5. World Business Council for Sustainable Development, *Trade and Environment: A Business Perspective* (Geneva: WBCSD, 1996).

6. Ibid., pp. 5, 10.

7. Rodney Chase, *Sustainable Development: Business Perspective and Opportunities,* speech given at the Global 500 Forum: Towards Corporate Environmental Excellence—Challenges and Opportunities in Asia-Pacific, Kuala Lumpur, 19 October 1995 (London: British Petroleum, 1995), p. 16.

WBCSD Working Group on Eco-efficiency

Chairmen

The Dow Chemical Company	Frank Popoff
3M	Livio D. DeSimone

Members

Anova Holding, A.G.	Frank W. Bosshardt
AT&T	Enrique Redondo
BCSD–Argentina	Raymond Florin
BCSD–Columbia	Maria Emilia Correa
BCSD–Czech Republic	Petr Horacek
BCSD–Gulf of Mexico	Holly Hammonds
BCSD–Indonesia	Prof. Otto Soemarwoto
BCSD–Latin America	Dr. Sylvia Pinal
The Boc Group Pic	Richard Burns
BP Chemicals	Christian Troussier
The British Petroleum Company pic	Charles Nicholson
Ciba	Martin Tanner
Ciba Pigments	Dr. Peter Donath
Confederation of Indian Industry	K. P. Nyati
Dow Chemical Company	Kenneth Koza
	Ric Olson
	Ben Woodhouse
Dow Europe S.A.	Peter Flueckiger
	Claude R. Fussler
	Kai Hockerts
	Michael Kolleth
	Hans Staeuber
DuPont Company, Inc.	Ross Stevens
ECOS/Fundes CH	Ernst A. Brugger
	Daniel Muntwyler
	Andres Romero
Ecotec	H. E. Williams

ESKOM/Environmental Industrial Forum of South Africa
Jonathan Hobbs

ERM, Inc.   Paul Woodruff

Hoffman-LaRoche AG   Manuel Glauser
                                         Dr. Peter Mueller

Interface Research Corporation   Nancy A. Gribble

John Laing Pic   Philip Rees

S.C. Johnson & Sons   Ken Alston
                                         Jane Hutterly

Monsanto Company   Dr. Earl Beaver

Nestle Ltd.   Irina du Bois
                                         Pascal Greverath

Norsk Hydro S.A.   Kjell Øren

Novo Nordisk   Peter Tang

PowerGen Pic   Dr. William S. Kyte

Proctor & Gamble   Dr. Deborah Anderson

Sandoz International Ltd.   Jean Jaques Salzmann

Shell   Alain Wouters

Sony Europe GmbH   Dr. Lutz-Günther Scheidt

Swiss Bank Corporation   Franz A. Knecht

TransAlta Corporation   Gord Lambert
                                         Jim Leslie

3M Company   Allen H. Aspengren
                                         Robert P. Bringer
                                         David A. Sonstegard

3M Italia SPA   Marcello Puccini

Western Mining Corporation   George White

Weyerhaeuser   Norman Johnson

Xerox Corporation   Jack C. Azar

**External Participants Involved in the Two Antwerp Meetings
and the Washington Workshop**

B&Q   Alan Knight

Bank Gdanski SA   Teresa Murat

Biofoam Corporation   Ed Altke

The Body Shop International	David Wheeler
Boston University	Jim Post
	Brian Walsh
Capitol Office	Kevin Mills
CEM	Dr. Jonathan Williams
Cofima SA	Gilbert Shoeni
Commission of European	
Communities	Robert Hull
Commission of European	
Union DG XII, D-5	Andrew J. Sors
Cookson Group	Lyn Holt
The Delphi Group	Nicholas Parker
Development Alternatives	Ashok Khosla
Digital Equipment S.P.A.	Michael Q. Adams
Domus Academy	Prof. Ezio Manzini
Environmental Conservation Service,	
Environment Canada	Robert W. Slater
GEM	Jonathan Williams
GISPRI	Tayzo Hayasi
	Katsuo Seiki
Gorbachev Foundation	Ludo van Oyen
Green Management Program	Martin Standley
The Greening of Industry	Kurt Fisher
Hallmark Cards, Inc.	Ed Van Leeuwen
Home Depot	Mark Eisen
IBM Corporation	Wayne Balta
IFC	Martyn J. Riddle
IMD	Annette Ebbinghaus
INSEAD	Prof. Robert U. Ayres
IRRC	Jonathan S. Naimon
Landis & Gyr	Dr. Donald Weir
McKinsey & Co.	Dr. Ulrich Guntram
Ministry of Environment, Norway	Paul Hofseth
Ministry of Environment and ·	
Natural Resources	Göran A. Persson

National Wildlife Federation	Barbara Haas
Nexus Television, Ltd.	Nick Hart-Williams
Novotex	Leif Norgaard
OECD	Jeremy Eppel
	Rebecca Hamner
President's Council on Sustainable Development	Molly Olson
Programme STD	Prof. Dr. ir. Leo A. Jansen
Science Application International Corporation	Tom Jensen
State of Minnesota Office of the Attorney General	Leroy C. Paddock
Stockholm Environment Institute	Prof. M. J. Chadwick
The Strategy Workshop	Dr. David Fleming
Sustainable Development Council on Environmental Quality	Keith Laughlin
UNEP IE/PAC	Jacqueline Aloisi de Larderel
US Department of Energy	Denise Swink
World Bank	David Hanrahan
World Resources Institute	R. Darrly Banks
	Dr. Rob Coppock
	Donna Wise
Writar	Mark Haveman
Wuppertal Institute	Prof. Dr. Friedrich Schmidt-Bleek
WWF UK	Dr. Richard Tapper

WBCSD Working Group on Sustainable Production and Consumption

Chairman

Waste Management International	Edwin O. Falkman

Members

Avenor Inc.	Wallace M. Vrooman
British Gas Plc	Michael J. Arnold
British Petroleum Company Plc	Charles Nicholson
CIBA AG	Hans Joerg Koch
Dow Chemical Company Europe	Claude Fussler
Hoffmann-La Roche SA	Hans Künzi
	Manuel Glauser
Fiat Spa	Salvatore Corso
ICI / Tioxide Group Services Limited	Phil D. Roberts
IKF / ESKOM	Jonathan Hobbs
International Paper Company	Wade Dyke
Johnson & Johnson	Brenda S. Davis
Henkel KGaA	Rolf Schnakig
National Westminster Bank Plc	Hilary J. Thompson
Nestlé Ltd.	Irina du Bois
Nippon Telegraph and Telephone Corporation	Masaaki Kasahara
Nurands Inc.	Frank Frantisak
Norak Hydro	Ole H. Lie
Ontario Hydro	Brian Kelly
Procter & Gamble	Deborah D. Anderson
The RTZ Corporation Plc	Sara Barnard
Samsung Electronics	Jin Taak Whang
C. Johnson & Son, Inc.	Jane M. Hutterly
Sony Deutschland GMBH	Lutz-Günther Scheidt
Thorn EMI	Ken Gray
The Tokyo Electric Power Company	Yasuo Hosoya
	Johannes Waltz

Toshiba Corporation	Masao Moro
Unilever N.V.	H. K. van Egmond
Volkswagen AG	Hermann Meyer
Waste Management International Plc	Miguel Veiga-Pestana
Xerox Corporation	James C. MacKenzie

Observers

OECD	Jeremy Eppel
BIAC	Sharon Bially

Index